Ethnographic Feminisms

Ethnographic Feminisms

ESSAYS IN ANTHROPOLOGY

edited by

Sally Cole & Lynne Phillips

Carleton University Press

Printed and Bound in Canada

Canadian Cataloguing in Publication Data

Main entry under title:
  Ethnographic feminisms : essays in anthropology

(Women's experience series ; 7)
Includes bibliographical references.
ISBN 0-88629-248-4

    1. Feminist anthropology. I. Cole, Sally
Cooper, date   .   II. Phillips, Lynne P. (Lynne
Patricia), date   .   III.   Series: Carleton women's
experience series ; 7.

GN33.8.E83 1995   305.42   C95-900225-1

Cover Illustration: Detail from *Reticent Red*, by Marcelle Blanchette (acrylic on paper, 1994).
Cover concept/execution: Carleton University Press/Coach House Printing
Interior: Cover to Cover Design Corporation, Ottawa

Carleton University Press gratefully acknowledges the support extended to its publishing programme by the Canada Council and the financial assistance of the Ontario Arts Council.

The Press would also like to thank the Department of Canadian Heritage, Government of Canada, and the Government of Ontario through the Ministry of Culture, Tourism and Recreation, for their assistance.

This book has been published with the help of a grant from the Humanities and Social Science Federation of Canada, using funds provided by the Social Sciences and Humanities Research Council of Canada.

Dedicated to the memory of

Melissa Knauer

d. June 16, 1985

and

Illah Patricia (Trish) Wilson

d. December 16, 1994

CONTENTS

Illustrations   ix

Acknowledgments   xi

1   The Work and Politics of Feminist Ethnography
    An Introduction   *1*
    Sally Cole and Lynne Phillips

PART I FIELDS OF DIFFERENCE AND UNITY

        Introduction   *17*
2   Difference, Indifference and Making a
    Difference: Reflexivity in the Time of Cholera   *21*
    Lynne Phillips
3   Feminism From Afar
    or To China and Home Again   *37*
    Ellen Judd
4   From Women's Point of View: Practising Feminist
    Anthropology in a World of Differences   *53*
    Marie-Andrée Couillard
5   Thank you, Breasts! Breastfeeding
    as a Global Feminist Issue   *75*
    Penny Van Esterik

PART II EXPLORATIONS OF GENDERED WORK

        Introduction   *93*
6   "Trading is a White Man's Game"
    The Appropriation of Navajo Women's Weaving   *97*
    Kathy M'Closkey
7   "A Little Free Time on Sunday"
    Women and Domestic Commodity Production   *119*
    Max J. Hedley

8   "Working at Home is Easy For Her"
      Industrial Homework in Contemporary Ontario *139*
      Belinda Leach

9   "I Know Now that You Can Change Things"
      Narratives of Canadian Bank Workers
      as Union Activists *157*
      Patricia Baker

PART III EXPERIMENTS IN ETHNOGRAPHY

      Introduction *179*

10   Taming the Shrew in Anthropology:
      Is Feminist Ethnography "New" Ethnography? *185*
      Sally Cole

11   Engendering the Mask: Three Voices *207*
      Rae Anderson

12   New Voices on Fieldwork *233*
      Clara Benazera, Elizabeth Houde,
      Marie-Hélène Bérard, and Renée Ménard

13   Conversation between Cultures: Outrageous Voices?
      Issues of Voice & Text in Feminist Anthropology *245*
      Judith M. Abwunza

14   Reading the 'Montreal Massacre': Idiosyncratic
      Insanity or the Misreading of Cultural Cues? *259*
      I. P. (Trish) Wilson

15   By Way of Conclusion *279*
      Sally Cole and Lynne Phillips

      Resource Bibliography *287*
      Some Questions for Discussion *294*
      Notes on Contributors *296*

ILLUSTRATIONS

1   "Pound" Blanket, circa 1905   *100*

2   Navajo Rug, circa 1975   *104*

3   *The Dance of the Scarecrow Brides*   *212*

4   *Snakebird and Egg*   *216*

5   *Belly Belly*   *218*

6   Mende *sowei* mask   *220*

7   *Volva Volva*   *222*

8   *I Sing. No One Hears Me*   *224*

ACKNOWLEDGMENTS

The editors would like to thank the contributors to this volume for their enthusiasm and their accommodating responses to our queries throughout the volume's preparation. Thanks are due to Jennifer Strickland, the Production Editor at Carleton University Press, Frances Rooney for copy editing and Pamela Pastachak for her comments on the conclusion. Thanks also to Concordia University for a small grant awarded from its general SSHRCC funds and to the Department of Sociology and Anthropology at the University of Windsor for helping to defray costs. Finally, we would like to thank Michael Huberman, Samuel and Isabella Cole Huberman, Alan Hall and Rachel Phillips Hall for their help and understanding. For our wonderful friendship, we thank each other.

CHAPTER 1

The Work and Politics of Feminist Ethnography

AN INTRODUCTION

Theory is exciting and the source of growth, but untested theory will in time turn a discipline into an art form.

Margery Wolf

*T*HIS VOLUME HAS ITS GENESIS IN DISCUSSIONS HELD BY the feminist caucus in the Department of Anthropology at the University of Toronto during the 1980s. At that time many of us were graduate students working on questions of women and work or international development. Influenced by research in volumes such as *Women and Colonization* (Etienne and Leacock 1980), *Feminism in Canada* (Finn and Miles 1982), *More Than a Labour of Love* (Luxton 1980), *The Politics of Reproduction* (O'Brien 1981), *Toward an Anthropology of Women* (Reiter 1975) and *Of Marriage and the Market* (Young et al. 1981), our goals at the time were to introduce gender consciousness to historical materialist analyses. Our theses focused, for example, on women and agrarian reform, transformations in women's work from "petty" commodity production to cheap labour for transnational factories, immigrant women and homework, and women's unionization. Our approaches offered an incipient critique of cultural analyses of gender which left gender ideologies unconnected to existing social relations of production, to women's lived experiences.

As we graduated, many of us moved across Canada to work as instructors and post-doctoral fellows, positions that enabled us to enter into dialogue with interdisciplinary feminist approaches and with women's concerns in our local communities. It was at this time that many of us were influenced by the writing of literary critics such as bell hooks (1984, 1989) and Mariana Torgovnik (1990), by the cogent critiques of women of colour (Anzaldúa 1987, 1990; Davis 1981; Moraga and Anzaldúa 1983) and by numerous postcolonial revisions of the social sciences (Mohanty 1984; Said 1978; Spivak 1988). Meanwhile, cultural anthropology was responding to postmodern critiques of ethnography — critiques that, to us, resonated with feminist criticisms of ethnographies that employed a neutralized authoritative ethnographic voice and homogenized people's lives.

Ethnographic Feminisms brings together the politics of representation with our feminist politics of fieldwork and research. The title refers to the theoretical grounding of feminism in fieldwork and to gender as an experience, process and identity which varies cross-culturally and within cultures. Ethnographic feminisms involves the dissection of power; it makes women visible without denying the problematics of writing about and representing women's lives. Pluralizing feminism acknowledges the reality of diversity, multiplicity and transformative possibilities of women's politics everywhere.

In "Out of Context: The Persuasive Fictions of Anthropology," published in *Current Anthropology* in 1987, Marilyn Strathern attributes the creative force of much contemporary feminist scholarship to the political commitment that moves scholarship from genre back to life. She recognizes that feminist anthropology, in its conscious play with context, is "akin to the postmodernist mood in anthropology":

Much feminist discourse is constructed in a plural way. Arguments are juxtaposed, many voices are solicited, in the way that feminists speak about their own scholarship. There are no central texts, no definitive techniques; the deliberate transdisciplinary enterprise plays with context. Play with context is creative because of the expressed continuity of purpose between feminists as scholars and feminists as activists.

The success of feminist scholarship, says Strathern, "lies firmly in the relationship as it is represented between scholarship and the feminist movement" (1987a:268).

As many authors, including Pat Caplan (1987), Joan Gero and Margaret Conkey (1991), Julie Marcus (1992) and Margery Wolf (1992) note, feminism and feminist critique are an essential, indeed integral part of anthropological study today. Yet the "awkwardness" in the relationship between feminism and anthropology (Strathern 1987b) indirectly points to the fact that the discipline continues to ignore feminist anthropology in contemporary debates. While feminist anthropology has criticized the discipline for its reification of culture, its objective (and objectifying) methods and its marginalization of women (Bourque and Warren 1981; Luxton 1980; O'Brien 1984; Shostak 1981), feminist perspectives in anthropology have remained unrecognized and are still considered illegitimate. This "management" of feminism, to use Deborah Gordon's (1988:8) term, means that practitioners often experience the relationship between anthropology and feminism as more akin to marginalization and silencing (Lutz 1990; Morgen 1989).

Moreover, post-colonial critics of anthropology have made a point of extending their concerns to feminist anthropology. Feminist anthropology has been criticized for both its essentialist assumptions which privilege the views of Western women and its tendency to homogenize the experiences of women in the "rest of the world" (Amadiume 1987; Mohanty, Russo and Torres 1991; Trinh 1989). Although by the end of the 1980s, feminist anthropologists were beginning to address these issues, for many the impetus came less from post-structuralist and post-colonialist critiques than from women themselves and from experiences "in the field." As we see in many of the contributions to this volume, women were telling anthropologists about their lives and were asserting that their models and interpretations were at least as valid as academic feminist ones.

That women's interpretations often challenge and contradict Western feminist theorizing contextualizes feminist projects in anthropology in the 1990s: to end the historical "muting" (Ardener 1975) of women in anthropology and ethnography. Feminist anthropological projects can now be characterized by attempts to listen (Myerhoff 1978), to translate (Behar 1993), to give women a voice (Patai 1988) and to provide a forum for the documentation and presentation of the conflicting, contradictory and heterogeneous experiences of women cross-culturally (Personal Narratives Group 1989).

Having said this, we acknowledge the difficulty, perhaps near impossibility, of this project. For the relative political and economic positions of Western feminists and anthropological subjects predetermine and mold the conditions for undertaking collaborative research. This dilemma has been much written about (see for example Daphne Patai's "U.S. Academics and Third World Women: Is Ethical Research Possible?" 1991) and the complexity is undeniable. It is the political goal of understanding, revealing and seeking to alleviate women's oppression, wherever it exists, however, that enables feminist anthropologists to believe in the absolute necessity of continuing this work. Not inclined to sidestep or ignore the difficult issues of power and cultural difference, feminist anthropologists seek to come to terms with them. By so doing, feminist anthropologists continue their practice of revealing the creative insights which emerge from the tension between feminist and anthropological perspectives.

SOME HISTORY

Feminist anthropologists are not, however, a homogeneous group. As the contributions to this volume indicate, there are important differences within feminist anthropology. This makes the writing of its history and its "project" both difficult and a little misleading; there are many projects to be continued and many histories to be told. Yet there is a history that many of us have experienced, a history that at times has supported, and at times constrained, our efforts to undertake fieldwork and write our ethnographies from feminist perspectives. The following history tells us something of our continuities, our roots and our transformations.

Pathbreaking in their time, the universal subordination of women arguments of the 1970s (Rosaldo and Lamphere 1974) characterize the literature of what was then known as the "anthropology of women." The precursor of feminist anthropology, the anthropology of women was primarily concerned with revealing and documenting androcentrism through ethnographic description and cross-cultural comparison of sex-gender systems. A search for the origins of gender inequality was also part of this project, with historical research focusing on the key differences between egalitarian and more hierarchical societies (Gailey 1985; Leacock 1978; Rapp 1977; Sacks 1979). The goal of such research was two-fold: to take gender seriously and to describe cultural differences and international diversity in women's status. The political impetus of this work was in part to convince colleagues within the discipline that anthropology that takes gender seriously is not only good anthropology but is in fact anthropology itself. By demonstrating how women's social and economic positions differed cross-culturally and historically from the positions of women in Western and advanced capitalist societies, such research was also undertaken to strengthen arguments against the supposed naturalness of women's domestic roles in our society.

However, there were important limitations to the anthropology of women literature. Difference and asymmetry were most often taken at face value as evidence of inequality and hierarchy, and the theoretical models employed tended to simplify gender/economy relationships and to underplay the multiple hierarchies upon which many societies are premised. Combining existing models of economic organization with a seldom questioned notion of women's status, such approaches went beyond the identification of single criteria for understanding gender relations but failed to recognize the extent to which societies are gender coded and how gender acts as the axis upon which other social inequalities turn (Alcoff 1988; Scott 1986).

The realization that the analytical possibilities for understanding women's lives were constrained by trying to make women visible within existing models permitted, and indeed encouraged, the development of feminist anthropology. An anthropology began to develop which had, and has, a more explicit acknowledgment of the political goal to expose the contradictory aspects of subordination in women's lives.

Critiques of assumptions about the universal subordination of women have shifted the focus from notions of "sameness" to critical rethinking of concepts of "difference" among women (Behar 1993; Moore 1988; Strathern 1987d; Abwunza, Couillard, Judd, Phillips, this volume). This research follows a number of different directions. Some writers are taking steps towards contextualizing the language of difference and inequality to see the different meanings that these keywords (Williams 1976) connote in different cultural contexts (Lederman 1989; Phillips 1990; Strathern 1987c). Others are concerned to reveal the complexity of power relations — how they change over time and how they vary from society to society — to appreciate how women may accommodate, negotiate and resist such power (Abu-Lughod, 1989; Boddy 1989; Ginsberg and Tsing 1990; Ong 1987; Silverblatt 1987). Still others are working on innovative methods to renegotiate the ways in which feminist anthropologists can understand and write about women's lives (Abu-Lughod 1993; Behar 1993; Cole 1991; Luxton 1980; Personal Narratives Group 1989; Shostak 1981).

Ethnographic Feminisms locates itself within this larger project of drawing out the complexities of what we mean today by feminist anthropology. The essays in this volume are bound by a common concern for rethinking the analytical categories and conceptual frameworks we use for understanding and writing about women's lives. Though the parameters of the categories of "work" and "politics" — and the theoretical approaches through which readers come to understand them here — differ considerably from essay to essay, a thematic thread that ties the volume together is the importance of unravelling and reworking these often related terms.

WORK: IN THE FIELD(S)

For some time feminists doing research within the area of the anthropology of work have concentrated on making women's work visible within existing models (Leacock 1981; Luxton 1980; Reiter 1975; Weiner 1976). More recent anthropological research on the United States has focused on the inter-relationships between gender, class and ethnicity to broaden our understanding of work in migrant and immigrant communities (di Leonardo 1984; Lamphere 1987; Zavella 1987). Feminist contributions to the discipline have helped to challenge traditional notions of work, which in turn has raised questions about the structural and ideological bases of the gendered divisions of labour that were once taken for granted. As evidenced by the essays in this volume, such research has encouraged a recognition of work as a *relationship* and helped to focus research on the relations between production and reproduction, between women's roles as mothers and wives and their economic activities within and beyond the household, and between capitalism and women's apparent linkage to domesticity. Critically analyzing the concept (and process) of domestication has meant distinguishing motherhood from mothering, differentiating women's identity as housewives from housework as a set of economic activities, and sorting out domestication as an ideology from domestication as a set of gendered relationships (see Benazera et al., Cole, Couillard, Hedley, Leach, M'Closkey, Phillips, Van Esterik, in this volume).

As the very different contributions of Pat Baker, Max Hedley, Ellen Judd and Belinda Leach suggest, our notions of work are constantly being challenged by the rapid social, economic and political changes occuring regionally, nationally and globally. This is one of the many contexts within which we can appreciate Penny Van Esterik's essay, for example which, by defining breastfeeding as work, opens up possibilities for new directions in the production-reproduction debate and helps to reveal the extent to which we have accepted capitalist-promoted distinctions between life and work. Similarly, Rae Anderson pushes at the boundaries of work in her analysis and practice of artistic production. The tragic ramifications of insisting that life, work and art are separate entities is seen particularly clearly in Kathy M'Closkey's contribution on the exploitation of Navajo women's work.

Essays in this volume also focus on the work (and politics) of anthropological fieldwork (Abwunza, Benazera et al., Cole, Couillard, Judd, Phillips). Viewing textbook advice for doing fieldwork with some skepticism, feminist anthropologists have sought out new methodologies to incorporate more egalitarian ways of learning with women and understanding their lives. Following the lead of sociologists such as Ann Oakley (1981), who has criticized the traditional interview as a masculine approach to knowledge production, feminist researchers have strongly questioned the characterizations of women's lives by both male informants and male anthropologists. Considerable research now exists on how the gender identity of the fieldworker shapes both their participation in and their analysis of social relations (Golde 1986; Okely and Callaway 1992; Roberts 1981; Warren 1988; Whitehead and Conaway 1986). The discipline of anthropology seems to be shifting away from the idea of fieldwork as a straightforward scientific activity of gathering data and moving towards an understanding of the social construction of the field, fieldwork and data. *Ethnographic Feminisms* takes this point one step further to ask how this more reflexive view of fieldwork figures in the development of an anthropology with women, not simply "of" women.

We recognize that what we have to say about feminist ethnography reflects our specific political, economic and cultural backgrounds. That we live and work in Canada shapes our political interests and our research agenda as feminist anthropologists. Many of us are conducting fieldwork in Canada on problems as diverse as male violence, women and unionization, immigrant women workers and domestic work (see the essays by Wilson, Baker, Leach, Hedley, M'Closkey, Anderson and Couillard). These contributors face the complex layers involved in developing a feminist reflexivity when working "at home" in our own society.

POLITICS: RESEARCH AND WRITING

A number of important anthropological studies in the 1970s and 1980s provided strong challenges to a discipline still rooted in a nineteenth century view of politics (Bell 1983; Weiner 1976; Van Allen 1972). Arguing that ritual, reproduction and sexual politics were central to an understanding not only of women's power but of the political in general, this research held considerable potential for transforming political anthropology. Curiously, though, this initial step has not been followed by the surge of literature on this theme that one might have expected. Perhaps the current stalemate between political anthropology and feminism is best explained by the fact that it is the politics of feminist anthropology (in particular, its political goals) that pose the greatest threat to cultural relativity, long the cornerstone of the discipline (Moore 1988).

Political issues have always been central to the concerns of feminist anthropology. Past research has revealed both the neglect of women's politics through skewed analytical perspectives and the active silencing of women's political voices in a wide range of societies (Ardener 1975; Caplan and Bujra 1979; Messick 1987; Ridd and Callaway 1986; Warren and Bourque 1985). Studies of colonization and development have showed that women have been forced to create separate spaces to express their specific political interests (Diane Bell 1983; Bourque and Warren 1981; Ong 1987; Silverblatt 1987). This work has helped to dispel the myth, reproduced within anthropology, that women are only important to politics insofar as they are a source of conflict between men or a commodity for which men compete (Levi Strauss 1969; Meillassoux 1975); women do indeed "rebel" — though seldom in the ways that male analysts, or feminist anthropologists, might expect. Many of the essays in this volume (see, for example, Abwunza, Anderson, Baker, Cole, Couillard, Hedley, Leach and Phillips) touch on these issues, some more directly than others, to address the thorny yet crucial question of how we analyze the relationship between women's multiple identities and women's political interests. These essays also hint at the enormous energy devoted to transforming women's socio-political interests into more individual, personal (and hence more dismissable) ones. The extent to which this occurs cross-culturally (including within academic disciplines), the different ways in which power is manipulated to ensure such control and the political implications of this process will likely be central questions in future efforts to develop feminist political anthropologies.

The politics of writing itself is the subject of a number of essays in this volume. How we write as feminist ethnographers is an integral part of how we approach fieldwork, since writing is one (for many anthropologists the only) goal of such work. To produce a written work which does not marginalize women's lives is a difficult feat within the disciplinary boundaries that silence feminist work. The politics of writing demands both a reflexive analysis of our role as authors in producing certain "truths" and an inclusive approach to the voices that must be heard. However, as many of the contributions to this volume clarify, it is also important for feminist ethnographers to go beyond mere dialogical exploration to write explicitly with a point of view. Our writing is motivated by our political interest in working toward a future when women's lives will be unencumbered by discrimination, injustice and oppression. Thus there are specific political objectives in the essays by Abwunza, Anderson, Baker, Cole and M'Closkey, who challenge traditional interpretations of women's lives by juxtaposing different voices in their writing. Abwunza, Couillard, Judd, Phillips and Van Esterik look at the global processes which determine whose voices get heard in an attempt to undermine those processes, not reproduce them. Trish Wilson's essay explores the politics of writing by tearing away the interpretations of feminism and male violence in the media, as evidenced in the tragedy of the "Montreal Massacre," well known to Canadians.

The politics of writing also raises the question of whose voices are heard within this volume. It is clear that a process of class and race privilege continues to prevail in universities, excluding many voices that are also not heard here. Though an even greater plurality of discourses would have been preferred, it is noteworthy that the contributors to this volume do offer an unusual, unmoderated dialogue between generations of feminist anthropologists, with voices from the next generation of feminist scholars often offering implicit critiques of the papers by other contributors who are now a few years from the experience of being graduate students. The juxtaposition of generational perspectives is presented here in the spirit of Strathern's characterization of feminist anthropology as deriving its creativity from having no definitive techniques and no central texts.

Ethnographic Feminisms exemplifies some of the work that feminist anthropology is pursuing now almost two decades after the emergence of the anthropology of women. The authors demonstrate a keen awareness of the problematic relationships between scholarship and feminist concerns, between the personal and the political, between women's lives and the texts that are written about them. As people with different backgrounds, different interests and different field experiences, each of the contributors has personally worked through the intersection of feminism and anthropology, of the politics of work and the work of politics. In the end, however, all our words are constrained and nurtured by fieldwork, by the concrete engagement with women's different experiences and struggles.

The essays in this volume are organized thematically and divided into three sections: reflexive critiques of fieldwork and global feminism; rethinking women's labour and politics in a world structured by capitalism; and experimenting with the interplay between voices and (re)producing women's experience in feminist texts. At the beginning of each of these sections a brief note introduces the individual essays.

□

We have dedicated this book to Melissa Knauer and Trish Wilson. Melissa Knauer was an active member of the feminist caucus at the University of Toronto. As a physical anthropologist who did research on breastfeeding, Melissa played an important role in encouraging us to think about our data and our lives from alternative points of view. Trish Wilson returned to university as a mature student and mother. She was a facilitator in the Women's Studies Program at McMaster University from its inception and received her M.A. in Anthropology in 1992. Trish and Melissa were exemplars of feminist humanism in the academy and are sorely missed.

BIBLIOGRAPHY

ABU-LUGHOD, Lila. 1989. "The Romance of Resistance: Tracing Transformations of Power through Bedouin Women." *American Ethnologist* 17(1):41-55.

———. 1990. "Can There be a Feminist Ethnography?" *Women and Performance* 5(1):7-27.

———. 1993. *Writing Women's Worlds: Bedouin Stories.* Berkeley: University of California Press.

ALCOFF, Linda. 1988. "Cultural Feminism versus Poststructuralism: The Identity Crisis in Feminist Theory." *Signs* 13(3):405-36.

AMADIUME, Ife. 1987. *Male Daughters, Female Husbands: Gender and Sex in an African Society.* London: Zed Books.

ANZALDÚA, Gloria. 1987. *Borderlands/La Frontera: The New Mestiza.* San Francisco: Spinsters/Aunt Lute.

———, ed. 1990 *Making Face, Making Soul: Creative and Critical Perspectives by Women of Colour.* San Francisco: Aunt Lute Foundation Books.

ARDENER, Shirley, ed. 1975. *Perceiving Women.* New York: Wiley.

BEHAR, Ruth. 1993. *Translated Woman: Crossing the Border with Esperanza's Story.* Boston: Beacon Press.

BELL, Diane. 1983. *Daughters of the Dreaming.* Melbourne/Sydney: McPhee and Gribble/Allen and Unwin.

BODDY, Janice. 1989. *Wombs and Alien Spirits: Women, Men and the Zar Cult in Northern Sudan.* Madison: University of Wisconsin Press.

BOURQUE, Susan, and Kay Warren. 1981. *Women in the Andes.* Ann Arbor: University of Michigan.

CAPLAN, Pat, ed. 1987. *The Cultural Construction of Sexuality.* London: Routledge.

CAPLAN, Patricia, and Janet Bujra, eds. 1979. *Women United, Women Divided: Comparative Studies of Ten Contemporary Cultures.* Bloomington: Indiana University Press.

COLE, Sally. 1991. *Women of the Praia: Work and Lives in a Portuguese Coastal Community.* Princeton: Princeton University Press.

DAVIS, Angela. 1981. *Women, Race and Class.* New York: Random House/Vintage Books.

DI LEONARDO, Micaela. 1984. *The Varieties of Ethnic Experience: Kinship, Class and Gender among California Italian-Americans.* Ithaca: Cornell University Press.

ETIENNE, Mona, and Eleanor Leacock, eds. 1980. *Women and Colonization: Anthropological Perspectives.* South Hadley, MA: Bergin and Garvey.

FINN, G., and A. Miles. 1982. *Feminism in Canada.* Montreal: Black Rose.

GAILEY, Christine Ward. 1985. "The State of the State in Anthropology." *Dialectical Anthropology* 9(1-4):65-91.

GERO, Joan, and Margaret Conkey, eds. 1991. *Engendering Archaeology: Women and Prehistory.* Oxford: Blackwell.

GINSBERG, Faye, and Anna Lowenhaupt Tsing, eds. 1990. *Uncertain Terms: Negotiating Gender in American Culture.* Boston: Beacon.

GOLDE, Peggy, ed. 1986. *Women in the Field.* 2nd ed. Berkeley: University of California Press.

GORDON, Deborah. 1988. "Writing Culture, Writing Feminism: The Poetics and Politics of Experimental Ethnography." *Inscriptions* 3/4:7-24.

HOOKS, bell. 1984. *Feminist Theory, from Margin to Center.* Boston: South End Press.

————. 1989. *Talking Back: Thinking Feminist, Thinking Black.* Boston: South End Press.

LAMPHERE, Louise. 1987. *From Working Mothers to Working Daughters: Immigrant Women in a New England Industrial Community.* Ithaca: Cornell University Press.

LEACOCK, Eleanor. 1978. "Women's Status in Egalitarian Society: Implications for Social Evolution." *Current Anthropology* 19(2):247-75.

————. 1981. *Myths of Male Dominance.* New York: Monthly Review.

LEDERMAN, Rena. 1989. "Contested Order: Gender and Society in the Southern New Guinea Highlands." *American Ethnologist* 16:230-47.

LEVI STRAUSS, Claude. 1969. *Elementary Structures of Kinship.* Boston: Beacon.

LUTZ, Catherine. 1990. "The Erasure of Women's Writing in Socio-Cultural Anthropology." *American Ethnologist* 17(4):611-24.

LUXTON, Meg. 1980. *More Than a Labour of Love: Three Generations of Women's Work in the Home.* Toronto: Women's Press.

MARCUS, Julie. 1992. *A World of Difference: Islam and Gender Hierarchy in Turkey.* London: Zed Press.

MEILLASSOUX, Claude. 1975. *Femmes, greniers et capitaux.* Paris: Maspero.

MESSICK, B. 1987. "Subordinate Discourse: Women, Weaving and Gender Relations in North Africa." *American Ethnologist* 14(2):210-25.

MOHANTY, Chandra. 1984. "Under Western Eyes: Feminist Scholarship and Colonialist Discourses." *Boundary* 2/3:333-58.

————, Ann Russo, and Lourdes Torres, eds. 1991. *Third World Women and the Politics of Feminism.* Bloomington: Indiana University Press, 51-80.

MOORE, Henrietta. 1988. *Feminism and Anthropology.* Minneapolis: University of Minnesota Press.

MORAGA, Cherríe, and Gloria Anzaldúa, eds. 1983. *This Bridge Called My Back.* New York: Kitchen Table, Women of Colour Press.

MORGEN, Sandra. 1989. *Gender and Anthropology: Critical Reviews for Research and Teaching.* Washington: American Anthropological Association.

MYERHOFF, Barbara. 1978. *Number Our Days.* New York: Dutton.

OAKLEY, Ann. 1981. "Interviewing Women: A Contradiction in Terms?" In *Doing Feminist Research,* ed. Helen Roberts. London & Boston: Routledge & Kegan Paul, 30-61.

O'BRIEN, Denise. 1984. "Women Never Hunt: The Portrayal of Women in Melanesian Ethnography." In *Rethinking Women's Roles: Perspectives from the Pacific*, ed. D. O'Brien and S. Tiffany. Berkeley and Los Angeles: University of California Press, 53-70.

O'BRIEN, Mary. 1981. *The Politics of Reproduction*. London: Routledge & Kegan Paul.

OKELY, Judith, and Helen Callaway, eds. 1992. *Anthropology and Autobiography*. London and New York: Routledge.

ONG, Aihwa. 1987. *Spirits of Resistance and Capitalist Discipline: Factory Women in Malaysia*. Albany: State University of New York Press.

PATAI, Daphne. 1988. *Brazilian Women Speak: Contemporary Life Stories*. New Brunswick, NJ and London: Rutgers University Press.

———. 1991. "U.S. Academics and Third World Women: Is Ethical Research Possible?" In *Women's Words: The Feminist Practice of Oral History*, ed. Sharon Gluck and D. Patai. New York: Routledge, 137-53.

PERSONAL Narratives Group, ed. 1989. *Interpreting Women's Lives: Feminist Theory and Personal Narratives*. Bloomington: Indiana University Press.

PHILLIPS, Lynne. 1990. "Rural Women in Latin America: Directions for Future Research." *Latin American Research Review* 26(2):294-310.

RAPP, Rayna. 1977. "The Search for Origins: Unravelling the Threads of Gender Hierachy." *Critique of Anthropology* 3:5-24.

REITER, Rayna Rapp, ed. 1975. *Toward an Anthropology of Women*. New York and London: Monthly Review.

RIDD, Rosemary, and Helen Callaway, eds. 1986. *Caught Up In The Conflict*. New York: Macmillan.

ROBERTS, Helen, ed. 1981. *Doing Feminist Research*. London and Boston: Routledge and Kegan Paul.

ROSALDO, Michelle, and Louise Lamphere, eds. 1974. *Women, Culture and Society*. Stanford: Stanford University Press.

SACKS, Karen. 1979. *Sisters and Wives: The Past and the Future of Sexual Inequality*. Westport, CT: Greenwood Press.

SAID, Edward. 1978. *Orientalism*. New York: Pantheon.

SCOTT, Joan. 1986. "Gender: A Useful Category of Historical Analysis." *American Historical Review* 91(5):1053-75.

SHOSTAK, Marjorie. 1981. *Nisa: The Life and Words of a !Kung Woman*. New York: Vintage.

SILVERBLATT, Irene. 1987. *Moon, Sun and Witches: Gender Ideologies and Class in Inca and Colonial Peru*. Princeton: Princeton University Press.

SPIVAK, Guyatri. 1988. *In Other Worlds: Essays in Cultural Politics*. New York and London: Routledge.

STRATHERN, Marilyn. 1987a. "Out of Context: The Persuasive Fictions of Anthropology." *Current Anthropology* 28(3):251-81.

———. 1987b. "An Awkward Relationship: The Case of Feminism and Anthropology." *Signs* 12(2):276-92.

STRATHERN, Marilyn. 1987c. "Producing Difference: Connections and Disconnections in Two New Guinea Highland Kinship Systems." In *Gender and Kinship: Essays Toward a Unified Analysis,* ed. Jane F. Collier and Sylvia J. Yanagisako. Stanford: Stanford University Press, 271-300.

————. ed. 1987d. *Dealing with Inequality: Analysing Gender Relations in Melanesia and Beyond.* Cambridge: Cambridge University Press.

TORGOVNIK, Marianna. 1990. "Experimental Critical Writing." *Profession* 90:25-27.

TRINH, T. Minh-ha. 1989. *Woman, Native, Other: Writing Postcoloniality and Feminism.* Bloomington: Indiana University Press.

VAN ALLEN, Judith. 1972. "Sitting on a Man: Colonialism and the Lost Political Institutions of Igbo Women." *Canadian Journal of African Studies* 6(2):165-81.

WARREN, Carol. 1988. *Gender Issues in Field Research.* Newbury Park, CA: Sage.

WARREN, Kay, and Susan Bourque. 1985. "Gender, Power and Communication: Responses to Political Muting in the Andes." In *Women Living Change,* ed. S. Bourque and D.R. Devine. Philadelphia: Temple University Press, 355-86.

WEINER, Annette. 1976. *Women of Value, Men of Renown.* Austin: University of Texas.

————. 1986. "Forgotten Wealth: Cloth and Women's Production in the Pacific." In *Women's Work,* ed. E. Leacock and H. Safa. South Hadley, MA: Bergin and Garvey, 96-110.

WHITEHEAD, Larry, and Mary Ellen Conaway, eds. 1986. *Self, Sex and Gender in Cross-Cultural Fieldwork.* Urbana: University of Illinois Press.

WILLIAMS, Raymond. 1976. *Keywords: A Vocabulary of Culture and Society.* London: Fontana.

WOLF, Margery. 1990. "Chinanotes: Engendering Anthropology." In *Fieldnotes: The Makings of Anthropology,* ed. Roger Sanjek. Ithaca and London: Cornell University Press, 343-55.

————. 1992. *A Thrice-Told Tale: Feminism, Postmodernism and Ethnographic Responsibility.* Palo Alto: Stanford University Press.

YOUNG, Kay, Carol Wolkowitz, and Roslyn McCullagh, eds. 1981. *Of Marriage and the Market: Women's Subordination in International Perspective.* London: CSE Books.

ZAVELLA, Patricia. 1987. *Women's Work and Chicano Families: Cannery Workers of the Santa Clara Valley.* Ithaca: Cornell University Press.

PART I

Fields of Difference and Unity

*I*N THIS FIRST SECTION THE AUTHORS TAKE up the problem of the gender differences and gendered difference feminist anthropologists meet when working in a global context. One of the key dilemmas for feminist anthropology today concerns the contradictions that arise from our training as anthropologists when we work with women in cultural contexts different from our own. It is when we do fieldwork that we find that the anthropological models we have internalized impede our understanding of women's experience. We are often forced to rethink not only our conceptual categories but our general approach to anthropology. Although often a frustrating process (see also the multivocal essay by Benazera, Bérard, Houde and Ménard), it is within this space that we can create new ways of seeing to develop what Donna Haraway (1988) refers to as "situated knowledges."

In this section we see how our feminisms — constrained as they are by Western cultural biases — are challenged by the contexts within which we work as anthropologists. Fieldwork often deeply challenges notions of universal sisterhood, but our close examination of the fabric of women's lives also offers us the opportunity to explore new political, ethical and theoretical ground for future feminisms. The essayists in this section are reflexive about their past feminist scholarship and write in an autobiographical mode, a kind of politically contextualized "confessional" (Visweswaran 1988).

By focusing on the cholera epidemic in Latin America, Lynne Phillips considers the processes which shape how we think about difference when considering women's political interests in other cultural contexts. Reflecting on her experience in coastal Ecuador, where her relationships with rural women were marked by important differences as well as commonalities, she exposes the ethnocentric implications of Western assessments of women's politics in Latin America. She argues that while this kind of critical awareness of who "we" are must be an essential component of feminist anthropology, it should not lead us into a reflexive mode of analysis which discourages us either from acting on issues of concern to rural women or from further exploring the possibilities of international feminism.

Ellen Judd highlights the paths different women choose in their struggles to make better lives for themselves. In particular she focuses on the difficulties of Western feminists in coming to terms with the apparently different goals of Chinese women and what Western feminists have perceived to be state control over the agenda of the Chinese women's movement. She argues that Chinese women's choices need to be understood within their concrete historical context, especially their experiences of war and poverty. She traces her personal history of coming to cross-cultural understanding through what she describes as a process of moving from romanticism to troubled disillusionment to reflexive critique.

Marie-Andrée Couillard's essay focuses on her research and development work in Malaysia, Africa and Quebec. Her role as a feminist anthropologist — and thus her relationships with women — differs considerably in these three ethnographic situations. Her reflections highlight how the problem of difference can take myriad forms and is not reducible to any predetermined set of analytical categories such as culture, race or class. She brings the question of feminist practice into the discussion by elaborating the notion of "women's agenda," the starting point she advises for all projects interested in understanding women's different interests. Like Judd, Couillard argues that feminist anthropologists need to recognize differences in women's agendas and especially that issues of gender relations and women's autonomy may not always be as central as Western feminists often expect them to be.

A breastfeeding advocate, Penny Van Esterik argues that feminist anthropologists' reproductive work has shaped and informed the arguments they make in their productive work as women in anthropology. She notes feminists' reluctance to identify breastfeeding as a feminist issue both because of fears of biological determinism and because of continuing feminist ambivalence to theorizing motherhood. She argues instead that a focus on breastfeeding forces rethinking on such basic theoretical issues as the sexual division of labour, the intersection of women's reproductive and productive lives and the role of physiological processes in defining gender ideologies. By focusing on breasts, Van Esterik reminds us that there are some aspects of women's experience that can at one and the same time vary widely yet be universal.

BIBLIOGRAPHY

HARAWAY, Donna. 1988. "Situated Knowledges: The Science Question in Feminism as a Site of Discourse on the Privilege of Partial Perspective." *Feminist Studies* 14(3):575-600.
VISWESWARAN, Kamala. 1988. "Defining Feminist Ethnography." *Inscriptions* 3/4:27-46.

CHAPTER 2

Difference, Indifference and Making a Difference:

REFLEXIVITY IN THE TIME OF CHOLERA

Lynne Phillips

But I won't mind if the box is empty — if all there is in it is some room, some time. Time to look forward, surely; time to look back; and room, room enough to look around.

Ursula LeGuin

THIS ESSAY EXPLORES THE RELATIONSHIP BETWEEN A reflexive understanding of women's politics and the development of a politics of feminist ethnography. I argue that, while reflexive analyses are essential for highlighting how ethnographies are linked to global power relations that may resonate in disturbing ways in women's daily lives, explorations of this kind from a feminist perspective have ethical and political limitations. This latter point has taken on special significance for me while conducting research on cholera in Latin America. The North American media and international health organizations have treated the cholera epidemic as a kind of natural disaster — a disaster which may be controlled by reminding women of their responsibilities as mothers and wives to maintain healthy families. Such an interpretation not only erases a long history of the North's role in shaping living conditions in the South but assigns

Latin American women the responsibility for improving people's health, as though the relations of class, race, nation and culture were irrelevant to how women regard such responsibilities and experience such conditions. For me this interpretation triggers questions about the impact of the North's hegemony on both our understanding of difference and our feelings of indifference. It raises concerns about the extent to which hegemonic interpretations may also be woven into analyses of women's politics and international feminism, and how this may shape feminist attempts both to understand — and to make a — difference.

Much of the recent literature on feminism and postmodernism has centred on the questions of difference and politics, and a debate has emerged which reveals two kinds of approaches to women's politics. What may be labelled the non-humanist position reflects efforts to appreciate the relativity of women's experiences. From this perspective there are no universal categories (such as Woman) which can be used as a common basis for political organization. Women's politics are always historically specific, involving varied dynamics of power, language and meaning. The notion of international feminism is therefore often criticized for being not only unrealistic but hegemonic: it imposes gender commonalities when none exist and ignores important differences among women. On the other hand, what may be considered the humanist position emphasizes that there are many experiences that women everywhere share and that the commonalities of women's lives within and between societies indicate the potential for at least an international sisterhood, if not a universal feminism. This perspective reveals how a focus on relativism tends to undercut feminist political action, since relativity always raises the question of how one can ever act for or with people one can never really understand. From the humanist position, relativism contributes too easily to political paralysis — perhaps encouraging a cultural interest in, but not promoting political concern about, the experiences of other women in the world.

Although this portrayal polarizes two points of view in a way which does not do justice to the complex argumentation of much of the literature on international feminism, it does highlight how easily we can find ourselves caught between two undesirable choices: we can either trivialize difference in our political analyses of other women's lives or we can assume our differences to be insurmountable and concentrate instead on something we think we can understand — ourselves. This essay attempts to interrupt this particular construction of the narrow options available to feminists by using fieldwork as a lens for rethinking some assumptions and arguments about the differences among women's politics. The discussion is centred on my research experiences in coastal Ecuador[1] in order to show how, in the dynamic tension of trying to understand women as "like us" or "not like us," we often become victims of our own categories, distorting the experiences of both "other" women and ourselves.[2]

REFRACTED REFLECTIONS

There are dangers involved in defining feminism. Problems are evident, for example, in the notion that the term feminism should be reserved for urban women's movements in Latin America and that rural women can only be said to have "politics," not feminism.[3] Arguments such as this highlight the problem of who should define feminism and the extent to which feminist movements are willing to accept the different politics of other women as other aspects of feminisms. They also hint at how North/South discourses might permeate how we (the varied lot of feminist academics in the North) think about other women.

Since Said's Orientalism there has been an increasing concern about the construction of the East/West dialogue and its influence on how Western analysts have assessed the Eastern woman (Burton 1990; Lazreg 1988; Spivak 1988). Equal concern has not as yet been expressed about how Northern constructions of the South shape our images of women in Latin America.[4] While the absence of veils and harems in Latin America deprives us of ethnocentric musings about these "obvious" symbols of male domination, there are nevertheless a few central images which form an important part of our gaze on Latin American gender relations. Here I will focus on two key symbols of the South which have been used as a basis for comparison with women's lives and politics in the North, a comparison which provides similar fuel for ethnocentric musings about the Latin American woman: machismo and motherhood.

The Machismo Gaze

When I arrived in Ecuador in 1980 to study the government's agrarian reform program for my doctoral disseration, I took with me literature-informed notions of gender relations in Latin America. An implicit goal in much of the early literature I had read was to explore machismo — often glossed as the Latin American version of male dominance — in terms of its influence on women. Drawing on the idea that there were discernable differences between the appearance and realities of women's lives in Latin America (Friedl 1967; Pescatello 1973), research during the 1970s had focused on the questionable image of the Latin American woman as passive, as accepting the basic tenets of machismo that women's lives ought to be centred on the needs of men and the family. Some analysts borrowed the public-private distinction (Rosaldo and Lamphere 1974) to argue that while women were devalued because of their seclusion to the domestic sphere, it was precisely because of this distinction that they were also generally respected and even feared by men (Paul 1973). Stevens (1973:91) extended this idea to argue that, thanks to the Catholic church, women had a counterpart identity in machismo ideology called marianismo, which linked female suffering (due to the power of machismo) with feminine spiritual superiority.[5]

Settling in the province of Los Ríos to begin a year of field research, I wanted to go beyond the two extremes of considering women as passive or superior; I wanted to understand Latin American women as social actors "in reality," as capable decision makers despite male dominance. Part of my project involved understanding how Ecuadorian women might use what I thought of as informal power to undercut male political and economic control (Chinas 1973; Rogers 1975). However, it is clear that I carried with me some important unanalyzed expectations, not the least of them being that I wanted these women to be a lot like me.

Relatively blind to the fact that I was looking for evidence of rural women's politics through urban North American eyes, the first months of research in Los Ríos were extremely difficult. All I could see was the women working very hard, getting only grudging recognition for their work and being so divided among themselves that there was little that I could identify as women's politics. They seemed so unlike me, and they confirmed this for me daily by their insistence that I be more like them. I received frequent lectures about how I should gain weight ("you have no hips to sway!") and that I should have children. One day I explained to a group of women that it was difficult to be productive in the university setting when one had a family and that I had decided to postpone having children so that I could do my work. This explanation seemed only to confirm to them that I was quite a pitiful creature.

At the same time, my interpretation of these women's lives during those early months was that their work, their productivity within the confines of separate households, was a serious obstacle to their political unity as poor rural women. Indeed in many ways it seemed to me that machismo had "won." My fieldnotes during this time drew on images of victimization: the scene of Marisol crying bitterly because her mate refused to let her walk into town with the rest of us to attend her father's funeral; Eva elaborately painting her face so that she could "hook" a man in town who would support her children; Graciela hiding her face so that I would not see that her nose had been cut during a fight with her partner the night before. I could not view women's daily lives, their work for the household, their emphasis on body weight or having children in dynamic political terms,[6] and I quickly distanced myself: I began to construct these women as very different from me. And as I denied them their humanity — their right to just *be* (Lazreg 1988) — they were all the while intimating the inhumanity of the political choices I had made in my own life.

After a year of fieldwork I felt that I could call many of the women who lived in the surrounding countryside friends. I had cooked, cleaned and watched soap operas with them. I had listened to their fears of men "wandering" to younger women, of not having enough food for the children to eat and of losing the daily battle to keep their families healthy. However, I had no idea how I was going to write about the women I thought I had come to know. Flying back to Toronto I wondered: could I write about women's lives in a way that would be considered acceptable not only to me, as a feminist analyst, but also to rural Ecuadorian women, who did not consider themselves feminists, and to an academic thesis committee generally disinterested in feminist ethnography?

The Motherhood Gaze

By the 1980s an emerging literature on the need to understand politics in more contextual terms had challenged traditional definitions of political anthropology.[7] Foucault and his oft-quoted phrase, "where there is power, there is resistance," had come to have an important influence on those social scientists who oriented their work around issues of social change, including some analysts of Latin American gender relations (Silverblatt 1987; Warren and Bourque 1985). It was this lens which again encouraged me to think about women in coastal Ecuador as more "like me." Even though I recognized that their gender identity took a different form than mine, I could begin to see the political character of their struggles as housewives and as mothers (see Phillips 1989). Viewing their lives in terms of their resistance to a system of domination made them more human for me; together we could become political actors who believed in the need to act on an unjust world. This perspective — developed in a university library far removed from the daily lives of the women I had come to know — enabled me, finally, to write a thesis.

But this interpretation clearly required some romanticism on my part. That this was the case was indirectly pointed out to me by the Ecuadorian women with whom I had worked. I have written elsewhere of the importance of flower gardens to *costenas* (Phillips 1990), indicating that I was constantly asked about why I did not cultivate and exchange flowers as did all the other women in the area. The revealing explanation of one woman to her daughter was that "she doesn't have to give gifts," a statement that I have always interpreted in terms of how important gift exchanges are to the women themselves. It now occurs to me that the statement also says something about these women's interpretation of *me:* "She is not like us." Viewed as socially and economically independent (unlike them), it did not seem to them that I needed social exchanges with other women. Thus, although once again Ecuadorian women's words hinted at my own inhumanity (how human can someone be when they don't need other people?), I was insisting on emphasizing our similarities at the expense of fleshing out the important differences in our political struggles.

Abu-Lughod (1990) has cautioned us that it is dangerous to romanticize resistance in a way that does not take into full account the existing power that makes such resistance necessary. As feminist ethnographers we can take her analysis one step further by recognizing that our power as analysts (the power to emphasize resistance in our analyses, for example) may become part of the power against which other women must struggle. This point becomes relevant when we consider the literature on the concept of motherhood in Latin America. For example, that women's politics are rooted in domestic concerns has been viewed as one of the barriers to feminist organization in much of Latin America. Analysts do not deny that motherhood can be combative (Molyneux 1985) in a way which takes women's political action beyond the confines of the household (e.g., the Mothers of Plaza de Mayo, The Bolivian Housewives Committees), but it is argued that this politicization of women's identity takes place at the cost of subordinating their specific gender interests: it is action for one's children, for one's community, for one's nation, but never for oneself. It is politics, not feminism, say the feminist academics, to which poor Latin American women, in their continuing struggles as mothers, respond by effectively saying "we are not like you."

On the basis of her analysis of Nicaragua, Molyneux (1985) has argued that we need to distinguish practical gender interests (such as the survival of one's family) from strategic ones (such as the abolition of the sexual division of labour) in order to transform the former into the latter. Such a transformation is necessary because women's actions around practical gender interests are politically limited, they "do not in themselves challenge the prevailing forms of gender subordination" (233). That strategic gender interests are "derived deductively" (232) by, we must assume, feminist scholars, is not seen as a problem for Molyneux even though it means that Latin American women must act politically like us, that is in terms of what we think of as strategic, if they are ever to get beyond the practical politics of being mothers.

This analysis does not sit well with Butler Flora's (1984) discussion about a feminist organization in the Caribbean which gave up work with poor women since it seemed to be easier to get women to think about their interests as women when they did not have "to deal with the ever-looming problem of providing sustenance for their families" (88). Strategic gender interests are, it seems, a luxury that only wealthier Latin American women can afford. The point to be emphasized here is that low-income women may be resisting such categorization not so much because their actions are non-feminist in any objective sense but because our gaze only allows for a limited definition of appropriate resistance for one's gender; in this case it ensures that the problems of economic survival and economic responsibility for others are erased as an integral aspect of women's political identities.

A similar kind of disagreement has taken place at international women's conferences around the issue of socialism and feminism. The tensions in the International Women's Day conferences in Mexico City (1975) and Copenhagen (1980) between Latin American socialists and North American feminists are now well known.[8] Accusations by the latter that Latin American women were failing to act in their own interests, that machismo, the church and male-dominated labour unions had got the better of them, clearly indicated that gender was the privileged category for North American feminists and from their point of view a necessary one if Latin American women were to become "empowered." For their part, Latin American women argued that they needed to define themselves in ways which took into account the pervasive impact of colonialism and underdevelopment on their continent. Autonomy was important to them, not as women but as a *people*.

This perspective was evident in a meeting to which I was invited of the Union of Working Women (UMT), an organization in Los Ríos that in the past I have categorized as a women's branch of the more male-dominated Union of Cooperatives. Sitting in silent objection, listening to this group of peasant women talk about how the problems experienced by women in the countryside were not caused by men but by capitalism and imperialism, I never considered the possibility that my presence might have precipitated such a discussion. These women may well have viewed the meeting as an essential aspect of my education about who I was to them — the anthropological byproduct of a (male-dominated) process of development emanating from the North. That this may be an accurate interpretation of the discussion in the meeting indicates the importance of exploring how our identities, and analyses too, may be bound up in the very power relations we, as feminist ethnographers, seek critically to reveal.

With this point in mind, two principal contexts within which the North understands the South need to be delineated: international development and the academic settings within which feminist researchers most often work. My argument in the following section is that these are two unspoken contexts within which feminist analyses about women's politics of empowerment must be placed if we are to become more cognizant of why we frame our differences and commonalities in the way that we do. It is an argument for contextualizing future feminist ethnographic research, for it is only when we understand our relationships to these (and other) contexts that spaces can be created for reconsidering existing ways of viewing the world.

OUR DISCOURSES, OUR POWER

The World Market as Development

Observations from the North about women's politics in the South take place within the powerful discourse of international development. This discourse involves ideas about the inadequacies of Latin America and the abilities of the North to remedy the situation (Escobar 1985, 1988). In the past the primary focus in the countryside has been on the need for capital, specifically the need for capital "penetration" in agriculture, so that countries such as Ecuador could freely produce for the market. Today within the discourse of a new world order, the language of development has become medicalized (Rahnema 1988), its tone reminiscent of (male) doctors discussing (female) patients who are not responding well to treatment. World market cures, even shock treatment in the more serious cases, are now proposed for the countryside which is perceived to be passively awaiting new remedies.

The projects of Women in Development (WID), the women's branch of the male-dominated development agencies, are constrained to reproduce this perspective (Mueller 1986; Staudt 1985) by defining development narrowly as economic growth and by stressing the need to enable — presumably disabled — women through income-generation projects and networking. By arguing, for example, for the elimination of global patriarchy so that women everywhere can act as free agents in the development process, WID feeds into a discourse of development which defines equality in terms of a total integration with the world market.

It is within this discourse that what is sometimes characterized as dialogue between nations takes place. Thus, while the South might emphasize poverty, impossible debt loads or the unfairness of quota systems, the North — its faith in the trickle-down benefits of the world market absolutely intact — is ostensibly concerned about the South's drug problem. Although the debt crisis and neo-liberal policies have taken their toll primarily on women and children, this point becomes almost irrelevant. The hegemony of the development discourse ensures that the South's concerns largely fall on deaf ears, the doctors of development being free to ignore the diagnoses of their patients.

The Struggle to Produce in Academia

A second context within which our analyses of Latin American women should be understood is the university setting itself. It is clear that much feminist analysis aims to challenge the patriarchy of academic disciplines: we want our disciplines to think differently about agency, politics and gender. The tendency to romanticize the resistance that is "discovered" in other women's lives must be understood at least in part in terms of what we consider to be admirable politics for ourselves. However, the search to find in the other what we find admirable in ourselves (a humanist tendency) becomes a problem if these apparent parallels in our lives are used as evidence for the universal oppression of women and thus as a basis for international sisterhood. Not only do such parallels tend to be overdrawn, as I have noted here, but they are likely to distort or erase the different *meanings* that women attach to such resistance.

A second point in this regard is that although cross-cultural research has been quick to note how women's accommodations to different aspects of their lives constrain their gender politics (as in the case of combative motherhood in Latin America), there has been a general unwillingness to apply the same analysis to our own lives as a means for developing other analytic possiblities. For example, the insistence that women's individual autonomy be a prerequisite for a feminist politics (as opposed to "just women's politics") seems somewhat misguided considering the extent to which notions of productivity monopolize so much of our lives as academic women. Emily Martin (1987) has described how as North American women we are likely to think of our minds, our bodies and our reproduction (including menstruation, pregnancy and menopause) in production terms. This example says something about the extent to which our economic context limits how we think of ourselves, and one of a number of good reasons for developing strong reservations about setting up our feminist vision of the world as a universal one to which others must measure up.

In the struggle to get degrees and employment, our work with women becomes an essential ingredient to our productivity and an important commodity in the academic marketplace.[9] We might feel ambivalent about and try to resist the commodification of our work with other women, but the power of a system based on the timely and efficient production of knowledge — the context in which we write as feminist ethnographers — cannot be denied. It is sadly ironic that when we identify as feminist only those politics which privilege the category of gender, we become rather like doctors of development ourselves, ignoring the significance of the economics underpinning women's lives. As the gatekeepers of categories, we share an indifference to the impoverishment of people whose lives secure our employment.[10]

THE LIMITS OF REFLEXIVITY

Reflexive exercises of this kind which question the practices and implications of feminist research and politics are imperative if we are to continue to try to understand the world. Like Ursula LeGuin's Pandora in the opening quote,[11] we too need more room and more time so that we can climb out of those boxes we have built around ourselves. But time and room are perhaps luxuries for all women, and the real catch is that only a Pandora from the North can afford to find the box empty. In this sense, to make self-critique the only purpose for reflexivity in feminist ethnography misses a major point: the underlying goal of feminist social science is to *make* a difference and not just understand it (Caplan 1990). Thus the question arises: how might we use our understanding of difference to make a difference?

This question must be contextually answered. Making a difference in the context of cholera, for example, depends at least in part on the deconstruction of a development discourse which silences the connections between "them" and "us." It shows that as feminist ethnographers we have a role to play in exposing the contradictions of a dialogue which emphasizes the North's interest in maintaining the illusion of world order by constructing cholera as a natural disaster which will be solved by improving the South's health habits. It also clarifies the necessity of revealing the complicity of Latin American governments in this process as they juggle with people's lives to ensure that foreign trade will not suffer. Finally, in making such a commitment we need to admit to our own form of hegemony and acknowledge that the strategic gender interests of Latin American women may come to the fore in such situations but that they may well take a form different than our own. Health care and adequate sewage systems, for example, tend to be the categories Ecuadorian women privilege in this situation rather than gender and autonomy. I have argued here that this does not mean that their actions are not feminist. Nor does it necessarily mean that those actions should be labelled feminist if this is a label against which the women themselves struggle. Rather, feminist visions and support should be grounded in the relative humanist "fact" that just as these political struggles are nurtured and constrained by local, national and global contexts, so are our interpretations of them.

Concluding Comments

Feminist ethnographers concerned about the problems involved in making a difference will always find divisions which connect us as women and connections which divide us, but it seems to me that the sorting out of this kind of process must be central to our thinking about what a non-hegemonic international sisterhood might look like. Rather than functioning as a meta-narrative, a gaze or a vision, international sisterhood becomes a kind of landscape — not immutable, but something which must accompany our work as a kind of insurance against our indifference, despite our differences.

I am tempted to speculate about whether the fact that I am now a mother will make me seem more female/human for those women I know in Ecuador. But as soon as I write this I realize that this kind of humanist connection is fraught with tension. In the past when I asked women how many children they had, they always listed those alive and those "in the grave." These same women and children haunt me in my thinking about what feminism is. These are the same women who have forced me to make connections between what I observe and who I am. They would not be surprised (as was I) by the slogan on the box for my daughter's first pair of shoes: "for the petite élite." They were not surprised when I didn't have to give gifts.

But surely we do have to give gifts. We could begin to think through the gift-giving character of ourselves by revealing the embodied-ness of our own feminism and not just that of others; by recognizing our own humanity at the same time that we recognize that of (different) others and by appreciating how women also inter- pret our lives as researchers and strangers ("others") to their com- munities; by exposing our complicity in the power relations against which other women often must struggle; by realizing that an accep- tance of feminisms means giving up our power to define what fem- inism is.

These are the kinds of landscapes which emerge at the intersec- tion of deconstructing difference and making a difference, at the intersection of reflexivity and politics. Both practices seem to be essential: if we don't make an effort to deconstruct difference, we will never be able to make a difference. And if we never attempt to make a difference, we leave intact our rage at just how much our lives as women are caught in the politics of constructing the world in particular ways.

□

I would like to thank Ruth Behar, Sally Cole and Jacinth Samuels for comments on earlier drafts of this chapter. I would also like to thank the women of UMT (Vinces) for their continuing friendship and encouragement. Versions of this chapter were read at the North Central Sociological Meetings, Dearborn, Michigan, April 1991, and at the Canadian Sociology and Anthropology Association Meetings, Kingston, Ontario, June 1991.

NOTES

1. Fieldwork was undertaken in Ecuador in 1980-81, 1982, 1985, 1986 and 1992.

2. It should be noted that it is with the aim of spilling the contents of images such as "the Latin American woman" and "the Western feminist" that such categories are employed throughout this essay.

3. Assumed (rather than investigated) political variations among women can take different forms depending on the interests of the researcher, as becomes clear later in this essay in the distinction between poor women's politics and middle-class women's feminism.

4. Poole (1988) successfully takes this approach for nineteenth century Peru. Bourque and Warren (1980) take issue with the contemporary stereotypes of rural Latin American women as either earth mothers or beasts of burden but do not consider how their own use of the rural-urban model (based on the North's obsession with modernization theory) reinforces other stereotypes about the South which distort women's politics in Peru.

5. The claim of Latin American women's superiority was further elaborated when Jacquette (1980), responding to Chaney's (1973) study (which revealed Latin American perceptions of women's inability to be good politicians), suggested that "mother-power" was the real power behind the more visible male "cockfights" that were called politics in Latin America. This argument is similar to that of Rogers (1975) for southern France.

6. Questions of weight for women also carry sexual connotations. The implication is that a thin woman is not as sexually active as she ought to be, an idea which I did not explore at all in political terms, perhaps because my socialist feminism was tinged with more than a little puritanism.

7. By this time feminist anthropology had considered politics in more contextual terms, but this perspective appeared to carry less weight in the discipline.

8. According to Cagatay, Grown, and Santiago (1986), the 1985 Nairobi conference was less hostile and there was greater acceptance by North American feminists of Third World economic issues.

9.   This hegemonic process is made even more suspect when we note the extent to which feminism in the North has either been depoliticized within the academic setting (Barry 1990; Currie and Kazi 1987) or subject to a kind of purdah (Papanek 1984).

10.   We then apparently proceed to erase those lives by failing to cite ourselves (as female anthropologists) when publishing within our discipline (Lutz 1990). The practice of citing the canon points yet again to the contradictions for feminist analysts, who in struggling for respectability within the social sciences, unwittingly take on many of the practices, concepts and methods of the very disciplines we characterize as patriarchal.

11.   The quote is from LeGuin's wonderfully creative ethnography *Always Coming Home* in the chapter entitled "Pandora Worrying about What She is Doing: She Addresses the Reader with Agitation."

BIBLIOGRAPHY

ABU-LUGHOD, L. 1990. "The Romance of Resistance: Tracing Transformations of Power through Bedouin Women." *American Ethnologist* 17(1):41-55.

BARRY, K. 1990. "Deconstructing Deconstructionism (or, Whatever Happened to Feminist Studies?)." *MS.* 1(4):83-85.

BOURQUE, S. and Warren, K. 1981. *Women in the Andes.* Ann Arbor: University of Michigan.

BURTON, A. 1990. "The White Woman's Burden: British Feminists and the Indian Woman, 1865-1915." *Women's Studies International Forum* 13(4):295-307.

BUTLER, Flora, C. 1984. "Socialist Feminism in Latin America." *Women and Politics* 4(1):69-93.

CAGATAY, N., C. Grown, and A. Santiago. 1986. "The Nairobi Women's Conference: Toward a Global Feminism?" *Feminist Studies* 12(2):401-12.

CAPLAN, P. 1990. "Studying Up Studying Down: Questions Raised by Similarities and Differences in Field-work in India and Tanzania." (A conference report on Practising Feminist Anthropology: Views from around the World, 4th International Interdisciplinary Congress on Women, Hunter College, The City University of New York, June 1990).

CHINAS, B. 1973. *The Isthmus Zapotecs.* New York: Holt, Rinehart and Winston.

CURRIE, D. and H. Kazi. 1987. "Academic Feminism and the Process of De-radicalization: Re-examining the Issues." *Feminist Review* 25:77-98.

ESCOBAR, A. 1985. "Discourse and Power: Michel Foucault and the Relevance of his Work for the Third World." *Alternatives* 19(3):377-400.

———. 1988. "Power and Visibility: Development and the Invention and Management of the Third World." *Cultural Anthropology* 3(4):428-43.

FRIEDL, E. 1967. "The Position of Women: Appearance and Reality." *Anthropological Quarterly* 40:97-108.

JACQUETTE, J. 1980. "Female Political Participation in Latin America." In *Sex and Class in Latin America,* ed. J. Nash and H. Safa. Brooklyn: Bergin, 221-44.

LAZREG, M. 1988. "Feminism and Difference: The Perils of Writing as a Woman on Women in Algeria." *Feminist Studies* 14(1):81-107.

LUTZ, C. 1990. "The Erasure of Women's Writing in Sociocultural Anthropology." *American Ethnologist* 17(4):611-24.

MARTIN, E. 1987. *The Woman in the Body: Cultural Analysis of Reproduction.* Boston: Beacon.

MOLYNEUX, M. 1985. "Mobilization without Emancipation? Women's Interests, the State and Revolution in Nicaragua." *Feminist Studies* 11(2):227-54.

MUELLER, A. 1986. "The Bureaucratization of Feminist Knowledge: The Case of Women in Development." *Resources for Feminist Research* 15(1):36-38.

NASH, J., and Safa, H. 1980. "Introduction." *Sex and Class in Latin America.* Brooklyn: Bergin.

PAPANEK, H. 1984. "False Specialization and the Purdah of Scholarship: A Review Article." *Journal of Asian Studies* 44(1):127-48.

PAUL, L. 1974. "The Mastery of Work and Mystery of Sex in a Guatemalan Village." In *Woman, Culture and Society,* ed. M. Rosaldo and L. Lamphere. Stanford: Stanford University Press, 281-99.

PESCATELLO, A., ed. 1973. *Female and Male in Latin America.* Pittsburgh: University of Pittsburgh Press.

PHILLIPS, L. 1989. "Gender Dynamics and Rural Household Strategies." *Canadian Review of Sociology and Anthropology* 26(2):294-310.

————. 1990. "The Power of Representation: Women, Households and Agrarian Politics in Ecuador." *Dialectical Anthropology* 15:271-83.

POOLE, D. 1988. "A One-Eyed Gaze: Gender in a Nineteenth Century Illustration of Peru." *Dialectical Anthropology* 13:333-64.

RAHNEMA, M. 1988. "A New Variety of AIDS and its Pathogens: Homo Economicus, Development and Aid." *Alternatives* 12(1):117-36.

ROGERS, S. 1975. "Female Forms of Power and the Myth of Male Dominance." *American Ethnologist* 2:727-56.

ROSALDO, M., and L. Lamphere, eds. 1974. *Woman, Culture and Society.* Stanford: Stanford University Press.

SILVERBLATT, I. 1987. *Moon, Sun and Witches.* Princeton, NJ: Princeton University Press.

SPIVAK, G. 1988. *In Other Worlds: Essays in Cultural Politics.* New York: Routledge.

STAUDT, K. 1985. *Women, Foreign Assistance and Advocacy Administration.* New York: Praeger.

STEVENS, E. 1973. "Marianismo: The Other Face of Machismo in Latin America." In *Female and Male in Latin America,* ed. A. Pescatello. Pittsburgh: University of Pittsburgh Press, 89-101.

WARREN, K., and S. Bourque. 1985. "Gender, Power and Communication: Women's Responses to Political Muting in the Andes." In *Women Living Change,* ed. S. Bourque and D. Devine. Philadelphia: Temple University Press, 355-86.

CHAPTER 3

Feminism from Afar

OR

TO CHINA

AND HOME AGAIN

Ellen Judd

What I want most to believe, though, is that we are all in this together.

Bronwen Wallace

We must start from the bourgeois world; there is nowhere else to start from.

Jean-Paul Sartre

ONE OF THE MOST EXTENSIVE BODIES OF LITERATURE IN the cross-cultural study of women concerns Chinese women and their movements for change during this century. The sustained interest, and even fascination, which has produced this literature derives from a tension between a presumed shared identity — as women in struggle — and the obvious and sharp differences between their lives and ours. The exotica of difference heighten a preoccupation with sameness; simultaneously, difference works as a magic glass through which aspects of our own culture, hitherto invisible, become revealed and problematic.

The pivotal issue is that of which paths women choose in their struggles to make better lives for themselves. The history of the Chinese women's movement[1] earlier in this century is one which has wide international resonances, resonances which were especially felt by re-emerging women's movements in the West about twenty years ago (see Croll 1978; Ono 1989; Smedley 1976). While Western women's movements have for the most part maintained an organizational separation from other movements and insisted upon the priority of feminist issues, the history of the women's movement in China shows a provocatively different choice. The Chinese women's movement split between a distinctly feminist trend which became isolated in an urban middle class and irrelevant to the lives of most Chinese women, and a trend which turned toward working women and gave priority to class and, during the Japanese occupation, to national issues. The vision of these women was one which included feminism as part of a wider revolutionary program, but did not give it priority. This choice is best seen within its concrete historical context, in which the actual suffering and needs of working women were less a matter of gender than of class, war and poverty, but it is a choice which has been perceived outside China as posing questions for women's struggles internationally.

My concern in these few pages is with the gaze through which we[2] examine across cultural boundaries what our culture loosely terms "feminism." Through examining that gaze it may be possible to take a fresh look at the problematization of feminism within our own culture.

My concern here will be primarily with women who identified themselves earlier as belonging to the women's liberation movement or later as socialist feminists and, among these, with those who have taken a particular interest in women in China. This is not, therefore, a comprehensive examination of feminism, but a reflection on the specific but influential effort of some feminists to find a historically grounded basis for an oppositional vision. This is a search which motivates and rests implicit in much cross-cultural exploration of women's lives. Here I will examine a process of cross-cultural understanding moving from romanticism to troubled disillusionment to reflexive critique.

THE ROMANCE

The romanticization of women's liberation in China is largely focused upon the early years of the People's Republic, when a number of significant changes were made in the interests of women. Attention has also been given to the preceding decades of war and revolution and to women's roles then, but social change was difficult to implement at those times, and Communist Party policy was distinctly moderate on women's issues in the formative Yan'an period (1936-47). Later thresholds such as the Great Leap Forward (1958) and the Cultural Revolution (1966-76) have been surrounded with greater controversy, and the dramatic years of the early Cultural Revolution (1966-69) were marked by an almost complete lack of initiative on women's issues. It has seemed that the major changes were made in the early 1950s, and this assessment is still generally accepted.

The initiatives taken then were certainly dramatic. The first law of the new People's Republic was the Marriage Law of 1950, a comprehensive family law which took equality between women and men as fundamental and directly attacked many of the familial and lineage-based sources of patriarchy. Although this law was not wholly directed toward women's interests (it also favoured the interests of children and of young men), it was a genuinely major initiative directed against some of the powerful forces oppressing women specifically as women. Other early policies included particular attention to women's interests: the land reform of 1947-52 allocated land to women as well as men, providing women with at least nominal ownership rights in land; the subsequent rural collective system incorporated women into the public work force; policies on factory work included specific provisions for women, such as paid maternity leave and childcare provided at the workplace; women who had been prostitutes were provided with medical care and offered employment in the expanding industrial sector; and so on. In short, the new People's Republic, under the leadership of the Communist Party and without an independent women's movement exerting pressure upon it, acted quickly in the interests of Chinese women in both the economic areas prioritized by the Communist Party and in areas which were the loci of women's specific oppression.

From the perspective of socialist feminists observing from outside China, this appeared to be an instance in which the women's movement had not only not lost ground in joining forces with other social movements, but had actually made very substantial gains. This was so despite the fact that the women who had joined the Communist Party or the struggles it led had not remained separately organized and had rarely made an issue of women's specific oppression.[3] The organizational structure of the Communist Party of China, while more open than that of some other Marxist-Leninist parties, has been consistent in refusing to allow any groupings to form within the Party, including women's caucuses. The only officially acceptable vehicle for women to organize (except for a few years in the 1980s) has been the network of Women's Federations. This constitutes a mass organization in the classical Marxist-Leninist sense of being a transmission belt through which Party policy reaches a specific constituency, in this case women. The Women's Federations can inform the Party of the views of their constituency, but their primary role is to mobilize women in support of the Party. This is a clearly weak position for the only recognized formal organization for women. Further, none of the mass organizations holds any direct power within the Chinese state,[4] nor are they bodies which recruit members from their designated constituencies. Rather, they are small professional bodies of quasi-officials responsible for promoting state policy in a given field. Consequently, the focus of almost all discussion outside China has been upon what was accomplished by the use of state power — in formulating constitutional guarantees, laws and policies — to further the interests of women as part of a wider revolutionary program. Women were very minor actors in the formulation of state policy, and the focus of these discussions has therefore been upon what change could be accomplished for women from above, without an independent women's movement.

The results of this approach have been real and impressive, although they have also been widely over-estimated by outside observers. The worst forms of oppression have been eliminated or significantly reduced, and Chinese women have in a few decades moved from an era of footbinding and nonpersonhood to an era of formal and legal — but far from realized — equality. Much in their world of gender relations and gender inequality is analogous to forms in our own, but the rate of change has been immeasurably faster. It is quite understandable that we have been deeply impressed by all that has been accomplished, even if we have not yet adequately comprehended the processes. Some of our difficulties in understanding have arisen from the long period of limited contact between China and the Western world, a period that included the initiation of most of the significant changes for Chinese women and restrictions on the nature of official Chinese discourse. The latter requires acknowledgment of state power and hierarchy and that explicit credit be given to the Communist Party and its policies. Problems of access to information and problems in interpreting discourse cross-culturally have surely contributed to the formation of our blind spots in understanding the Chinese women's movement.

The extent of these blind spots was only brought home to me when, long after my student years in China, I returned in the 1980s to study the reconfiguration of gender in the wake of rural decollectivization. I was no longer limited to urban and intellectual circles, and I asked women who had been responsible for woman-work in their villages in earlier decades about their experiences. I was surprised to find that they made virtually no reference to the official campaigns which have been so prominent in public discourse on the subject and in the Western feminist literature.[5] Indeed, no one made any reference to the major campaign to implement the 1950 Marriage Law (see Johnson 1983) unless and until I specifically asked about it. Nevertheless, they did talk about changes which had occurred, including the major change of women initiating divorce. What was especially important was that these women presented none of these changes as the implementation of a campaign from above and from outside. Instead, they described concrete cases in which individual women took steps to improve their lives and created new precedents within their communities. These steps were enabled by the altered political climate, including new laws and policies, but were not reduced to a matter of implementing policy. Rather, women were making active use of opportunities provided in an altered political climate to make major changes in their lives. There are complex issues here involving questions of who was able take such action effectively — the information I have suggests that women comparatively well placed in the emergent political order were better able to do so — but I am in no doubt about the need to shift our perspective from that of policy and its implementation to women and their agency.

Oversight of these elements in Western feminist accounts of the lives of Chinese women constitutes a form of colonial discourse (see Mohanty 1988). We have been more adept at discerning differences among Western women and at perceiving Western women as subjects than we have been in relation to Third World women, who tend to appear in our discourse as undifferentiated and as passive victims of forces beyond their control. At least in the case of China, I would argue that we have also been more likely to see Third World women as simplistically dependent upon state-driven programs for promoting their interests.

A SECOND LOOK

The increased direct contact between Western and Chinese societies during the 1980s has enabled a confrontation with earlier romanticized, or simply inaccurate and inadequate, concepts about Chinese women which had been widespread outside China. There is still a long road to be travelled before we will have a more satisfactory understanding of the processes through which women in China have been changing their lives. This is not the subject of the present paper, and I will here only observe that the overreaction that denies significant change for women in China in recent decades is as surely wrong as the earlier misconceptions. What is at issue is not a measurement of change (according to what yardstick and in whose hands?), but a knowledge of the dynamics in the process.

Closer contact had other consequences as well, when Western feminists were more widely and more directly brought into contact with Chinese women and with the Women's Federations. This had the effect of generating a shock — the women's movement in China was difficult to recognize as feminist in terms that were familiar to Western women who considered themselves feminists, and a large portion of Chinese women, including most of those in the Women's Federations, rejected any identification of themselves as feminist. Did feminism not exist in China, or was it constituted in a very different way?

It will help here to review some of the aspects of the Chinese women's movement which are most difficult for Western feminists to accept or even to recognize as feminist:

Chinese women, in the Women's Federations and more generally, widely recognize shared interests among women (although what these interests are or what it means to be a woman have their own Chinese meanings), but not shared interests as feminists. The Chinese term for the feminist movement, *nüquan yundong,* refers precisely to the movement to win more power for women, and is used only in reference to the West. In China, the Western women's movement is widely understood to have this narrow, and in its historical context essentially bourgeois, meaning. Chinese women involved in analogous struggles by no means reject this goal — it is a high priority at present — but consider that their contrasting category of woman-work, *funü gongzuo,* is much more inclusive and far reaching.

Woman-work does have a broader scope than feminism. The work involved includes actions to protect and promote the interests of women, but also education in early childhood care, promotion of harmonious family relations, matchmaking, fashion services, and mobilizing women to support Party (or state) policies and programs. It could be described as work in the service of women, rather than work with a specifically feminist agenda. But it would most accurately be described as the work of the Women's Federations and, in this sense, it is internally defined through its relation to the state.[6]

Staff in the Women's Federations (who are not very numerous) and women designated as women's heads in their villages or with similar designations in urban settings (often in unions) do woman-work as their job. Nobody else does woman-work, by definition. Occasionally a woman may be officially asked to volunteer some special skill or prestige, but there are effective informal mechanisms which prevent women from meddling in woman-work. Woman-work is constructed as an aspect of the work of the state, and is not open to any woman who wishes to do it. Staff in the Women's Federations do not acquire their positions through demonstration of interest or volunteering work for feminist goals — no channels of that nature are available.

Organizing independent women's groups without state approval is illegal. This has been most clearly the case since June 1989, when all spontaneously formed popular groups came under renewed pressure, and groups which had appeared during the more open years of the 1980s could at best seek official review and affiliation, perhaps to a Women's Federation at some level. Despite the relaxation of the 1980s, state control over women's organizing and denial of legitimacy to independent women's organizations has been a continuing feature of the Chinese state. This owes something, perhaps, to the Marxist-Leninist tradition of recognizing the power of organization, but also a great deal to the imperial Chinese state's long-standing distrust of heterodoxy, especially when organized.

Women in China, within or outside the Women's Federations, who wish to accomplish anything in the interests of women must take the state into account, and do so as a matter of course. This can only sometimes take the form of criticism, and then usually only in a muted or indirect way, as explicit criticism of current state policy is known to be counter-productive. Occasionally some opportunities do present themselves: Zhao Ziyang had been known before his fall from power in 1989 to be opposed to women holding political power. His fall in 1989 — for very different reasons — has allowed the Women's Federations to talk openly about the reduced role of women in the state since the CCP Thirteenth Congress of 1987 and to pressure the present authorities to reverse this trend. In taking such actions, the advocates of an increased role for women become enmeshed in larger political issues in which compromise is difficult to avoid. This lays them vulnerable to criticisms from Western feminists who have usually tried to maintain a greater distance from state power and have only recently confronted the problems attendant upon partial incorporation of the women's movement into the structure and operations of the state.

From the perspective of Chinese women, as I understand it, operating outside state power is simply not possible, and this view is difficult to dispute given the historical context of their society. Although not explicitly linked to this point, another view raised (no longer always in explicit class terms, but with the implications still clear) by at least some Chinese women activists with an acquain-

tance with Western feminism is the association of our feminisms
with the bourgeois societies in which they are embedded. In other
words, Chinese women activists may have points in their practices
which are problematic in terms of their relation to the state —
although they also have a highly sophisticated view of state power
— just as we have problems in terms of our relations with market
forces.

In recent years our examination of the struggles of Chinese
women has been afflicted with a blindness similar to that described
elsewhere by Mernissi: "Is there a nascent female liberation movement in the Middle East and North Africa similar to those appear-
ing in Western countries? For decades this kind of question has
blocked and distorted analysis of the situation of Muslim women,
keeping it at the level of senseless comparisons and confounded
conclusions" (1985:7).

CRITIQUE

When the question of critique has arisen in relation to Chinese
women's struggles it has commonly been in terms of what Chinese
women might or should have done differently. It has also involved
an element of critique of our own inadequate knowledge of Chinese
women's struggles. However, the critique has remained focused on
Chinese women and their lives and practices. A fundamental change
can be made in the construction of critique if our gaze is shifted
elsewhere.

What if Chinese women and Western women did not engage in
dialogue about the possibilities of feminism based primarily on discussion of the Chinese experience, but found a fundamentally altered
basis for a shared ground? Lynne Phillips has already addressed one
other approach, focused upon the relationship between women in
different societies and concentrated upon the inequality structuring
that relationship. Much of her argument is applicable here, but the
specifics of the Chinese women's movement have prompted thought
in another avenue.

The history of Chinese women in struggle is less closely tied to
a colonial or post-colonial dependency than is the case for many

other histories. China has maintained a degree of relative independence for most of the period since the founding of the People's Republic in 1949, although it is now becoming increasingly incorporated into the global market-oriented political economy. China's women's movement has had a similar history of relative independence, and its recently increased contact with Western feminism has taken place as a meeting of distinctly different movements. Chinese women have available to them a set of values on women's issues and a history of struggle on those issues from which they view our feminisms with an interested and highly critical eye.[7]

An appropriate meeting ground for Chinese and Western women is one which lies in the exclusive area of neither but the shared area of both, the ground of critique and critical practice directed in each case toward oneself. It is first of all on the basis of a critique of our own practices that we can find a shared ground of difference with Chinese (and other) women. This difference is not a static, comparative one of "their" experience and "our" experience, but rather difference in a sense of movement. Through critique and critically altered practices this difference consists of movement away from whatever or wherever we are toward some more adequate feminism (if we still choose to use that term).

On this ground, it is possible to generate cross-cultural encounters which are not internally structured by the dynamics of global inequality. We might then be able to address that inequality in a fundamental manner, and reduce the risk of inadvertently reproducing it. The basis of this practice would not be a negotiation of differences between cultures, but a common project of becoming different from each of our current situations. Cultural specificity will remain, but difference will be transformed from something which divides to something which unites, without any requirement of identity.

We might well choose at the same time to continue our endeavour of understanding the lives of women in other cultures, and we might also strive to alter the terms of the relations we are enmeshed in when we come into contact with women in other cultures. But I suggest that neither of these endeavours will lead us directly to understand the contradictions within our feminisms, and it is these that are at the root of our difficulties in thinking about feminism cross-culturally. Before we examine our encounters with others, perhaps we should examine the selves we bring to this encounter.

Such an examination requires a shift of attention from the specially marked moments of cross-cultural contact to the everyday worlds (see Smith 1987, 1990) in which we live our own lives. It immediately raises questions about personal politics, knowledge and power, violence and a host of other issues, all of which need to be addressed if this critique is undertaken. Here I will limit myself to some of the questions specific to women who are professionally engaged in understanding women and feminism cross-culturally. Most of us somehow do this from positions located within the academic world, and I will address the particular problems which this brings to our efforts to conceptualize feminism.

If we leave aside wishful thinking about what the academy might be, and professional ideologies which obscure what we are actually doing, we may be able to see the social and cultural conditions of both our intellectual production (see Benjamin 1970) and our constructions of ourselves as feminist. The academic world in our society is, of course, deeply imbued with the operations and the ethic of the market. Many aspects of this are commonplace and the general issue hardly requires mention. For the purpose of this argument, however, I will draw attention to one particular dimension of our bourgeois world. While most of us would prefer, and do strive, to pursue knowledge through research and teaching, this substantive activity is often subsumed to more immediate processes of evaluation. One need only calculate the portion of each day which is spent in processes connected with evaluation or preparation for it, whether of students, of peers or of oneself. The nature of the evaluation done in this context is characteristic of market-oriented competition. For example, while we may exert ourselves to make helpful and constructive comments on student papers, we are professionally required to assign grades, and grades are a very important part of the evaluation, considering that one of the central operations of educational institutions in our society is exclusion: "Since there is too much talent around, someone must decide who is talented and who is not. And this decision, when it is made among narrow ranges of difference, is a political decision" (Wallerstein 1988:105). While we may not value these processes and may seek to reduce our involvement in them, we cannot entirely do so, and even opposition involves an engagement with this evaluative structure which we cannot escape. I suspect that it has permeated our consciousness more thoroughly than we have realized.

The parallel with some aspects of our encounters with feminisms elsewhere is striking. Discussion of what is and is not feminism, here or elsewhere, partakes of similar processes of competitive exclusion. These procedures surely have a value within a market context, but it is less certain that they have any value for women struggling to improve the conditions in which they live.

In place of this approach, which is not only pointless but harmful to prospects for building a global sisterhood, we could substitute two simple guideposts to the handling of difference. The first of these is affirmation of the standpoint that supports practices which are in the interests of all women. The critical point here is the qualifier "all," which requires that difference be encompassed within our vision and that the only women excluded be those who deny inclusion to other women. This effectively opens doors toward women of all cultures, classes, ethnicity and so on, while keeping adequate watch against tendencies — colonial, élitist, racist and other — which harm women. It allows for a diversity of conceptualizations of feminism (whether called that or not), organizational forms, activities and choices of priorities and strategies.

The second of these is a commitment toward critical, reflexive processes of becoming different. This is perhaps the only irreducible common feature to be found among the diversity of possible feminisms. To the extent that we can bring our critique home and realize it as the basis of our own practices, we will be able to encounter others as equals on a shared voyage of difference.

> Here, where it seems impossible
> that one life even matters, though
> like them, I'll argue
> the stubborn argument of the particular,
> right now, in the midst of things, *this*
> and *this*.
> (Wallace 1987:111)

□

My first direct encounter with Chinese women was as a student in China, from 1974 to 1977, on a Canada-People's Republic of China Exchange Scholarship. This paper more immediately arises from a series of fieldtrips in 1986, 1987-88, 1989 and 1990. This research was made possible by a generous series of grants from the Social Sciences and Humanities Research Council of Canada: Exchange Grants with the Chinese Academy of Social Science, 1986 and 1987; a General Research Grant, 1986; a Canada Research Fellowship at the University of Western Ontario, 1987-89, and at the University of Manitoba, 1989-92; and a Research Grant, 1990-91.

I would like to acknowledge the patient teaching of innumerable Chinese women over these years, and also my debt to women and feminist organizations in Canada and England.

NOTES

1. I will use this broad umbrella term in order to avoid placing prior limits or definitions on the diversity of movements being discussed here. When I refer to feminism or feminisms I am also including diversity within that narrower term.

2. The division between "we" and "they" is partly a rhetorical convenience. There is a cultural distinction between Chinese and Canadian women and the encounter between these gave rise to this paper. I am making no assumption of any rigid distinction, and in common with most people who have lived in more than one culture, I am aware of carrying a shifting and ambiguous mix of cultures within myself.

3. The most prominent exception is the case of Ding Ling in the early 1940s.

4. I am using the term state to refer to the entire apparatus of governing, including the government, political parties, the armed forces and mass organizations.

5. This is a classic example of the convergence between official and anthropological models criticized by Bourdieu (1977).

6. One illustration of the relation of the Women's Federation to the state concerns birth control, or, as it is termed in China, planned reproduction *(jihua shengyu)*. Like other plans, these too are made by the state — people do not speak of their own choices in quite the same terms. Specialized formal structures for implementing China's planned reproduction policy exist, but in practice the Women's Federations are called upon to support

and to help implement this very unpopular policy. As components of the state, they are not permitted to oppose its policy, and they do not do so. They have been willing and able to take action on some consequences of the policy which are especially damaging to women — especially female infanticide and the beating and murder of women who give birth to daughters.

It is worth noting that while the consequences of China's birth control policy fall most heavily upon women, Chinese culture is strongly pro-natalist, and the one-child policy is widely opposed by both women and men. The preference of most Chinese for more than the one child (or, in some cases, the two children) permitted in the plan conflicts with state policy designed to reduce population pressure. In this context, the issue of birth control has become more a conflict over the legitimate reach of the state than a question of women's control over their own bodies. The Women's Federations do not organize for women's right to control reproduction. See Potter and Potter (1990).

7.   We can also learn from the critiques Chinese and other women make of our feminisms. The argument presented here owes much to what I have learned from Chinese women.

BIBLIOGRAPHY

BENJAMIN, Walter. 1970. "The Author as Producer." *New Left Review* 62:83-96.

BOURDIEU, Pierre. 1977. *Outline of a Theory of Practice.* Cambridge: Cambridge University Press.

CROLL, Elisabeth. 1978. *Feminism and Socialism in China.* London: Routledge & Kegan Paul.

JOHNSON, Kay Ann. 1983. *Women, the Family and Peasant Revolution in China.* Chicago: University of Chicago Press.

MERNISSI, Fatima. 1985. *Beyond the Veil: Male-Female Dynamics in Modern Muslim Society.* rev. ed. Bloomington: Indiana University Press.

MOHANTY, Chandra. 1988. "Under Western Eyes: Feminist Scholarship and Colonial Discourses." *Feminist Review* 30:61-88.

ONO Kazuko. 1989 [1978]. *Chinese Women in a Century of Revolution, 1850-1950.* Joshua A. Fogel, ed. Stanford: Stanford University Press.

POTTER, Shulamith Heins, and Jack M. Potter. 1990. *China's Peasants: The Anthropology of a Revolution.* Cambridge: Cambridge University Press.

SARTRE, Jean-Paul. 1976 [1973]. *Sartre on Theatre.* Michel Contat and Michel Rybalka, eds. Frank Jellinek, trans. New York: Pantheon.

SMEDLEY, Agnes. 1976. *Portraits of Chinese Women in Revolution.* Jan MacKinnon and Steve MacKinnon, eds. Old Westbury, NY: The Feminist Press.

SMITH, Dorothy E. 1987. *The Everyday World as Problematic: A Feminist Sociology.* Toronto: University of Toronto Press.

SMITH, Dorothy E. 1990. *The Conceptual Practices of Power: A Feminist Sociology of Knowledge.* Toronto: University of Toronto Press.

WALLACE, Bronwen. 1985. *Common Magic.* Ottawa: Oberon.

———. 1987. *The Stubborn Particulars of Grace.* Toronto: McClelland & Stewart.

WALLERSTEIN, Immanuel. 1988. "The Bourgeois(ie) as Concept and Reality." *New Left Review* 167:91-106.

CHAPTER 4

From Women's Point of View

PRACTISING FEMINIST ANTHROPOLOGY IN A WORLD OF DIFFERENCES

Marie-Andrée Couillard

RACTISING FEMINIST ANTHROPOLOGY IMPLIES AN agenda,[1] the content of which may vary according to the practitioner. To me it has meant trying systematically to see things from the point of view of women.[2] It has also meant that, as a follower of Leacock (1975, 1981), I have been trying to identify spheres of autonomy into which women have been able to realize some of their aspirations rather than focus on oppression and its numerous manifestations. I am more interested in differences and their richness than in similarities. Like most of us, I am confronted with the problem of how to theorize differences in a way which will be useful to those with whom we work (so as not to generate racism for instance) as well as enlightening to the activists who wish to "change" them. If, like Moore (1988:197), we start with gender as the primary concept to deal with differences, I fear we might fall directly into the path of the relativism associated with "culture," a relativism often glorified in postmodernism. If, on the other hand, we stress social relations and the social rather than the cultural construction of gender relations, we are soon faced with other theoretical and methodological difficulties.

It is generally agreed now that it is not for middle-class white women to set the agenda for women from differing backgrounds. But what tools do we have to appreciate the agendas other women set for themselves? As translators not so much of culture but of struggles are we equipped to identify what is at stake in social contexts that are radically different from ours?[3] For instance, what do we do when the very notion of social equality is foreign to the women we work with? What do we do when their most urgent desire is to become a housewife ?

In my work, both applied and theoretical, I recognize power relations and try to understand them, but not in broad abstract terms. Rather I focus on their specific manifestations and their interplay in actual settings. In other words, my thinking has evolved in direct interaction with people who have to solve problems in concrete situations (whether in local or international "development"). I am writing here as someone who has been and is still confronted with action and this in spite of my position as a university lecturer (I have been part of the regular staff of the Department of Anthropology, Laval University, Quebec, since June 1987). Hence my understanding of gender necessarily informs my work with real women who face real contradictions and vice versa. My work with women from developing countries is coloured by the fact that my first contacts with them was not as an outside expert, but as a peer, while I was doing my master's degree at Universiti Sains Malaysia in Penang, Malaysia (1975-78). I then learned not only to speak Malay women's language, but also to appreciate their cultural parameters. Later I went to rural areas of Malaysia as a local development agent working on a UNICEF-funded project for women and children (1979-80). In 1982 I went back to Malaysia to do field research for my Ph.D. Then in 1989 I went to Burkina Faso, Africa, as an outside expert, head of the research group Femmes-Sahel from the Sahel Centre of Laval University. This was a very different point of view and indeed a very different experience. And my current research on women's groups in Quebec City is even more ambiguous: here I am a native, more educated and never pretending the contrary; I sometimes become the "on call" intellectual and play my role as such. Most of the time however I am learning to read situations and develop pragmatic responses to them. Having a child and forty odd years behind me brings me close to the majority of the women I work with in this context. Yet my long experience abroad (more than ten years in the States, Europe and Asia) gives me the distance I need to appreciate the various agendas of the women involved in volunteer work and consciousness raising groups. For all these reasons, my approach is rather pragmatic, though not necessarily empiricist.

In these various contexts, I have been confronted with numerous "differences," some of them terribly difficult to deal with for a feminist. In this paper I will present some of these differences — not as entities existing in themselves but as the product of particular conceptual tools used to decode reality. These are summarized in the following section. I hope to show that our lenses define relations of significance which are not necessarily those of the women we work with. This in itself is not new, but a brief discussion of the implications this has for a feminist standpoint and for research with women should contribute to the current debate on relativism and politics. My experience with rural Malay women, urban Burkinabè women and urban Québécois women will be used to illustrate my point. This will be done in three steps, each of them pointing out differences and questions to which we need to address ourselves as practising feminist anthropologists.

THEORETICAL TRAVERSES

As a feminist inspired by Marxism, I came to anthropological research with parameters meant to help me order the chaos I faced in the field. In this perspective, where "the economic is determinant in the last instance," one had to explore whether or not women had access to the means of production, including land, and to identify their role in the organization of production (Sacks 1979; Stoler 1977). With these data, one was supposed to assess women's position in their society.

It soon became obvious that economic data, though interesting and relevant to the understanding of the overall context, were not sufficient to grasp men-women relations.[4] Feminist researchers from England, followed by Americans and Canadians also sharing the Marxist tradition, were then looking for an equivalent to the notion of social relations of production to explain men-women relations (for instance Edholm et al. 1977; Beneria and Sen 1981; Mies 1986; Stichter and Parpart 1988). Returning to Engels (1964), they privileged the notion of reproduction as the central concept to analyze men-women relations. Reproduction was conceived of as having three facets: biological (on this subject they joined the more radical feminists who had been denouncing biological reproduction as the site of women's oppression [Firestone 1972]); generational, including the reproduction of the labour force (this refers to the domestic labour debate which tried to establish who — the husband or the capitalists — was the main "enemy" [Delphy 1977, for instance]); and social reproduction, or the learning of one's place in the overall system (here the work of feminists more influenced by the structuralist stream, e.g., on culture and language, was relevant). The desire to parallel Marx's methodology led to the identification of a central axis: for the understanding of society the determinant is the economy, for men-women relations it would be reproduction. This axis was to be integrated into a general theory of men-women relations which would be parallel to that of society and not reducible to it (Bryceson and Vuorela 1984).

The link between the two entities (the social form emerging from the social relations of production and men-women relations) was not problematized at this point, and it seems to me that most of these investigations leaned toward a universalistic bias. This universalistic trend is encompassed in the expression "patriarchy," which ties in closely with radical feminist discourse. It postulates that it is in reproduction that patriarchy expresses itself as the main social relation between men and women and that this relation is necessarily one of oppression. In such an analysis the socio-historical specificities of this relation are not clarified: we are not told whether the "system" is "capitalist," "feudal" or "pre-capitalist" to speak by analogy, patriarchy being applied to all forms. Instead patriarchy is assumed to be a universal, though the content or the form might vary. In all cases, then, oppression is postulated to be rooted in reproduction, even if oppression manifests itself differently and in various locations. We are not even told how these variations are tied to the wider social form.

In my own work, I have tried to bridge this gap by offering an interpretation of men-women relations among Malay peasants that did not start from a postulate concerning oppression, and did attempt to show how the rules in the wider society set limits to men-women relations. In other words, I tried to account for differences by rooting them in a specific social form. This in turn was to help me understand the process of social transformation in Malay rural communities since the colonial period.[5]

In academic circles, attempts to correct what seemed to be an overly universalistic and therefore potentially imperialist interpretation of gender relations (Ong 1988) has given rise to a relativist approach and a systematic "deconstruction" of current theoretical tools (for diverging opinions on the relevance of this development see Nicholson 1990; Barrett and Phillips 1992). With postmodernism, we were to swing away from such "structural" readings of reality and toward "genealogies," individual particularities and "cultural" specificities. Detailed studies of individual itineraries, interior journeys and blossoming "realities" became the focus of research. Such a perspective, pushed to its limits, portrays everything as having similar importance, since everything can be reduced to subjective readings of an evanescent reality. The danger, however, is that differences may be reified, leaving us with a very superficial understanding of social processes. Yet some deconstruction was needed to put our studies into proper perspective.

For instance, Foucault's (1972, 1984) deconstruction of the notion of power, central in this new trend, has been enlightening in more ways than one. The notion of "complex strategies," rather than binary oppositions between those who have power and those who don't, seems a useful approach to study men-women relations.[6] It also allows for the reading of a certain hierarchy in the observed facts: the strategies are not simply the result of random actions (though not necessarily consciously organized by each social agent).

To decipher power, then, we need to understand that the meanings produced by actions and discourses are not all equal in their results. This inequality has to be accounted for, which brings us to the relevance of differences and their constructed meaning in social contexts.

Yet I feel more at ease with a methodology that leaves room for structuring principles rather than with an approach denying them or any referents outside the immediacy of data. These principles themselves should be considered for what they are, that is, constructions whose origin can be traced to modernity and tied to a dichotomy between thought and action (Mitchell 1990). As such they are but another way of exerting power since they allow us to define reality for those we work with. The consequences for women of what Mitchell calls "framing" (1990:569 ff.) should be carefully studied, certainly within the context of international development but also within our own society, as it refers to practices which must be constantly renewed to be effective (hence there is room for change if we understand the "framing" mechanisms). In such an approach we are far from a conception of social actors as puppets of an abstract structure.

Gender, then, is only one of those concepts we use to account for relations of power and differences. It is only one of a number playing the same role in our intellectual constructions. Individuals and researchers also use class, ethnicity and age (or generation) to define the parameters of particular strategies (Connell 1984). Social scientists may use these terms to define reality, as feminists use gender to discuss power relations between men and women, but what is the link between these categories? As feminists can we allow ourselves to conclude that gender is not a central difference in a particular context? When questions of bread and butter occupy all of one's energy, what priority can be given to the control over one's body or interpersonal violence? Can gender be seen as a central principle when the socio-cultural identity of a people is perceived as threatened or when the initiatives of youth are systematically blocked?

ISLAM AND AUTONOMY

In 1979 and 1980, I spent one year in a Malay village on the north-western coast of the Peninsula working with rural Malay women on a development project. I was hired as local staff on a UNICEF-funded project using a participatory research approach. I was to identify with these women the reasons for the failure of so many projects, their conception of a better future and the means to realize it. I spoke fluent rural Malay and I was familiar with Islam, the religion of the majority of the population. I had been in the country since 1975, and I felt comfortable dressing like the rural folk. I took plea-sure in learning to do things as they did, and this minimized differ-ences at the beginning.

Yet as I learned to live "like" a villager, I also researched land titles, land occupation and types of cultures. Simultaneously, I had to probe into project failures and avenues for development. I also wanted to understand the position of women in this community to assess what could be done to better it eventually. So I was clearly not a villager. And I was a woman. It was uncommon for a woman, especially a foreign one, to do this kind of work in a Malay rural area at that time. I had to hold meetings with the whole population addressing the men from a position of authority. Outsiders always query me on that. But it was not a problem, as far as I was aware, within the village limits. I was treated with affectionate respect by all, young and old, men and women, Malays and Chinese, poor and rich. My main advantages were "knowledge" and my status, both of which permitted me to interact easily with civil servants. The fact that I was a Caucasian probably played a role, since the Malays have been colonized by the British, though this was not obvious, either to me or to friends who visited me. I did not have money to spend on projects or on goodies. My salary was paid according to local standards (for equivalent type of work), so I was not a rich expatri-ate dispensing wealth, and I was not seen as such.

As I pointed out above, I began my research with the belief that men-women relations had an economic basis. In order to assess the position of women I tried to measure their involvement in the pro-duction process and their access to land ownership. But I found that rice cultivation was much more than an economic activity. In this area not submitted to the so-called Green Revolution, women played an important role in that production as its labour force but they were also engineers of the whole production process. I also found that up to recently rice was more than a staple food for the Malays; it had a soul and women were its guardian. Even in the 1980s, some women talked about the spiritual dimension of rice agriculture with great emotion. Village women were and are also involved in rubber tapping and fruit cultivation. They own rice fields (40 percent of the surface belonged to women), rubber small-holdings, fruit orchards and village land. They traded and managed their income. All of this was fine as I, like others, believed that participation in social production was the key to women's liberation. Malay women enjoyed high "status" in their community and they worked hard. But to my dismay most of them (young and old) were dreaming of becoming housewives, *seri rumah tangga,* "queens of the home" (Couillard 1988, 1990). Development to them is thought to mean having leisure, and having leisure is associated with having wealth. It is as if today's technology was an equivalent of slaves and servants who did domestic chores for wealthy women of the old days. Then as now trade was seen as a good occupation for women who could afford it (those who had time and capital). Housewives in this perspective have little in common with domesticated women produced by "development." Rather than being defined (in the discourse) as outside something (social production for instance), they are defined as central to a process (child education and family consolidation). From a feminist perspective this might appear to be a very tenuous distinction, but for those concerned it seems to have important consequences. This is also a radically different way of defining oneself from that provided by Islam as taught in fundamentalist circles.

Indeed, an increasing number of young women (especially those living in town) are becoming fundamentalist, covering themselves as their mothers never did, refusing contraception while their mothers had often used some traditional or modern forms, staying home while their mothers had diversified income-earning occupations (including trade). To them, development coming from the West and supported by the Malaysian state[7] is seen as bad (some of them refuse television and Western literature). It endangers their souls. Islam, rather than custom, is seen in this context as providing the means to identify oneself in a legitimate language while protecting this identity from Western "invasion."

What does a development agent do in such a case ? Either she plays on the state's messages and opposes one authority to another (state versus Islamic authority), and in so doing takes the side of the state (the one who pays her salary, perhaps). Or she takes the feminist standpoint, analyzing the "objective" causes of women's oppression and concluding that a form of false consciousness (here understood to come either from images of modernity in the media or notions of gender in Islamic discourse) makes village women blind to the "real" alienation lived by housewives elsewhere. The manifestations of patriarchy, somehow more easily recognized in Islamic discourses but just as important in modern "education," are then seen as the main enemy. A deliberate and systematic denunciation of these manifestations (especially in the sphere of reproduction, which as I indicated above has been the conceptual tool used to read reality) as well as "consciousness raising" through discussion and group work would be used, in the good Western feminist tradition. According to the laws of progress, rational arguments should eventually win over irrational practices.

I was not at ease with either of these avenues. I preferred to try to understand what was at play in this process from within: why should one wish to be a housewife? What did the term mean to the village women? What was Islam to these women (and not the scriptures' rules concerning women in abstract terms)? To me "the point of view of women" was that of specific women with specific social characteristics: some were well off, others poor, some educated, others not, some were well connected to urban centres, others not, and so on. This brought me to confront the social construction of meaning: what is a housewife, what is a good Muslim woman?

The understanding of this construction is in fact the key to an eventual deconstruction of these cultural elements. Village women tend to rule out abstract broad statements (about patriarchy for instance) because they view these statements as irrelevant to their understanding of the world. They even offer a terrible "resistance" to all that is defined as irrelevant to their construction of meaning and/or threatening to their identity as Malay women.

Those who do not, those few who have been seduced by Western feminist precepts, often have studied abroad, come from well off families who have brought them up in a "modern" manner, and are already quite "dislocated" with regard to their cultural identity when compared to village women. Their referents are not those of rural women, and communication between them and rural women is sometimes quite difficult, even more so if the feminist activists are not from the same ethnic community.

It is a challenge for a non-Muslim to enter into the logic of Islam with respect. It may be easier if it is done through actual practice rather than in abstract terms, that is by slowly absorbing the structuring effects of Islam on daily practices of women rather than memorizing precepts and scriptures. In doing the former, it becomes possible to identify the priorities in the agenda of the women we work with. It is then possible to decipher the language into which this agenda is formulated and the terms of reference. It is not necessarily because they were conforming to Islam that the women with whom I worked wanted to become housewives. More often it was because to be a housewife means having leisure and having leisure means having wealth. Modern women on TV seem wealthy, they do not work in the fields or estates, they are well dressed, clean and they are housewives. This ambiguity in the demands of Islam and those of modernity are central to Malay women's agendas. Surely that can only be because, in Malaysia today, Islam and modernity share something basic concerning women and their place in society. If we stand outside rural Malay women's referents we cannot grasp this ambiguity and we fail to decipher their struggle. Most rural Malay women wish to become "modern" women and fit with images of modernity to which they are exposed. But they also want to be good Muslim women.

On the other hand, some Malay women, most often younger women who are educated and live in town, refuse modernity as it is presented to them (in the media, in secular schools, in the state's messages). They choose Islam, in its fundamentalist version, as a means to define themselves outside the logic of efficiency, productivity and consumerism. This rejection is quite difficult to understand for Western-influenced feminists. Yet, I believe we should ask why and how, rather than judge and attack their strategies. They are telling us something through their choices, and as feminists should we not be listening? They are not passive victims of male conspiracy; most of them freely choose this path. What seems "sacrifice" to us clearly has another meaning to them. Shouldn't we try to understand this other way of defining reality while placing it in a wider context?

This necessarily means going further than locating differences in "cultural traits." The notion of "cultural traits" implies that differences among people are simply elements which can be assembled and reassembled and are of equal value in the construction of meaning. Hence we might argue that women are the same everywhere but for minor cultural traits which, with proper "education," can be modified without having a major impact on the individual's identity. In contrast what I am arguing here is that Islam for Malay women is not a "cultural trait." It is a structuring "difference." Such differences come from complex choices in the construction of reality and the meaning given to it. Women's agendas have to be understood within this frame of reference and not with regard to our own. Their struggles, within this context, are real and as worthy of support as any.

Working with women as an anthropologist then would mean understanding their agendas, and translating their objectives. Women should be seen as competent social agents within the parameters they define as relevant, rather than incompetent actors to be transformed to our image. Superficial references to "culture" should be left to those who are not equipped to grasp the complexities of social processes. Culture is not something above us, like clothing which can be rearranged to suit fashion, it is the very core of our being in society, as well as of our individual identity. In other words, I do not think we have much choice but to start from where women are.

WOMEN AND MULTIPLE HIERARCHIES

My contact with Burkina Faso, in 1989, was of a different nature. I went to Ouagadougou, the capital, as a representataive of a University Center of Excellence funded by CIDA (Canadian International Development Agency), to identify partners for eventual research projects. I had to do quite a lot of what I call "public relations" work, meeting people involved in planning development and researchers. My position here was perceived as that of a potential fund raiser. My stay was brief, around ten days, but contacts were kept thereafter through researchers from the group who made a number of field trips. Preliminary research with women's groups of Ouagadougou and the periphery was carried out in this manner. This means that part of what I say was filtered through intermediaries: this is, in fact, the kind of relation to others which is more prevalent among university lecturers, including anthropologists, than we like to admit in the academy (Kay 1990).

I do not speak More, the language of the majority of the population of Ouagadougou, so my contact was with French-speaking people. This means I also interacted mostly with Western-educated urban women who told me about the hardships of their rural sisters and the need for foreign aid. Here I was clearly confronted with a group of women who serve as intermediaries between the international agencies and the local population. Seeking foreign funds, administering them and eventually making linkages with the population has become a business which can be quite lucrative in some quarters. The relationship between rural people and the state apparatus being one of mistrust, a profusion of NGOs (non-governmental organizations) handle a good share of the foreign aid.

I do not intend to discuss the integrity of the women handling these funds, nor the relevance of the various disconnected projects planned to suit agencies from various Western countries with different priorities. Because of CIDA policies, for instance, all projects with Canadian funds must take women into account *(volet femmes)*. Many of the local men administrators I met complained about this saying they had to find women to administer these projects while they could very well have done that on their own. They certainly did not see the relevance of "gender in development," but then in that they are not alone.

What I want to discuss here is the relation women entertain with other women. Feminists have made it a point to question power structures and hierarchies. When working in international development, they somehow tend to think that women as partners will share this ideal.[8] This is clearly not the case in Burkina Faso. Here, our partners often use our support to confirm their higher status and their authority vis-à-vis their "sisters." Rather than taking for granted that this power game is similar to those we know in our own context, shouldn't we try to "deconstruct" it to understand its roots ? Burkinabè women are in fact applying the rules of their society, which is in all sectors highly hierarchical. They play according to the rules, but can we decipher those rules if we start from our ideals?

In this highly structured context, gender relations are far from central. Age groups, ethnic belonging and rank of one's family are terribly important in constructing meaning and colouring interpersonal relations. Women's solidarity, then, rather than being taken for granted must be problematized and investigated in specific contexts. This is specially crucial when projects are planned on the basis of mutual help and self-training. Both these strategies which may, in some cases, yield fruitful results, might also be the basis for exploitation and oppression of women *by* women. The often noted shyness of rural women when confronted with educated urban leaders tells us more about social relations than about personal problems in expressing oneself.

So what can a well-intentioned community organizer do? If she encourages women's personal expression, those involved might be punished for breach of rules (younger women expressing themselves in front of elders, women speaking up when men should, and so on). How does she organize? How does she reach the women? What about methods like action or participatory research which presume that all participants can be involved and formulate their opinion equally? These techniques have been developed in a setting governed by the great myth of equality. Are they relevant here? The failure of so many projects over the last twenty years clearly answers this question and should force us to confront power relations rather than deny them in the name of a feminine utopia.

When Burkinabè women say "we are all sisters," we should never forget that age groups are structured hierarchically and that some members of the "family" are better off than others. Moreover some "sisters" manage better than others vis-à-vis the "brothers" who hold power positions. And some "sisters" will not hesitate to manipulate "brothers" to their own ends while preventing other "sisters" from having access to knowledge, skills and financial resources. After all, who said "sisters" had to support each other? Playing on ethnic affiliation, age groups and family status, each social actor plans complex strategies to better his or her position. And in that "game" most women are fierce competitors.

Such scenarios, when placed against a background in which most of the population hardly manages to feed itself on a daily basis and in which women pay the heaviest price, seem both desperate and terribly cynical. I would argue that we cannot cope with this kind of "difference" without seeking to unravel its meaning.

I have heard Burkinabè women say that in Canada we can afford to be generous with our time to help other women (as in volunteer work in women's groups) because we are all well off. The same women did not see the relevance of organizing against family violence or providing support to rape victims. This was a luxury to them. Bread and butter were the real issues, and to be involved in a women's group meant getting an opportunity to have access to resources (financial, technical, and other). The very notion of working without material rewards to help others seemed not to make sense to them. Some work is needed for us to appreciate their ordering of the world.

In this context a straight economic approach to understanding "other" women is doomed to failure. We need tools to grasp strategies of power, cultural constructions not only of gender, but of ethnic affiliation, age group solidarity and strong hierarchical relations (Couillard 1989; Piron 1990; Piron and Ringtoumba 1991). If one enters this universe equipped with a concept like "reproduction," chances are that these women's struggles will not be identified and only those related to our own will be perceived. If we focus only on similarities and deny differences, we will not be able to follow these women in their struggles as their own agendas define them.

WOMEN'S GROUPS, FEMINISM AND
WOMEN'S POINT OF VIEW

With these two experiences in mind I decided to seek the roots of feminist theories in our own practices. I began research with women's groups in Quebec City, funded by the Social Sciences and Humanities Research Council of Canada starting in 1990. The approach is interactive, and we participate in the activities of ten groups.[9] Among these groups some qualify as radical feminist-inspired collectives, others are Christian-based volunteer groups, yet others are mixed. I purposely chose not to focus only on groups defining themselves as feminist so as to be able to appreciate the whole range of discourses and practices of women in my own society. These groups catered to women with various backgrounds, some well off, others very poor and so on. As the project is still in progress, I cannot yet discuss the conclusions. Nevertheless, my activities with the project so far allow me to put my other experiences into perspective.

The main objective of this research is to investigate power relations within women's groups. I would like to understand how women give themselves the means to realize their goals and whether or not they do reach them. This project focuses on relations between women. It studies their agendas, their resources, their linkages and their style in discourse and practice in reaching their goals. Taking this approach, I stumbled on the relation of these women to the state apparatus and discovered that within the groups, those who worked on a volunteer basis and those who are paid constitute two distinct categories, with a high potential for tension between them. On the other hand, volunteers guided by moral precepts and activitists inspired by a political agenda often work together on specific issues. Between these groups I do not perceive the unbridgeable gap I had expected (Couillard 1991).

At an abstract level I might say that all these groups aim at helping women, in various ways, to realize themselves as individuals within the parameters of modernity. Self-respect, self-esteem, autonomy and financial independence all seem to be prerequisites to the smooth functioning of our modern society. Our socio-economic system is a normalizing one in the sense that a whole panoply of leveling mechanisms (from the bureaucracy to medical practices, school systems and so on, cf. Foucault 1972, 1975, 1984) are at work to discipline social agents and force them to interiorize parameters of individuality. Idiosyncrasies in such a context are seen as threatening and they are often defined as pathologies to be cured for the good of society. Combined with this tendency to homogenize the population is an obsession with the self, the individual seen as responsible for or guilty of deviations (in opposition to collectivities defined as responsible for the well being of their members). In this context "wounded egos" have to be helped to resume normality. Such support is terribly costly for the state and not always successful. Women have needs in this domain and women's groups serve as a protected space for them to try to find both their identity as persons and the means to take care of themselves without falling prey to a system which "neutralizes" them. Hence the activists talk about the three "autonomies" that must be developed in every woman: psychological, emotional and financial. Then and only then will women be able to cope with social and individual demands in a "healthy" way, that is as responsible citizens and not as puppets in the hands of bureaucrats.

In Quebec, as in North America in general, physical and psychological violence is less and less tolerated, and women need help to resist aggression and move out of reach of aggressors. Sexual abuse, rape and incest all directly assault one's integrity, and the victims often must face such trauma alone. These women are seriously in need of support to recover self-esteem, and the family cannot play this role as it is often scattered and at times the origin of the problem itself. Simultaneously, we are confronted with the fact that medical science, in spite of its victories, has also contributed to alienate women from their bodies. Some of the groups I work with assist women who wish to regain control over their health and their reproductive functions. North American women's alienation from their bodies is not understood by many women from the developing countries who, in spite of harsh conditions, have often managed to control sufficient knowledge concerning their bodies and their health not to feel dislocated from themselves. Furthermore, in our

rich country, numerous women find themselves in difficult economic situations following divorce, serious sickness or simply
because of family origin. Support groups help these women seek
adequate training, find their ways through our bureaucracy and legislation, and regain sufficient self-confidence to search for employment.

Most of the work in these groups is carried out by volunteers
who receive minimum training when they are not specialists (social
workers, psychologists, lawyers, or nurses). Most of them deeply feel
the need to get involved and do something to help women. Even
those who are paid receive relatively low salaries when compared to
the current market value of the work they do. A few use this
involvement to familiarize themselves with the broader context and
eventually find a better job, to introduce themselves to local politics
or decision-making positions. Some make such choices out of selfish ambition, but others do it to better serve their ideal of helping
the cause of women.

The agendas of Quebec women, like those of women elsewhere,
cannot be appreciated if we do not know about the overall context.
All the far-reaching transformations Quebec society has undergone
over the last thirty years have left the population searching for its
"identity." They have left its women in need of redefining their relations to men, to other women, to the state apparatus and to science
in general. Quebec is far from the highly integrated communities of
rural Malaysia or Burkina Faso. There is a cost to modernity, and
Quebec society is as good an example as any in that domain. As elsewhere in the "postmodern" world, ruptures and not continuity
inform the construction of meaning. This creates paradoxes for
women who wish to create for themselves a protected space, cush-
ioned by sisterhood and mutual respect. The splitting of the
women's movement into cells with diverging agendas is but one of
these paradoxes. But the glorification of differences, a reaction to
the normalizing drive of the surrounding context, may lead to a
dead end if differences are not tied to wider issues, including political ones.

Hence the agenda for women in Quebec seems to reveal a preoccupation with one's integrity and confidence in a normalizing

context which tends to "disorganize" and destabilize individuals, especially women. From the point of view of activists one has to add to all these challenges a will to reach the younger women, the daughters of the "feminists," who often want to work with men rather than against them and who shy away from the label "feminist." Activists also find it problematic to include immigrant and Native women in their groups (though some cater specially to immigrant women). Coping with these kinds of differences, then, does not seem easy for Quebec activists. I would suggest it is because the agendas of the women of these different cultural backgrounds are not at all the same ...

SUMMARY

If we cannot resolve such difficulties in our own context, how then can we think of reaching out to other women, both here and abroad? I note that activists who work with women from developing countries often work with urban, educated women who have become feminists. These women often belong to the urban élite, a by-product of the expansion of international capital. As such they share in modernity to the extent that they adopt its myth of equality, the glorification of the individual, rationality and science. These urban mediators tend to blur deep-seated differences. Women are everywhere the same, they say, they all have the same problems. Do they really? More important, do they have similar resources to solve them?

Of course as we export our economic system and its accompanying "science," we also export our reading of reality and with it the centrality of gender relations. It should be clear by now that I do not believe in a universalistic model to account for these relations, though I obviously admit a prejudice in favour of "women's point of view." This does not imply that I defend a relativistic position praising differences for differences' sake. At this point, I think it is more relevant to retain the notion of "agenda," very much a pragmatic approach, but one which allows us to deal with differences.

In every context — social and historical — women have agendas which define their ideals and their struggles. Today, I do not believe that the notion of social production in a Marxist sense is sufficient to grasp the complexities of these agendas. It remains a central tool for understanding women's position in society but not for translating the specificities of gender. Nevertheless, some of women's priorities are economic, and a class analysis will help us disentangle their strategies. On the other hand, I do not believe that the notion of reproduction, with its three layers, brings us closer to understanding other women's agendas. While this concept is useful in our own context, because reproduction constitutes a central means of control of women here, it loses its analytical potency when applied to other "cultures" in an uncritical manner, since it often assumes more than it reveals. "Deconstruction" in this case, as in so many others, is useful and necessary. Deconstruction assists us in refining our tools for getting closer to understanding diverse women's realities. Rather than assume we understand, we search for meaning and for the context of its construction.[10]

Hence women as social agents are involved in power relations whose meaning has to be defined and whose origin has to be traced. Yet these power relations imply a social construction of gender, but also of class, ethnicity and age groups. With these parameters, we can account for specificities in all their complexities without falling prey to relativism.

The point of view of women, then, is that which is to be found in their "agendas." It probably includes but certainly cannot be reduced to, elements of gender, since class, ethnicity and age also inform their strategies. Point of view identifies struggles, but also ideals and victories. As an anthropologist, I should be able to translate these, I should be able to make them intelligible to others, and in so doing create a space for more tolerance in a world of ever changing differences.

NOTES

1. In this text the term "agenda" translates the French expression "enjeux" which has no English equivalent.

2. I do not wish to get into a discussion on the meaning of the expression "point of view of women" at this point (Hartsock 1987, Smith 1987). I use the terms here in a broad sense to refer to an effort to take into account the opinions, visions and struggles of women with respect for class, ethnicity and age diversity. It comes as a pragmatic counterpart to a universalizing

approach which very often takes the men's point of view to be everyone's. I will provide a clearer definition in the conclusion of the text.

3.   I am talking here as a white intellectual who wishes to understand women from different backgrounds. I am not so much concerned here with providing them with tools to understand us, though the approach used here could very well help them do so if they wish to. In this text I always refer to our agendas (white middle-class feminists' agendas) as differentiated from other women's differing agendas to be appreciated in their own terms. This opposition (ours/theirs) does not imply that I set ours as the ideal. It only specifies the point where I stand.

4.   I retain in this text the expressions "men-women relations" and "gender relations" and use them according to the theoretical premises I discuss. Here for instance, I am discussing the Marxist feminist position so I retain the expression "men-women relations" as it is closer to the Marxist representation of social agents. On the other hand, later I will use the notion of "gender relations" to stress the cultural construction of meaning associated with men and women in society. These two expressions are not theoretically equivalent and should not be confused or used interchangeably.

5.   This analysis is found, along with all the ethnographic underpinnings, in Couillard 1987.

6.   Feminists do not agree as to the relevance of Foucault for the study of gender. On this see the debates in Diamond and Quinby 1988.

7.   The Malaysian state recognizes Islam but tries to prevent the development of a radical fundamentalist movement within the country. Such a movement is seen as a threat to balanced ethnic relations and the competitive development of the Malays.

8.   A good number of women involved in international development do not share this ideal at all and use their position to satisfy their own need for power. I witnessed this in our research group and could follow the unravelling of a conflict between one of our Canadian coordinators and her Burkinabè partners who were determined not to let anyone overtake them in this domain.

9.   This is a university-based project with one full-time researcher as coordinator and four students as research assistants. Each of us has been integrated in more than one group to participate in its activities for between six and twelve months, according to schedules and group activities. Field notes are shared and experience discussed among us. During the second year, in-depth interviews were carried out with selected women to follow some avenues identified during the first year. All of us had to do volunteer work for the groups in which we were involved as part of a reciprocity process. Our observations are regularly discussed with interested women so as to allow for adjustment, and in some cases their comments have forced us to modify significantly our objectives and our research agendas. The funds were provided by grant number 410-90-0529 from the Social Sciences and

Humanities Research Council of Canada.

10.   For a discussion of this approach with regard to gender and anthropology in the context of postmodernism, refer to di Leonardo 1991.

BIBLIOGRAPHY

BARRETT, M. and A. Phillips, eds. 1992. *Destabilizing Theory: Contemporary Feminist Debates*. Stanford: Stanford University Press.

BENERIA, L., ed. 1982. *Women and Development. The Sexual Division of Labor in Rural Societies*. New York: Praeger.

———, and G. Sen. 1981. "Accumulation, Reproduction and Women's Role in Economic Development: Boserup Revisited." *Signs* 7 (2):279-98.

BRYCESON, D., and U. Vuorela. 1984. "Outside the Domestic Labour Debate: Towards a Theory of Modes of Human Reproduction." *Review of Radical Political Economics* 16 (2 & 3):137-66.

CONNELL, R.W. 1984. *Gender and Power*. Stanford: Stanford University Press.

COUILLARD, M.A. 1987. *La tendresse, le discours et le pouvoir. Les rapports hommes-femmes et les transformations sociales chez les paysans malais du nord de la péninsule malaise*. Ph.D. thesis, Université Laval.

———. 1988. "De l'autonomie relative à la dépendance: les femmes malaises et le développement." *Recherches féministes* 1(2):69-89.

———. 1989. "Le développement avec les femmes ou le pouvoir renégocié." In *A Propos de la coopération féministe et du pouvoir des femmes au Sahel*, ed. S. Champagne, F. Piron, and L. Maiga. Notes et travaux no.14, Centre Sahel, Université Laval, Québec, 10-21.

———. 1990. "The Pangs and Pitfalls of Development for Malay Women: From the Rule of the Domestic Sphere to Its Downfall." *Kajian Malaysia* 8(1):68-93.

———. 1991. "Bénévolat ou militance, simple question de terminologie? Les défis méthodologiques d'une incursion à la 'base'." Paper presented at the section Études feministes, Association canadienne française pour l'avancement des sciences (ACFAS), Université de Sherbrooke, Sherbrooke, Quebec.

DELPHY, C. 1977. *The Main Enemy*. London: Women's Research and Resource Centre.

DIAMOND, I., and L. Quinby, eds. 1988. *Feminism and Foucault: Reflections on Resistance*. Boston: Northeastern University Press.

DI LEONARDO, M. 1991. *Gender at the Crossroads of Knowledge: Feminist Anthropology in the Postmodern Era*. Berkeley: University of California Press.

EDHOLM, F., O. Harris, and K. Young. 1977. "Conceptualizing Women." *Critique of Anthropology* 3(9 & 10):101-30.

ENGELS, F. 1964 (1884). *The Origin of the Family, Private Property and the State.* New York: International Publisher.

FIRESTONE, S. 1972. *The Dialectic of Sex.* New York: Bantam.

FOUCAULT, M. 1972. *The Archeology of Knowledge.* London: Tavistock.

———. 1975. *Surveiller et punir.* Paris: Gallimard.

———. 1984. "Deux essais sur le sujet et le pouvoir." In *Michel Foucault: Un parcours philosophique,* ed. H. Dreyfus and P. Rabinow. Paris: Gallimard, 297-321.

HARTSOCK, N.C. 1987. "The Feminist Standpoint: Developing the Ground for a Specifically Feminist Historical Materialism." In *Feminism and Methodology,* ed. S. Harding. Bloomington: Indiana University Press, 157-80.

KAY, H. 1990. "Research Note: Constructing the Epistemological Gap: Gender Divisions in Social Research." *The Sociological Review* 38(2):344-51.

LEACOCK, E. 1975. "Class, Commodity, and the Status of Women." In *Women Cross Culturally: Change and Challenge,* ed. R. Rohrlich-Leavitt. La Haye: Mouton, 601-16.

———. 1981. *Myths of Male Dominance: Collected Articles on Women Cross-Culturally.* New York: Monthly Review Press.

MIES, M. 1986. *Patriarchy and Accumulation on a World Scale: Women in the International Division of Labour.* London: Zed Books.

MITCHELL, T. 1990. "Everyday Metaphors of Power." *Theory and Society* 19(5):545-77.

MOORE, H. 1988. *Feminism and Anthropology.* Cambridge: Cambridge University Press.

NICHOLSON, L.J., ed. 1990. *Feminism/Postmodernism.* New York: Routledge.

ONG, A. 1988. "Colonialism and Modernity: Feminist Representations of Women in Non-Western Societies." *Inscriptions* 3/4:125-49.

PIRON, F. 1990. *Le pouvoir des femmes au Sahel: Analyses et discussions.* Séries Notes et travaux no.17 Centre Sahel, Université Laval, Quebec.

———, and F. Ringtoumba. 1991. *Les savoirs des femmes au Sahel: Vers une valorisation des compétences locales.* Séries Dossier no. 23, Centre Sahel, Université Laval, Quebec.

SACKS, K. 1979. *Sisters and Wives.* Urbana: University of Illinois Press.

SMITH, D.E. 1987. "Women's Perspective as a Radical Critique of Sociology." In *Feminism and Methodology,* ed. S. Harding. Bloomington: Indiana University Press, 84-96.

STAMP, P. 1989. *Technology, Gender and Power in Africa.* Ottawa: International Development Research Centre.

STICHTER , S. B., and J. L. Parpart. 1988. *Patriarchy and Class: African Women in the Home and Workforce.* London: Westview Press.

STOLER, A. 1977. "Class Structure and Female Autonomy in Rural Java." In *Women and National Development: The Complexities of Change,* ed. Wellesley Editorial Committee. Chicago: The University of Chicago Press, 74-89.

CHAPTER 5

Thank You, Breasts!

BREASTFEEDING AS A FEMINIST ISSUE

Penny Van Esterik

I NFANT FEEDING DECISIONS ARE NOT ABSTRACTIONS for mothers, including many authors writing in this text who integrate the practice of mothering with the practice of anthropology.[1] Although I have not had an opportunity to speak with all the mothers whose work appears here, it is difficult to imagine that their reproductive work has had no impact on their productive work in anthropology. In other publications, I viewed the relation between women's productive and reproductive work as a scheduling problem, stressing the difficulty of integrating breastfeeding with other work commitments (Van Esterik 1990). Perhaps the experience of mothering and doing anthropology can provide models for interpreting other aspects of our own lives and others' lives.[2] Mothering has helped me understand many abstract concepts in anthropology — reciprocity, anticipatory socialization, mind-body dualisms. While preparing for this paper, one memory of mothering and anthropology kept coming back.

Part of this myth that is "me" concerns the moment when having successfully completed my doctoral exams in anthropology and defended my thesis proposal, the milk for my three month old daughter let down and ejected forcefully across the seminar table at the committee's suggestion that we adjourn the exam for a celebratory beer. Through those three tense months of preparation for the exams combined with first-time motherhood, I began to associate the ritual of going to a comfortable rocking chair and greeting my daughter after a few hours separation with the cold beer my husband always brought to me for extra liquid, relaxation and pleasure. My "breasted experience" (cf. Young 1990) mingled the pleasure and relief of breastfeeding with the joy of seeing my daughter's response and the enjoyment of a cold beer after thirsty hours in the library. My committee member's mention of a cold beer at the end of a successful examination was too much for my overworked brain to sort out, and my breasts took over, expressing relief and anticipatory pleasure, as they had been trained.

Looking back over my selective memory and use of this anecdote in my life, I wonder what concepts it has informed, what arguments it has shaped. As another woman has expressed it: "My breasts have taught me about giving" (Ayalah and Weinstock 1979:182). I think the memory was directing me to include bodily experience and maternal praxis in what otherwise might have been a review of why feminists ignore breastfeeding and the pros and cons of various feminist approaches to motherhood. Thank you, breasts.

FEMINISM, MOTHERHOOD AND BREASTFEEDING

Although breastfeeding is recognized as a women's issue, it is seldom framed as a feminist issue. In fact, it is most often ignored by feminists. This paper argues that breastfeeding is a paradigmatic feminist issue for anthropologists because it requires rethinking some basic issues in anthropological theory, such as the sexual division of labour, the fit between women's productive and reproductive lives, and the role of physiological processes in defining gender ideology.

This paper reviews what feminists have said (or left unsaid) about breastfeeding, presents breastfeeding as an issue of empowerment for women and argues for its inclusion in definitions of feminist praxis. Most of the feminists cited here are not anthropologists, although many are social scientists trained in interdisciplinary women's studies.

I have argued elsewhere that breastfeeding should be considered a feminist issue for the following reasons:

1. Breastfeeding requires structural changes in society to improve the position and condition of women.

2. Breastfeeding confirms a woman's power to control her own body, and challenges medical hegemony.

3. Breastfeeding challenges the predominant model of woman as consumer.

4. Breastfeeding challenges views of the breast as primarily a sex object.

5. Breastfeeding requires a new definition of women's work — one that more realistically integrates women's productive and reproductive activities.

6. Breastfeeding encourages solidarity and co-operation among women at the household, community, national and international level. (Van Esterik 1989:69-76)

But this brings us face to face with one of the most persistent dilemmas of contemporary feminism, the place of motherhood in feminist theory. Rothman writes: "Feminists are caught in an awkward position facing these new definitions of motherhood. The old definitions were so bad. We fought them for so long, and now the newer ones are worse. We have not yet claimed a language of our own for motherhood, a woman-centered way of looking at it" (1989:22).

In her review of Rossiter's book, *From Private to Public* (1988), Lundberg reveals her conflicting feelings toward her dual roles as feminist and mother: "We are not comfortable about feeling proud to be mothers, about giving it priority. Even non-feminists have difficulty resolving the conflicts between personhood and womanhood under capitalist patriarchy" (1989:95).

Feminism is dominated by seemingly contradictory approaches to motherhood. Some feminists ignore it; others critique the institution, finding within it the source of women's oppression; others celebrate and glorify it. Liberal feminists fought for increased opportunities for women in order for them to "catch up" with men and participate more fully in the mainstream of modern society. They are concerned with ensuring that women have full access to the benefits of industrial society, and they approach this objective primarily through the passage of new laws and regulations. Liberal feminist arguments inform policy initiatives that remove conditions discriminating against lactating mothers such as the lack of facilities for nursing couples to feed in comfort and privacy in the workplace or other public locations or inadequate paid maternity entitlements.

De Beauvoir (1961) generally devalues reproductive work and stresses how reproduction alienates women from their bodies biologically and socially. Lazaro picks up on this point of alienation, and argues that "technology provides a partial solution to female natural alienation," although it "opens unsuspected doors which are potentially — although in fact not necessarily — liberating" (1986:101). This approach to technology as liberation partially explains the feminist silence around breastfeeding and the source of the idea of bottle feeding as liberation.

Rothman explores ideology and technology in a patriarchal society in her book *Recreating Motherhood* (1989). In it, she critiques capitalist, technological approaches to pregnancy, birth, abortion, adoption and infertility from a feminist perspective. She explores midwifery and surrogate motherhood as feminist praxis, and concludes with suggestions for a feminist social policy. Although she makes anecdotal reference to breastfeeding, in fact it would have made a fine focus for her argument that capitalist technology is commodifying process into product and treating people like commodities (1989:19). Jagger carries this idea of biological reformulation even further: "This transformation might even include the capacities for insemination, for lactation and for gestation so that, for instance, one woman could inseminate another, so that men and nonparturitive women could lactate and so that fertilized ova could be transplanted into women's or even men's bodies" (1983:132).

Ursula Franklin reminds us that technology reorders and restructures relations between social groups, between nations and individuals, and between all of us and our environment (1990:13). Her elegant and essentially feminist argument contrasts holistic technology where an individual controls his or her own work from start to finish, with prescriptive technologies, where the task of doing something is broken down into clearly identifiable steps that could be carried out by separate workers. While the latter become designs for compliance, the former are tasks that cannot be easily planned, co-ordinated and controlled: "Any tasks that require imme-diate feedback and adjustment are best done holistically" (Franklin 1990:24).

Breastfeeding is a good example of a holistic growth model dependent on context and thus not entirely predictable and con-trollable. Some breastfeeding promotion programs and lactation management courses run the danger of becoming prescriptive when they provide rules and techniques from authority figures, and lose sight of the goal of empowering women to breastfeed. Bottle feed-ing is an excellent example of a prescriptive technology, where every effort is made to follow a sequence of steps under controlled condi-tions determined by others and to eliminate the need for decision-making and judgment on the part of the user. Everything appears controllable and predictable, a comforting (but utterly false) assump-tion for new mothers.

The heart of the dilemma of feminist motherhood lies in the fear of biological determinism: "The starting point of feminist inter-est in biology was, and is, a critique of biological determinism" (Birke 1986:10). Birke also argues that since feminists want to change society, biological arguments cannot serve feminist causes (Birke 1986:11). Women's biology is either ignored by feminists or assumed as given by others. But, as Lazaro points out: "A feminist analysis which wants to escape biologism must account for the fact that the data of biology are differently valued in different societies.... There is nothing inherently good or bad in the capacity to bear chil-dren; rather, society assigns a value to it and different societies assign different values" (1986:96). Others see this as a challenge to femi-nism: "The understanding that biological particularity need not be antithetical to historical agency is crucial to the transformation of feminism" (Diamond et al. 1990:xi).

This in part accounts for the ambivalence in the way feminists approach motherhood. But much harder to understand is the fact that even feminist analysis of motherhood ignores or minimizes breasts and lactation as uniquely female. As Oakley points out, feminists have been interested in breasts, but not in breastfeeding: "The natural feeding of children poses an incurable dilemma for those asserting the autonomy of women, their right to exist as full members of society. To be social means to repudiate the natural world, where life is governed by animality" (1986:86).

Lactation as a process smacks of essentialism and biological determinism. For radical feminists who locate women's oppression in their bodies and their reproductive capacities, lactation could hardly be explored as empowerment. A more gynocentric view is represented by the work of O'Brien (1981, 1989), whose arguments are also problematic. Her attempt to recover motherhood for feminism offers a deep challenge for feminists (Lazaro 1986:88). Lazaro claims that O'Brien's mishandling of biology "leads her into the view of reproduction which she criticizes, namely, one which opposes nature to history and which suggests, against her own views, that women must overcome their natural condition as childbearers in order to become feminists" (1986:94).

Although socialist feminists do not directly address breastfeeding, their approach takes a broader historical examination of institutions in class societies which oppress women. They consider the experiences of different groups of women to observe the interaction of class and gender relations in specific historical and cultural contexts and how they reinforce each other. Socialist feminists would probably place the contradiction between productive and reproductive work in the expansion of capitalist modes of production into developing countries rather than in the personal infant feeding decisions of individual mothers. Helsing locates the origin of the oppression of women in industrial capitalism which forced women to compete with men without adjustments to meet the special requirements of women (1979:72). This argument, combined with the devaluation of women's productive and reproductive work under industrial capitalism is the current direction of socialist feminist analysis.

But socialist feminists, too, "are extremely reluctant to acknowl-edge any role for biological differences in determining women's social position" (Brenner and Romas 1984:47). My argument is that the physiological process of lactation must be included in any analy-sis of the relation between production and reproduction. This is not biological determinism but common sense. The biological facts of pregnancy, birth and lactation are not readily compatible with cap-italist production unless profits are expended on maternity leaves, nursing facilities and childcare. Thus when mothers enter the work-force, they are forced to seek marginal, low paying kinds of work. "Women's skills are less 'valued' not because of an ideological deval-uation of women, but because women are less likely to be union-ized, less mobile in making job searches, more constrained in general by their domestic duties" (Brenner and Romas 1984:55).

The most recent stream of feminist theory grew out of the shared concerns of ecologists and feminists for the future of the earth and the life forms she supports. Ecofeminism reasserts metaphors of weaving, webs, and nurturance to stress the interconnectedness of systems and the biological and cultural diversity that sustains life. In such a discourse, breasts and breastfeeding are useful images for describing symbiotic relations and nurturance. Since ecofeminism grew out of radical feminism rather than liberal or socialist femi-nism (Diamond et al. 1990:5), it is supportive of breastfeeding, cel-ebrating the woman–nature connection rather than repudiating it. Ecofeminism, like gynocentric radical feminism, sees women's bod-ies as sources of spirituality and power rather than as sites of oppres-sion. In its manifestation as female spirituality and Goddess worship, ecofeminism may over-romanticize maternal principles and breast-feeding, but unlike some feminist theories, it is less likely to devalue or ignore them. Ecofeminists claim to be developing non-dualistic theories, and building bridges between nature and culture. However, in glorifying female body and nature, radical ecofeminism perpetu-ates the dualities it seeks to overthrow (Merchant 1990:102).

Another stream in ecofeminist thought may prove to be more useful for a feminist examination of breastfeeding and lactation. This stream is more compatible with socialist feminist theory and action. Women who have taken on various causes such as the breast-bottle controversy have come to see their own place in the world in a different way. Quimby writes that "struggling against specific sites of power not only weakens the juncture of power's networks, but also empowers those who do the struggling" (1990:124). Yet ecofeminists have not seriously addressed the breast-bottle controversy from an ecological perspective (cf. Radford 1991). The Brundtland Report of the World Commission on the Environment and Development, *Our Common Future* (1987), made no mention of lactation or breastfeeding. Such omissions should be unthinkable from an ecofeminist perspective. This silence on the subject is all the more surprising since ecofeminists are sensitive to the way women's bodies reflect environmental stress. Using our children as canaries to test pollution levels is a key theme in ecofeminist writing, although it is miscarriages and not mothers' milk which are usually cited: "Because of women's unique role in the biological regeneration of the species, our bodies are important markers of the sites upon which local, regional, or even planetary stress is often played out" (Diamond et al. 1990:xi).

It is in the conjunction of women's productive and reproductive lives where ecofeminist theory could be most useful for thinking through environmental hazards in the home and workplace. Here the work remains to be done. Environmentalists publicize radioactivity and dioxins in breast milk without considering the effect this knowledge will have on breastfeeding mothers. While it is true that breastmilk is a concentrator of what is in the environment of the mother, without an ecofeminist critique of the wider problem, including the existence of dioxins in water and food, the "answer" may be presented as a shift to the use of infant formula without an examination of the contamination of those products. Concerns about contamination should lead to struggles against chemical companies, not from a consideration of politically correct theory but from the practice of mothering.

While the body represents a universally available antecedent object for symbolic elaboration, in recent work on the body, certain products, people and processes are privileged over others — for example, menstrual blood and menopause over lactation and breastmilk. Feminists want to avoid privileging mothers over other women, or, we might add, breastfeeding mothers over other mothers. Menstrual blood and semen express the essential nature of male and female sexuality in many parts of the world. In research on women's health, menstruation (or PMS) and menopause are privileged over lactation, for example. Perhaps this is because women cannot easily choose not to go through the former processes, but can choose to suppress the latter. The absence of breasts in the following works is surprising. Does *The Woman in the Body* (Martin 1987) not have breasts? In Shorter's *The History of Women's Bodies,* are we to conclude that breasts have no history (cf. Oakley 1986)? Surprisingly, lactation forms no part of O'Brien's brilliant analysis, in *The Politics of Reproduction* (1981) (cf. Kahn 1989), of the moments of reproduction which belong or could belong solely to women. Mary Daly's *Gyn/Ecology* (1978), for example, does not have an index entry on breasts or breastfeeding, but focuses attention instead on breast surgery. She links breast surgery to "the breast fetishism of the entire culture" (1978:244), and attacks the excesses associated with mastectomies and cosmetic breast surgery to alter the shape of breasts. Silicone breasts receive more attention than lactating breasts.

Feminist theorists have preferred to ignore lactation and breastfeeding rather than engage the many inherent contradictions its examination entails. But the avoidance of engaging in the analysis of breastfeeding whether for theoretical or practical reasons can have serious consequences.

DANGERS OF IGNORING BREASTFEEDING

The theoretical perspectives of alternative feminist approaches render visible certain problems, while leaving others invisible and unexamined. With the lack of feminist analysis of breastfeeding, the lack of informed feminist critique of the breast-bottle controversy and the wide diversity of feminist approaches to maternity, there is a danger that feminist discourse will be co-opted on the issue, to produce so-called woman-centred views that are not in the least woman centred.

Business and government are particularly skilled at co-opting feminist arguments. The arguments that follow in the next section of this paper come from an address by Dr. Nafis Sadik, Executive Director of the United Nations Population Fund at the policy makers inter-agency Consultation on Breastfeeding in the 1990s held in Florence, July 30, 1990. They highlight the themes of personal choice, guilt, convenience and modernity. These misappropriations of feminist discourse at worst hide non-feminist or anti-feminist arguments, and at best send mixed messages that undercut breastfeeding.

Personal Choice

The theme that individual women make a "personal" decision regarding infant feeding based on what is best for them overstresses the individualism so characteristic of Western liberal feminism. This is not a concept that explains women's choices in much of the developing world. Talk of personal decisions by individuals stresses notions of women's "right to choose," again a strongly Western notion. Choice, of course, only exists when options are fully available, including information regarding possible consequences of different methods of infant feeding. Yet the "risk" of bottle feeding may be very difficult to communicate, particularly in contexts where bottle-fed infants seldom die as a direct result of feeding practices, as in Canadian cities and among the élites in developing countries.

The demands of the women's movement included the right to self-determination. But as Mies points out, the utopia of an independent, isolated, autonomous individual woman is not attractive to all women (Mies 1989:51). In the case of infant feeding decisions, women appear to be practising self-determination when they have the freedom to choose between different brands of infant formula. "For people trained to choose between packaged formulas, mother's breast appears as just one more option" (Illich 1981:67). Is this the feminist utopia envisioned by the woman's movement?

Lessening Guilt

A second theme in co-opted feminist discourse is often used against breastfeeding promotion: breastfeeding should not be promoted nor its advantages stressed lest women be made to feel guilty and to blame themselves for not breastfeeding or for breastfeeding failure:

"She should not be made to feel guilty, or less of a woman if she does not breastfeed" (Sadik 1990:3). Letting women know of the health risks involved in choosing not to initiate breastfeeding and using a particular brand of infant formula should be a normal part of informed consent. Patients are told of the risks of heart surgery in order to inform them, not to make them feel guilty for not choosing that option. Why should artificial feeding not be treated in the same way? This is not to say that overzealous or insensitive service providers or health promoters may not occasionally make women feel guilty for not breastfeeding. In fact, this will be a serious problem if women feel they are being made to breastfeed "for the sake of the baby." A brief response is that a feminist task should be to turn that guilt into anger — anger at the lack of information to make fully informed choices, at the lack of support and lactation management skills in training health professionals, at patriarchal institutions such as work environments and patriarchal families, that make it difficult to exercise one's choice.

Convenience

In our awareness of women's double and triple burden, arguments that present breastfeeding as yet another burden or obligation women must bear are often presented as "pro-woman." Thus, artificial feeding is supposed to lighten women's burden, not add to it. Spurious appeals to women and co-opted feminist arguments make reference neither to the burdens of purchasing and preparing breast-milk substitutes nor to the burden of a sick or dying infant. The arguments about convenience pick up on the language of "scientific motherhood" common at the turn of the century — breastfeeding as moral obligation, a burden mothers must endure. Advancements in technology are presented as if they relieve women of time-consuming duties. A higher priority on many feminist agendas is co-parenting and the need for more male involvement in the nurturing process. One task for both practitioners who wish to support breastfeeding women and feminists who should take up the task of a feminist analysis of breastfeeding is to show how, by increasing the interdependence between parents, breastfeeding supports rather than breaks down co-parenting strategies.

Escaping Traditional Roles

While direct consumer advertising for infant formula used to contrast "traditional" breastfeeding with "modern" bottle feeding, such
tactics are rare today, thanks in part to the WHO/UNICEF Code for
the Marketing of Breastmilk Substitutes. To discuss breastfeeding as
a chain tying women to a traditional role, as Sadik does, reveals both
a lack of understanding of the context of infant feeding choices in
developing countries and insupportable biases about breastfeeding
as a "traditional" act. Yet more subtle messages continue to reinforce
an inappropriate association between bottle feeding and modernity,
as if it is more modern for women to desire to escape the responsibilities of child nurturance. Not all women want to be freed from
those responsibilities, particularly in countries where children are a
source of women's power and status in the community.

WHY ARE THERE NO BLACK LACE NURSING BRAS?

Over fifteen years ago, Kelly argued that "feminist social thought is
just beginning to overcome the dualisms it inherited to account sat-
isfactorily for sex, class, and race oppositions within a unified social
theory" (1979:224). Although feminist discourse has remained sensitive to these dualisms, it has also operated within them to a considerable extent.

Theoretically, breastfeeding requires negotiating a number of
socially constructed dualisms that have dominated Western thinking. These discursive categories that have shaped and continue to
shape the way we experience and understand the world include
oppositions such as:

> production *vs* reproduction
> public *vs* private
> nature *vs* culture
> mind *vs* body
> work *vs* leisure
> self *vs* other
> maternal *vs* sexual

These dualisms are embedded in Western discourse, and are both ethnocentric and pervasive across the social sciences. Each opposition

deserves an essay to explore the implications for anthropology and feminism. Breastfeeding in theory and practice bridges many of these oppositions and dissolves others. For example, Marxist analysis forced the production-reproduction split and privileged production over consumption. Marxist feminists still struggle with the production (public), reproduction (private) split. But Mies argues that women's bodies were the first means of production — of children and food. Women consciously appropriated their own bodily nature to give birth and produce milk, forming not only units of consumption, but of production as well (Mies 1986:54). The production–reproduction opposition parallels the division between the public and private or domestic spheres. What is consigned to the private sphere should be done in private. But in what sense is breastfeeding a private act? Public-private oppositions underlie controversies surrounding breastfeeding in public, often leading to analogies between breastfeeding and excretion. Gaskin writes, "It is strange indeed that countries which so pride themselves on their fastidiousness should make social rules which often force their most vulnerable members to eat in places designed for the excretory needs of the other members of society" (1987:20).

Breastfeeding is solidly body based. It is therefore consigned to the nature half of the nature-culture divide — an example of the immanence of women as opposed to the transcendence of men, in de Beauvoir's terms. It is critically important that we find a way to support breastfeeding women without reducing them to their breasts. But breastfeeding as a process is strongly affected by emotional and cognitive states, and thus is very vulnerable to social context. As a total social fact, breastfeeding is also the first means of enculturating and transforming a human life.

Even the work/leisure opposition breaks down when applied to breastfeeding as it does for much of the work of mothering — work that is always a burden and a pleasure at the same time (Mies 1986:216-18). I have argued that lactation should be redefined as productive work (Van Esterik 1990:48); but there is still ambiguity regarding its relation to leisure. In many work contexts, breastfeeding is either accomplished while doing other things (joint production), or is a truly pleasant and restful respite from other tasks.

Because of its potentially sensual nature, breastfeeding is qualitatively different from child care which is often calculated by economists as a leisure activity.

Finally, the subject/object opposition cannot be usefully applied to intersubjective activities such as breastfeeding (cf. Benhabib and Cornell 1987:2). The experience of breastfeeding blurs body boundaries, as women experience continuity with their infants. It is this continuity — this experience of other-as-self — that makes breastfeeding a powerful transforming experience for some women, a terrifying loss of personal autonomy for others — or both at the same time.

If feminist theorists took up breastfeeding as an issue as Kahn (1989) suggests, they might well be able to use it to reformulate a nondualistic feminist problematic that would draw together a wide range of theories and practices that go beyond breastfeeding and mothering. These include practices related to care and nurturance in particular.

The answer to the intriguing question posed by the title of this section is partially answered by Young who writes that "breasts are a scandal for patriarchy because they disrupt the border between motherhood and sexuality" (1990:190). Women who breastfeed toddlers or who admit to experiencing sensual pleasure while breastfeeding may even find themselves accused of sexual abuse. This horrifying experience happened to a mother in New York State who had her daughter taken from her and was jailed for sexual abuse ("mouth to breast contact") (Davidowitz:1992). The male gaze has forced women to deny any sexual pleasure associated with breastfeeding because one cannot be maternal (madonna) and sexual (whore) at the same time. In this discourse, women cannot be nurturer and seducer simultaneously; one precludes the other. Thus in Western society the sensual pleasure of breastfeeding has been repressed, leaving breastfeeding as simply a part of "this tamed, pleasureless, domesticated world of maternal duties" (Sichtermann 1986:57).

Ayalah and Weinstock produced a unique assemblage of photographs and stories in a popular work entitled *Breasts: Women Speak about their Breasts and their Lives* (1979). The subjects were American women of different ages and origins speaking informally about their breasts and how they influenced their lives. Women included in their breast histories a discussion of breastfeeding or their decision not to breastfeed. Women who breastfed occasionally mentioned pleasure and sensuality. These women spoke of "total orgasm, the highest moment of satisfaction," "a spiritual experience," "very sensual ... even erotic," "a fantastic high," "It's sensual, even sexual, but not in the regular way one thinks of sex; It's like a different department in my mind" (1979:165-66). The last quote reveals the compartmentalization of Western thought and experience that encourages women to deny any highly charged sexual feelings associated with breastfeeding. The denial of sensual feelings, or even of the pleasure of relaxed intimacy enhanced by the hormones prolactin and oxytocin, is a patriarchal distortion of the maternal body. Kahn writes, "When we advocate androgyny, women atone for entering male gendered time and space by making impermissible the riches of the maternal body" (1989:35). It is the responsibility of feminist anthropologists of the future to reclaim that maternal body, "to muck about in the ambiguities of the lived body" (Young 1990:14), and demonstrate the unity of theory and practice that would emerge from defining breastfeeding praxis.

NOTES

1. This paper does not address the breast = bottle controversy per se. I have explored the controversy in another book (Van Esterik 1989). However, my biases here are obvious. As a breastfeeding advocate and an anthropologist, I am constantly challenged to consider the the cultural context of infant feeding decisons, the dangers of Western authorities' prescribing breastfeeding, and the importance of transnational processes. These issues, however, are not explored in this paper.

2. My work has benefitted enormously from research assistance and numerous conversations with Kathy M'Closkey, Ph.D. candidate in Anthropology at York University, Toronto.

BIBLIOGRAPHY

AYALAH, D., and Weinstock, I. 1979. *Breasts: Women Speak about their Breasts and their Lives.* New York: Summit Books.

BENHABIB, Seyla, and Drucilla Cornell. 1987. *Feminism as Critique. On the Politics of Gender.* Minneapolis: University of Minnesota Press.

BIRKE, L. 1986. *Women, Feminism and Biology.* Brighton: Wheatsheaf.

BRENNER, J., and M. Romas. 1984. "Rethinking Women's Oppression." *New Left Review* 144:33-71.

BRUNDTLAND Report. 1987. *Our Common Future.* World Commission on Environment and Development.

DALY, Mary. 1978. *Gyn/Ecology: the Metaethics of Radical Feminism.* Boston: Beacon.

DAVIDOWITZ, Esther. 1992. "Breastfeeding Taboo." *Redbook.* July:92-95.

DE BEAUVOIR, Simone. 1961. *The Second Sex.* New York: Bantam.

DIAMOND, Irene, et al., eds. 1990. *Reweaving the World.* San Francisco: Sierra Club.

FRANKLIN, Ursula. 1990. *The Real World of Technology.* Montreal: CBC Enterprises.

GASKIN, I. M. 1987. *Babies, Breastfeeding, and Bonding.* South Hadley, MA: Bergin & Garvey.

HELSING, E. 1979. "Women's Liberation and Breastfeeding." In *Lactation, Fertility and the Working Woman,* ed. D.B. Jelliffe et al. London: International Planned Parenthood Federation.

ILLICH, Ivan. 1981. *Shadow Work.* Boston: M Boyars.

JAGGAR, Alison. 1983. *Feminist Politics and Human Nature.* Totowa, NJ: Rowman and Allanheld.

KAHN, Robbie Pfeuffer. 1989. "Mother's Milk: the 'Moment of Nurture' Revisited." *Resources for Feminist Research* 18(3):29-35.

KELLY, J. 1979. "The Doubled Vision of Feminist Theory: A Postscript to the 'Women and Power' Conference." *Feminist Studies* 5(1):216-27.

LAZARO, Reyes. 1986. "Feminism and Motherhood: O'Brien vs Beauvoir." *Hypatia* 1(2):87-102.

LUNDBERG, Norma. 1989. "A Feminist Exploration of Early Mothering." Review of Amy Rossiter's *From Private to Public. Resources for Feminist Research* 18(3):95-96.

MARTIN, E. 1987. *The Woman in the Body.* Boston: Beacon Press.

MERCHANT, Carolyn. 1990. "Ecofeminism and Feminist Theory." In *Reweaving the World: The Emergence of Ecofeminism,* ed. I. Diamond and G. Orenstein. San Francisco: Sierra Club, 100-05.

MIES, Maria. 1986. *Patriarchy and Accumulation on a World Scale.* London: Zed Press.

———. 1989. "Self-determination: The End of a Utopia?" *Resources for Feminist Research* 18(3):41-51.

OAKLEY, Ann. 1986. *Telling the Truth About Jerusalem.* Oxford: Blackwell.

O'BRIEN, Mary. 1981. *The Politics of Reproduction.* Boston: Routledge.

————. 1989. *Reproducing the World.* Boulder, CO: Westview Press.

QUIMBY, Lee. 1990. "Ecofeminism and the Politics of Resistance." In *Reweaving the World: the Emergence of Ecofeminism,* ed. Irene Diamond and G. F. Orenstein. San Francisco: Sierra Club, 122-27.

RADFORD, Andrew. 1991. *The Ecological Impact of Bottle Feeding.* Cambridge: Baby Milk Action Coalition.

ROTHMAN, B. 1989. *Recreating Motherhood: Ideology and Technology in a Patriarchal Society.* New York: Norton.

SADIK, N. 1990. "Statement" at the Interagency Consultation on Breastfeeding in the 1990s. July 30, 1990. Florence, Italy.

SAMUALS, S. E. 1982. *Socio-cultural Obstacles to Breastfeeding in an American Community.* Ph.D. thesis, University of California, Berkeley.

SICHTERMANN, Barbara. 1986. *Femininity, the Politics of the Personal.* Minneapolis: University of Minnesota Press.

VAN ESTERIK, Penny. 1989. *Beyond the Breast-Bottle Controversey.* New Brunswick, NJ: Rutgers University Press.

————. 1990. "Women, Work and Breastfeeding." Background paper for UNICEF. Institute for Social Research, York University, Toronto.

YOUNG, I. 1990. *Throwing Like a Girl and Other Essays in Feminist Philosophy and Social Theory.* Bloomington: Indiana University Press.

PART II

Explorations of Gendered Work

R ESEARCH ON GENDER AND WORK HAS BEEN one of the strongest contributions of feminist scholarship to anthropology (Benería and Roldán 1987; Fernandez-Kelly 1983; Leacock and Safa 1986; Stoler 1985). The contributors here share a common heritage in the theoretical contributions of Marxist and socialist feminist orientations to the understanding of women, work and development (Barrett 1980; Mies 1986). Challenged by the current theoretical concern to understand the fragmented sub-jectivities which are intrinsic to contemporary social relations (Ulin 1991), these essays move in new directions by considering women's lives as they are grounded in the contradictory conditions of labour-ing in Western society.

As Luxton (1980) noted more than a decade ago, both the invisibility of women's work and the complexity of women's politics are part of the hegemony of capitalism. Building on this contribu-tion, the authors in this section emphasize the need to dissect taken-for-granted analytical categories, recognizing the necessity of delineating the politics of the social construction of gender. The essays show both how women's everyday praxis is shaped and con-strained by a world structured by capitalism and how women's lives and labours vary under diverse and historically specific circum-stances. By exploring the links between different kinds of produc-tion relations and women's abilities to contest the constraints of those relations these authors are specifically concerned to work out and through the nexus of politics and work.

Kathy M'Closkey's essay on Navajo women weavers highlights the disparity between the merchants' view of women's weaving as a generic commodity and Navajo women's view of their weaving as life work. In this essay we see how Western views of "art" versus "craft," patriarchal notions of women's "place" and the development of mercantilism with North American aboriginal peoples intersect to disadvantage Navajo women. M'Closkey raises the question of why it is that anthropologists have remained silent on this issue, despite their awareness that traders were purchasing Navajo women's intricate woven designs "by the pound." This haunting question points to the need to conceptualize the practice of feminist anthropology in terms relevant to and useful for those who experi-ence the double oppression of racism and sexism in our society today and the legacy of colonialism.

Max Hedley's essay delineates the role of women's labour in fishing, farming and trapping households in rural Canada. Where the literature has tended to emphasize the economic consequences of the involvement of these domestic commodity-producing house-holds in a global capitalist economy, Hedley's concern is with the activities that fall outside the commercial realm, in particular the work of women. In contrast to "real" work, women's labours have been largely ignored because they have been primarily viewed as noncommercial. He uses the autobiographical text of a Labrador woman, Elizabeth Goudie, to bring to light the many activities of women which, although seldom discussed, are basic to the creation and reproduction of the way of life of rural households.

In case studies of industrial homeworkers in southern Ontario, Belinda Leach examines social and ideological constructions about what work is and what it is not. The study of industrial work has tended to privilege certain kinds of labour, in particular male blue-collar factory work, rendering other kinds of work invisible. The separation of home and work has also been assumed in these studies. De-centring concepts of "work" and "family," Leach examines how they developed historically and how they are used to organize the worlds of homeworkers for whom home and work come together. She explores how the relations of production in homework are organized to permit a tension-ridden convergence of the two spheres.

Pat Baker's discussion focuses on the origins and nature of women wage workers' empowerment. Considering the question of why Canadian bank workers historically have had difficulty organizing, Baker's starting point is the narratives of Canadian women bankworkers themselves. The politicization of women bank workers is found to be both constrained and supported by their relations of community and family, thereby revealing the specificity of the potential for women's empowerment — both inside and outside the workplace.

BIBLIOGRAPHY

BARRETT, Michele. 1980. *Women's Oppression Today.* London: Verso.

BERNERÍA, Lourdes, and Marta Roldán. 1987. *The Crossroads of Class and Gender.* Chicago and London: University of Chicago Press.

FERNANDEZ-KELLY, Maria Patricia. 1983. *For We are Sold, I and My People: Women and Industry in Mexico's Frontier.* Albany: SUNY Press.

LEACOCK, Eleanor, and Helen Safa, eds. 1986. *Women's Work.* South Hadley, MA: Bergin & Garvey.

LUXTON, Meg. 1980. *More Than a Labour of Love.* Toronto: Women's Press.

MIES, Maria. 1986. *Patriarchy and Accumulation on a World Scale: Women in the International Division of Labour.* London: Zed Press.

STOLER, Ann. 1985. *Capitalism and Confrontation in Sumatra's Plantation Belt, 1870-1979.* New Haven: Yale University Press.

ULIN, Robert. 1991. "Critical Anthropology Twenty Years Later: Modernism and Postmodernism in Anthropology." *Critique of Anthropology,* 11(1):63-89.

CHAPTER 6

"Trading is a White Man's Game"

THE POLITICS
OF APPROPRIATION:
THE LESSONS FROM NAVAJO
WOMEN'S WEAVING

Kathy M'Closkey

T HIS PAPER EXPLORES THE IDEA THAT THE WESTERN distinction between art and craft legitimized the global devaluation of textiles woven by indigenous people. It focuses on the textiles created by Navajo[1] women, which were the most valuable trade items in the Southwest United States prior to the formation of the reservation in 1868 (Dockstader 1978:99). As pastoralists, Navajo women continued to own the means of production, but they lost control of the marketing of their textiles. Autobiographical evidence of this devaluation is poignantly expressed in the following translation from Navajo weaver Nancy Woodman (1980:np):

I learned to weave when I was 13 years old, and weaving became my trade. When I learned it, I gained my independence. I got so I could support myself by my work and I kept it up. I made fairly good rugs,

and still do ... I've made a great many rugs. I just take them to the
trading post, where I have always just taken them out in trade.
I get food for my rugs ... it is now 49 years since I learned to weave ...
and back there in the days of my innocence I merely took them to the
trader accepting whatever he offered for them ...

There is not a trader here amongst us who pays cash. I ask for even
so little as a nickel in cash, but they won't give it to me.... As I now give
thought to this matter, I wonder why this is true ... why is it? Could
there be some law which makes it that way? Maybe there's a regulation ...
it's for this reason that even when I take a little rug to the trader I feel
sort of unhappy at letting it go. I put a great deal of effort into my rugs,
and it is this fact which causes me to be a bit unhappy at letting them go
to the traders hereabout.

Merchant capital articulated with patriarchy and the art/craft
distinction to distort the economic contributions of Navajo weavers.
Under the ethnocentric guise of Western aesthetics, artistic imperialism overshadowed the silent and unrecognized transformation
that took place when Native production was appropriated by colonial merchants. The Western distinction between art and craft
served to legitimize the devaluation of indigenous creations that
accompanied their commodification. Many textiles woven by
indigenous people centuries ago are today viewed as "art" and avidly
purchased by dealers, artists and collectors (Berlant and Kahlenberg
1977; Witherspoon 1977:174). Yet when these articles were produced after the initial period of commoditization (circa 1870), they
were treated as renewable resources and sold by the pound (Dockstader
1978:472; Hubbell Papers [ledger books]). The articulation of several critical dichotomies: art/craft, public/private, civilized/savage
and masculine/feminine served the interests of the traders. Ironically,
they are depicted in the literature as "saving" Navajo weaving. This
paper is an attempt to untangle the threads that have rendered this
tale invisible.

HISTORICAL CONTEXT OF NAVAJO WEAVING

The Navajo are the largest indigenous group in North America, and currently occupy an eighteen-million-acre reservation in the southwest United States. More than 160 thousand Navajo share a geographically diverse but agriculturally poor area. Overgrazing remains a serious and chronic problem because of increasing population growth of both the Navajo and their flocks. Recent extraction of coal and uranium has augmented tribal coffers, but the Navajo remain impoverished. Per capita income has remained at 20 percent of the national average for decades (Weiss 1984).

Archaeologists date Navajo arrival in the region between 1000-1500 A.D. (Vogt 1961:288). Prior to the appearance of the Spanish in the sixteenth century, the Navajo were nomadic hunter/gatherers who eventually borrowed a number of farming techniques and religious ceremonies from their sedentary Pueblo neighbours. The Navajo acquired livestock (especially sheep) from the Spaniards. Fields and herds became closely identified with women (Underhill 1956:156). Grazing land became an integral part of family property. Children received lambs from birth.

The flexibility of Navajo social organization is remarked upon in a wide variety of literature. Ownership and control of animals has not changed, although external environmental factors (drought, floods and frosts) and political policies affecting access to land have altered subsistence patterns for many Navajo. Kin relations in Navajo society favour female autonomy (Aberle 1962; Witherspoon 1975; Lamphere 1977). Navajo society is matrilineal and matrilocal, although residence patterns have shifted to more diverse patterns in recent history. Even in the most recent studies such as those by Witherspoon (1975) and Lamphere (1977), matrilocality continues to predominate, especially in the more remote parts of the reservation. As long as a woman has living kin organized into an "extended outfit," she is assured access to cleared land, even if she never married, was divorced or widowed. Her flock of sheep are hers from birth.

Archaeologists have determined that Navajo women learned weaving during the seventeenth century, probably during the

Figure 1

"Pound" Blanket, woven circa 1905

Pueblo Revolt when Spanish reprisals drove many Pueblo peoples westward to Navajo country. Eighteenth century Spanish documents note that the Navajo wove with more delicacy and taste than their neighbours, and that their textiles became highly desired by Spaniards, Mexicans and many other Indian tribes (Amsden 1975:133). By the early nineteenth century, the products of the Navajo loom were the single most valuable trade item produced in the Southwest (Dockstader 1978:99).

Many anthropologists and interested observers writing about Navajo life have noted how weaving was integrated into Navajo daily life (Amsden 1975; Berlant and Kahlenberg 1977; Reichard 1934, 1936, 1939; Underhill 1956; Witherspoon 1977). Until school attendance became compulsory, most Navajo girls learned to weave from a female relative, although some weavers were self-taught. Most Navajo men are thoroughly familiar with nearly all stages of the production process and often perform tasks such as sheep shearing, collection of dye plants, loom construction and related tool-making activities (Reichard 1939, Hedlund 1989). Navajo women own the means of production, for they cull the best wool from their animals before the wool clip is taken to the trading post. The preparation of the wool, which includes shearing, carding (brushing out the wool fibres), washing and/or dyeing and ultimately the spinning, may take more time than the actual weaving process. Although a weaver may receive help from relatives at various stages of the preparation process, she will usually weave the textile herself. Navajo weavers currently have access to pre-spun or dyed yarn for warp and weft, but many weavers continue to spin wool from their own animals (figure 1).

When the United States assumed control of the area in 1846, government officials and Anglo ranchers perceived the Navajo as "the most aggressive raiders" in the Southwest. To halt raiding and open the area to colonization, the government dispatched Colonel Kit Carson in 1864 to kill all Navajo men resisting arrest, round up women and children, and destroy peach orchards and cornfields. Eight thousand Navajo were eventually driven four hundred miles into eastern New Mexico and incarcerated at Bosque Redondo. Floods, insect infestation, hail and drought thwarted attempts to turn them into plow farmers. After four years of misery and promises to refrain from raiding, the government allowed the six thousand survivors to return to their beloved Canyon Country. The Department of the Interior created a 3.5 million-acre reservation for them, far less land than they had occupied previously (Vogt 1961:315). Federal authorities issued livestock and household goods, including aniline dyed Germantown yarns, to encourage weaving.

The first traders with the Navajo had been sutlers, frontier individuals who supplied the army with food and clothing. When Navajo flocks began to increase after Bosque Redondo, some sutlers bought the excess Navajo wool. Indian agents encouraged this, and by 1889 there were fifteen posts on the reservation and thirty posts surrounding it, which were outside government control (Weiss 1984:50). Patronage and politics often determined who received a trading licence. Competition for licences, obtained from the Commissioner of Indian Affairs for an annual fee, was spurred by the knowledge of recent fortunes made by western entrepreneurs.

During their incarceration at Bosque Redondo, the Navajo had acquired a taste for government-issued rations. Bartering for staples with blankets and wool became the basis for the symbiotic relationship between Navajo and traders that continues in remote portions of the reservation even today. Yet the trader occupies an ambivalent place in Navajo history. Numerous authors (Adams 1963; Reichard 1936; Underhill 1956; Utley 1961) see him as an individual who aided the Navajos' transition into the modern world. Others (Lamphere 1976; Ruffing 1978; Weiss 1984) picture him as often unscrupulous and profit oriented. Some traders befriended the Navajo acting as interpreter, doctor, lawyer, banker and sometimes mortician (Underhill 1956). But many were unscrupulous and casually justified a number of inimical trading practices. Navajo killed more than twenty traders between 1901 and 1934 (McNitt 1962:322). Underhill (1956:184) refers to the trader as "the Navajos' Shogun": "He had the touchstone of friendly personal contact which opened the hearts of the Navajos. While the government was striving to civilize the Navajos by issuing orders that they should cut their hair and cease their heathen dances, and while the missionary was trying to convince them of their errors, the trader simply laid before them the possibilities of a new life."

Underhill noted that trading was doubly profitable because of the mark-up on staples sold to the Indians and the handsome profit gained selling Navajo products. Probably the most famous trader associated with the Navajo was Lorenzo Hubbell, who over a fifty-year period owned or held interest in more than thirty businesses on the Navajo reservation. To Hubbell the trader was "everything from merchant to father confessor, justice of the peace, judge, jury, court of appeals, chief medicine man and de facto czar of the domain over which he presides" (Underhill 1956:184).

Hubbell and a few of his contemporaries played a pivotal role in Navajo weaving history. They succeeded in destroying the blanket weaving (except for saddle blankets) by bartering cloth which the Navajo quickly adopted, in addition to importing the well-known Pendleton blanket, which replaced the native product. They sold string which weavers began to use as warp instead of their own laboriously spun wool warp, and garish aniline dyes. A number of traders initially encouraged Navajo women to weave "fast and loose" in their haste to establish a viable market in the east. By 1890 borders began to appear in designs and the Navajo blanket became a rug, sold to tourists or shipped to eastern cities. The arrival of the railroad in 1882 facilitated the removal of Navajo weaving in larger quantities from the reservation. Within twenty years of the traders' appearance, the Navajo had ceased weaving for intertribal trade and no longer wove bed coverings, body shawls, doorway closures or blankets for themselves. Instead, nearly all loom products left the reservation as rugs (figure 2). Only saddle blankets and belts continued to be used by the Navajo. In 1902 (McNitt 1962:210), Hubbell retailed rugs from 50 cents to $2.50 per pound. Prior to their commoditization, textiles averaging sixty to eighty weft threads per inch were common; afterward, weft count decreased ten-fold and weavers were paid strictly by the pound and averaged the equivalent of three cents an hour for their labour. By 1920 Navajo weaving had reached its lowest level of quality (Dockstader 1978:101). There was no cash remuneration; traders utilized the credit system, advancing groceries to weavers until the spring wool clip or fall lamb. Textiles were bartered all year. Many traders issued tokens with the name of the post stamped on the back, which were redeemable only at their store(s).

Figure 2

Navajo Rug, woven circa 1975

There is no question that wool and rug production were seen as the backbone of the traders' businesses (Hubbell Papers; McNitt 1962; Underhill 1956). Traders sought to monopolize weavers' production and all other products such as wool, hides and piñon nuts. A few traders, including Hubbell (1902), published pamphlets illustrating handmade items for sale. The largest pamphlet was published around 1911 by J. B. Moore, who traded at Crystal, New Mexico. Moore (1987) writes in the Foreword:

In the beginning I had stubborn and conservative workers in these Navajo women, and a discredited product to contend with ... resistance, stubborn, hurtful, and senseless opposition on the part of the weavers has given place to cheerful co-operation, good natured rivalry and friendly strife for excellence in their work.... I saw in their dormant skills and patience a business opportunity provided they could be aroused, encouraged and led on to do their best; and a market for their product could be established.

Both Moore and Hubbell pushed for quantity and quality despite the fact that such goods were paid for by the pound. Moore was the only trader who actually organized a workshop and had thirteen weavers weaving for him. The vast number of rugs were woven by women in their homes, miles away from any workshop or trading post, and taken to the post and bartered for groceries.

One of the most remarkable relationships in Navajo trading history involved Lorenzo Hubbell and Fred Harvey, Sr., founder of the famous "Harvey Houses." Harvey founded the company in 1876 to manage the eating houses and later the dining cars for the Santa Fe Railway. Eventually over seventy hotels dotted the landscape from Chicago, St. Louis, westward through Kansas to San Francisco, Los Angeles, Arizona and New Mexico. Henderson (1969:33) notes that "Harvey helped to populate and civilize the West." Hubbell was Harvey's major rug supplier from 1907 to 1920 (B. Harvey 1963:37). Tourists travelling by railroad were treated to a visual ethnographic feast since baskets, pottery, rugs and jewellery adorned the walls, floors, tables and display cases of the impressive "Indian Rooms" located in many of the hotels. To augment the attraction Herman Schweizer, Harvey Company manager, arranged for Hubbell to send him "reliable" Indians who would weave and make jewellery at the railroad stations and the larger hotels located in resort areas and national parks.[2] The Harvey family eventually acquired over 4,000 choice Indian artifacts currently valued at over $1 million as part of their personal collection. Major museums in the United States owe the nucleus of their ethnographic collections from the Southwest to buyers for the Harvey family.[3] By 1930 Harvey was serving fifteen million meals per year on the trains, and by 1965 Harvey Houses were the sixth largest restaurant retailer in the United States (Henderson 1969:37).

The most powerful indictment of Navajo/trader relations remains William Adams's detailed study (1963), titled *Shonto: A Study of the Role of the Trader in a Modern Navajo Community.* Adams's field investigations for his doctoral research in anthropology took place in 1955 at Shonto, a post located in a remote area of the reservation. The regular clientele consisted of about 100 Navajo families. Fifty percent of the adults could not speak English, and fewer than 10 percent could read or write. Shonto was located 132 miles from the nearest town and seventy-five miles from paved roads. Because the owner/trader lived in town, he hired Adams to work full-time at the post. Adams (1963:24) admits to engaging in: "credit saturation, delaying checks, tampering with the mail, misrepresenting the outside world, and all other devious devices by which the trader maintains his position in the community ... if I had not done these things I would not have been a trader — and this study could never have been made."

Adams (1963:182) admits that people from outside the Shonto area paid less for groceries when they bought for cash; credit was advanced against all predictable earnings by the Indians in order to profit from "credit saturation." The trader at Shonto was budget director and financial manager for the whole region since he was fully informed about the financial situation of all Navajo families who traded at his post (thanks to social workers and his position as "agent" for hiring railroad workers). Because of credit saturation, no more than 1 percent of all welfare income was returned to the Navajo as cash in any one year (1963:137).

As welfare and social security checks increased after World War II, weaving decreased dramatically in importance as a trade item.

Adams (1963:154) and McNitt (1962) note that by 1910 large accounts were built up against rugs (thus assuring the traders of a continual supply). By 1955 no credit was allowed against rugs at Shonto, as they were considered to be an "unavoidable nuisance." Because of fluctuating wool prices on the international market, amounts paid for Navajo wool constantly varied. The Navajo received 80 cents per pound for their wool in 1950, and 25 cents per pound in 1956. During that decade Shonto weavers averaged 4 cents an hour for their labour (Adams 1963:121).

Thus weaving (along with wool production) has declined from its position as the backbone of the native economy until after World War I to a peripheral income source or intermittent "windfall" for the weavers. This contrasts with the memoirs of an earlier Shonto trader which indicate that there were tens of thousands of pounds of Navajo rugs in Hubbell's warehouse at Third Mesa in New Oraibi during the 1920s (Hegemann 1963:127).

Adams (1963:211) notes that in 1955 he took clean fleece on credit at 25 cents per pound, single saddle blankets traded for $4.00 worth of groceries, double saddle blankets for $8.00, and rugs brought in around $14.00. The following quote describes typical trader behaviour when bartering for a rug: "Look it over in silence for a minute or more, without touching it ... or measuring it. The trader can then come out in a firm voice with the first figure that enters his head and stick resolutely to it. The trader who examines a proferred rug closely weakens the authority of his judgement since he is supposed to be able to spot ... defects at a glance ... trading is a white man's game" (200, 211).

Although Adams's monograph on Shonto was published in 1963, and the government had received numerous complaints from reservation residents for decades, the Federal Trade Commission failed to investigate abuses until 1971. Then the National Federation of Independent Businessmen came to the defense of the traders, saying that they operated in the "American Way" (*Akwasasne Notes* 1972:5).

Spicer (1962:224) states that per-family income gradually declined from 1900 to 1930. Welfare and government work projects began during the Depression. Trade was geared to what the Navajo were producing, so they became more integrated into the general American economy than any other Indian group. Most traders admitted that their greatest profit lay in the annual wool clip. Amsden (1975:236) notes that for a while raw wool prices were higher during World War I than rug prices per pound during the Depression. When wool prices were down, women increased rug production in a vain attempt to augment their financial return. Adams (1963:295) admits that

Expansion of the Navajo economy under the aegis of the trader has produced neither capital nor wealth, but simply a much higher level of material consumption. The economy of Shonto community today remains essentially a vast redistribution system in which the trader is the direct or indirect source and also the ultimate recipient of all of the financial benefits derived from contact with the White world ... and works to further its own purpose of maximum sustained profit.

This profit-making activity had the most devastating impact on Navajo women who wove. In a more recent article, Adams (1968: 148) maintains that traders had "managed the process of economic change so that it did not, as among many other tribal peoples, have disastrous repercussions in other areas of life." Given the above discussion, this is certainly a debatable statement in relation to weaving.

NAVAJO WOMEN AND THE APPROPRIATION OF THEIR WEAVING

For nearly a century, traders sold goods by the pound to the Navajo: machine-made cloth, potatoes and flour, sugar and coffee. Everything the Indians pastured, hunted or grew was bartered by the pound to the traders: piñon nuts, wool, sheep, pelts, corn and textiles. Weavers' abilities, the quality of their work, their industriousness, all were remarked upon by traders, dealers, missionaries, Indian agents and educators. It is evident from the available documents and texts that Navajo women were not purchasing or trading trinkets for their textiles. They had their own wool and weaving accounts with the traders. A check of ledger books and other documentation provided in anthropological and ethnohistorical literature underscores that their production was a necessity for the economic well-being of their families. Yet for decades they averaged less than five cents an hour for their weaving while living in the richest country in the world. How could this kind of exploitation remain unchallenged for so long?

Unlike the 100 thousand lacemakers of Narsapur described by Mies (1982), who are "invisible" because they are part of a vast network of women in purdah labouring under the putting out system, the production of Navajo weavers was visible and incorporated in annual government reports and traders' records. Men like Harvey and Hubbell responsible for "civilizing" the Southwest used these women at trading posts, national parks and hotels to attract tourists (Babcock 1990:404). Navajo women wove "in the public eye" for over a century, indeed they were used as a major drawing card to attract business. Their abilities were acknowledged at Indian fairs and museums. They were studied by a pantheon of anthropologists including women anthropologists Gladys Reichard (1934, 1936, 1939), and Ruth Underhill (1956).[4] The Navajo are reputed to be the most studied aboriginal group in the world (White 1983:281). An old joke states that many Navajo hogans (their mud and log homes) had an extra room added on for the "visiting anthropologist." Yet there is silence in the literature about the marketing of their weaving by the pound for more than sixty years.

Marxist scholar Weiss (1984:154) comments that rug weaving gave such low returns to the weavers because merchant capital skimmed everything off the top that "it wasn't worth it to the potential [merchant capital] investors to set up workshops." Navajo women on the reservation were "almost all engaged in the weaving of rugs for sale or trade to traders. While this produced income, the activity is not included in this analysis since it was not a formal wage in the sense of industrial labor" (Weiss 1984:92).

Thus Weiss, who has written the most comprehensive study of the development of capitalism on an Indian reservation, commits a serious blunder. Through an ideological sleight of hand, Navajo weavers became privatized and domesticated. The signifier "woman," regardless of race or place, became the signified "domestic." Sacks (1982:111) critiques this kind of analysis in the following comment: "When Marxists focus on precapitalism (or even capitalist) modes of production, they consign women to a domestic sphere and append both as an afterthought or forget about them altogether."

Prestigious dealers of Navajo rugs have done the same, trivializing women's weaving by failing to consider it "real work":

A dealer friend of mine once placed an expert Navajo weaver on his payroll at $1 an hour. For her he bought hand spun vegetal dyed yarns. He told the woman to do two pieces of weaving: a better than average twill weave double saddle blanket (30 x 60 inches), and a 3 x 5 foot quality rug. The saddle blanket was completed in 140 hours, the rug in 238 hours.... The two pieces of weaving were sold at the going market price (in 1955) of $35 for the saddle blanket and $65 for the rug. This compares with the $140 which my friend paid for the saddle blanket and the $238 which he paid for the 3 x 5 foot quality rug. Which brings up a very important point: although weaving is an essential part of the reservation economy, it is not exercized as a full-time occupation. Hence there can be no wage scale. A Navajo woman will do most of her weaving in her spare time as some of our non-Indian ladies will knit a wool dress in their spare time. (Maxwell 1963:19-20)

Decade after decade, the importance, the necessity, even the survival of the Navajo rested primarily on women's textile production and the wool from their sheep. Government tables, if carefully read alongside other reports by military personnel, missionaries, educators and agents, demonstrate that the more goods (especially textiles) that left the reservation, the poorer the Navajo became (Bailey and Bailey 1989:153, 159). This enormous amount of textile production fed capitalist accumulation. Gary Witherspoon (1987:41) estimates that approximately one million blankets and rugs have been woven by Navajo weavers during the past two centuries. As with the lacemakers Mies (1982) described, the entire trading nexus was dominated by men. Navajo women were the producers, and women in distant locations were the primary consumers. Traders like Hubbell evaluated, controlled and dominated the textile markets and it is their names that are recalled with nostalgia, while the weavers remain anonymous. The continuation of Navajo weaving is attributed to the traders, as are the design changes. To fully acknowledge the importance of weaving to Navajo economic well-being would have directly counteracted the prevailing Western attitudes about what constituted "appropriate behaviour" and the proper sphere for women in general (Leacock and Etienne 1980:1). Recognizing Navajo women's economic contributions would directly have challenged the dominant ideology in Western society concerning women's role as domestic helpmate and mother. Missionaries, traders, government personnel and educators, all men who came into contact with Navajo women, participated in the reproduction of this bourgeois world, effectively silencing Navajo women's point of view. We also find parallels of this silencing within the Western art world. Although it is beyond the scope of this paper to explore how women were written out of art history in the Western world, some of the distinctions made are relevant to the Navajo case because they form part of the cultural baggage that traders brought with them in their encounter with the Navajo.

HOW WESTERN IDEAS ABOUT ART CONTRIBUTED TO THE APPROPRIATION OF NAVAJO WOMEN'S WEAVING

The making of art during the Renaissance required the learning of specific techniques and skills within an institutional setting.[5] Because of the organization of the art academies, and their adherence to social conventions, it was impossible for women to achieve excellence or success equal to that of men regardless of how talented they were. The most important aspect of any artist's training required the attendance at drawing classes which focused on the male nude; women were excluded from such classes until the end of the nineteenth century, when drawing from the female nude was common. Consequently, women who did become artists were daughters, mistresses or wives of famous painters. Although burdened by many constraints, women did manage to paint, and a few became famous. Yet in this century, major art history texts failed to include the biographies of any women painters (Parker and Pollock 1981). Women have been evident as subjects in art, but as creators their records are scattered and few (Pollock 1988).

During the nineteenth century realism reigned supreme in art, and all types of geometric patterns were deemed inferior forms of design — they were considered an expression of the feminine, purely decorative spirit in art. Victorian art critic and historian John Ruskin (1911) noted that women's intellect was not for invention or creation. One of the ways women failed to measure up concerned their predilection for geometric forms (graphically represented in quilt, coverlet and aboriginal textile and basketry designs). In the early twentieth century, two historians of Neolithic art noted:

The geometric style is primarily a feminine style. The geometric orna-
ment seems more suited to the domestic, pedantically tidy and at the
same time superstitiously careful spirit of woman than that of man. It is,
considered purely aesthetically, petty, lifeless, and, despite all its luxuri-
ousness of colour, a strictly limited mode of art. But within its limits,
healthy and efficient, pleasing by reason of the industry displayed and its
external decorativeness — the expression of the feminine spirit in art.
(quoted in Parker and Pollock 1981:68)

Placed on beds, bodies or floors instead of walls, textiles simply were not and could not be "seen" as art — they were located outside the frame of reference and contextual space created for and dominated by the art world. The way in which art has become institutionalized in the last three hundred years has distorted our perceptions and shaped our recognition of "art" created outside the domain of the art world. The language developed by classical art historians and aestheticians has told us who made art (and by omission, who did not), and what was art (and what was not). Exclusion is a very pow-erful means of control. The absence of any textiles from art history books speaks volumes about how such work was perceived.

In non-Western societies, the individual who *wove* the textile almost always *designed* it. The exception occurred in highly stratified societies (such as the Inca) in which a class of weavers produced tex-tiles designed by a master weaver for royalty. Nearly all weaving techniques in use today were practised in prehistoric times by vari-ous societies (Bird 1963:47). Textile production in one form or another was practically a global phenomenon — surely the antithe-sis of the production of "rare art." Most weaving produced by pre-literate peoples requires a unique combination and co-ordination of conceptual and manual skills, especially since neither drawings nor other preliminaries are created before weaving begins. This ability, achieved after years of conscious manipulation of materials, has been trivialized and dismissed in the literature. My survey of over 100 papers in art and anthropology revealed few articles referring to this unique ability (Weltfish 1967, Witherspoon 1977, 1981).[6]

CONCLUSION

Artistic imperialism incorporated in the art/craft distinction held by European colonizers has led to the destruction of indigenous expression since Native handwork has been reduced to a trinket industry in many areas (Hirschmann 1976). Textile production in many areas will continue to deteriorate as small-scale societies increasingly industrialize. Because of the Western view that painting, sculpture and prints are the only legitimate art forms in the West, individual artists from a few minority groups may enjoy financial success in catering to an elitist market, while their Native associates who continue to weave, pot and make baskets supply the ubiquitous craft markets.

Unfortunately, anthropologists have worked within the framework of this conceptual dualism. The deterioration in quality which occurred in post-contact situations when indigenous trade networks were disrupted or destroyed by colonial merchants failed to trigger a response by anthropologists (and others) because Natives were thought to have produced only functional "crafts." A number of prominent U.S. anthropologists were actively doing research in the region while this massive appropriation occurred. The weight of art history, aesthetics and the structural relations of art and craft production in the West obscured the parallel processes involved in producing art or craft. Just as non-literacy implies a pathological condition in contemporary society, indigenous peoples were perceived by colonizers as being artistically illiterate since they did not draw, nor did they produce within recognized fine arts media. Without a formal mechanism in place to dictate design, each indigenous artisan was compelled to develop the ability necessary to conceptualize and produce many items necessary for personal and/or tribal use or trade. The words of Mali historian Amadou

Hampate Ba (1976:17) poignantly summarize the position of indigenous artisans perhaps everywhere:

We live in a very curious age. The amazing development of science and technology goes hand in hand, contrary to all expectations, with a worsening of living conditions. Along with the conquest of space has come a sort of shrinking of our world which has been reduced to its material and visible dimensions alone, whereas the traditional African craftsman, who had never moved from his little village, had the feeling of participating in a world of infinite dimensions and being linked with the whole of the living universe.

Many of the world's most "valuable" textiles today were produced by the ancestors of some of the poorest people on earth. Aesthetics and economics have been and remain inextricably linked. Because of the importance of trade in the earlier years of colonization, many articles fashioned by indigenous weavers were treated like renewable resources. Many Navajo textiles marketed by the pound for decades now sell for thousands of dollars on the auction block. But investors need not worry, for dead weavers are unlikely to collect their due.

□

I wish to thank the editors and in particular Mané Arratia, for their helpful comments and suggestions. Research funding was provided by a Social Sciences and Humanities Research Council of Canada pre-doctoral fellowship.

NOTES

1. Although some Navajo call themselves Diné, other Navajo prefer to retain the name. A name change has not been approved by the government of the Navajo Nation.
2. See Babcock (1990:400-37) for insightful and salient discussion regarding the creation of the "exotic other" within the continental United States.
3. Yet the Navajo Tribal Museum struggles to remain open. Sotheby's auctioned a nineteenth century Navajo satillo serape in 1984 for $114,000,

and in 1989 one of four First Phase Chief's Blankets (circa 1840) still in private hands sold for a record-breaking $522,500.

4. Reichard (1936) and Underhill (1956) commented upon but never criticized trader relations with aboriginal producers since traders were considered to provide the only outlets for their products. The Boasian paradigm privileged the gathering of all the "facts." As his students, these women produced a wealth of information on many aspects of tribal life. The monographs they wrote describing the production of various crafts have become classics in the discipline. In historical particularism, change was never discussed except in terms of acculturation. Specific cultures were viewed as "wholes" — totalities. As a result, structural conflict remained invisible and irrelevant.

5. The mind/body dualism so prevalent in Western thought was extended to the realm of art during the Renaissance. The creation of painting and sculpture became an intellectual activity. Only painters received formal drawing lessons. This training increasingly came to include knowledge of architecture, geometry, perspective and anatomy (Pevsner 1940:84). The great Renaissance crafters lacked a key qualification — they had no training in math. Through their studies of perspective, painters laid the foundations of projective geometry in math, mapmaking and draftsmanship used by architects and engineers (Random House Encyclopedia 1977:1445). Production of crafts (including weaving) was demoted to manual labour and became an unpleasant activity, attractive only because a wage was involved (Kant 1951).

6. Weltfish comments on how the organization of work in industrialized societies is inimical to the creation of "art." In 1967 (207) she wrote: "When we consider that even a small tribe [the Pima] of several hundred Indians has the creative vigor to evolve and develop a living style of design, while in our own culture, neither the whole nor the several parts of our 150 million people shows an equivalent creative vigor, we must ask ourselves, Why?" The worry over unemployment, speed-up, etc. in industrial production "inhibits the aesthetic possibilities that could be realized" (209).

BIBLIOGRAPHY

ABERLE, David. 1962. "Navajo." In *Matrilineal Kinship,* ed. David Schneider and Kathleen Gough. Berkeley: University of California Press, 96-201.

ADAMS, William Y. 1963. *Shonto: A Study of the Role of the Trader in a Modern Navajo Community.* Bureau of American Ethnology. Bulletin 188. Washington: Government Printing Office.

———. 1968. "The Role of the Navajo Trader in a Changing Economy." In *Markets and Marketing in Developing Economies,* ed. R. Moyer and S. Hollander. Holmwood, IL: R. D. Irwin, 133-52.

AMSDEN, Charles A. 1975. *Navajo Weaving, its Technique and History.* Salt Lake City: Peregrine Smith.

ANONYMOUS. 1972. "Navajo Testimony Reveals Treatment at Hands of Traders." *Akwasasne Notes* 4(Autumn):5.

BABCOCK, Barbara. 1990. "'A New Mexican Rebecca.' Imaging Pueblo Women." *Journal of the Southwest* 32(4):400-37.

BAILEY, Garrick, and Roberta Bailey. 1989. *A History of the Navajo: The Reservation Years.* Santa Fe: School of American Research.

BERLANT, Tony, and Mary H. Kahlenberg. 1977. *Walk in Beauty.* New York: Little Brown.

BIRD, Junius. 1963. "Technique and Art in Peruvian Textiles." *Technique and Personality,* ed. Margaret Mead, Junius Bird, and Hans Himmelheber. New York: Museum of Primitive Art.

DOCKSTADER, Frederick J. 1978. *Weaving Arts of the North American Indian.* New York: Thomas Y. Crowell.

HAMPATE BA, Amadou. 1976. "African Art, Where the Hand Has Ears." New York: *The UNESCO Courier,* 12-17.

HARVEY, Byron. 1963. "The Fred Harvey Collection 1889-1963." *Plateau* 35 (Spring):2.

HEDLUND, Ann. 1989. *Perspectives on Anthropological Collections from the American Southwest.* Proceedings of a Symposium. Anthropology Research Papers No.40. Phoenix: Arizona State University.

HEGEMANN, Elizabeth C. 1963. *Navajo Trading Days.* Albuquerque: University of New Mexico Press.

HENDERSON, James D. 1969. *Meals by Fred Harvey.* Fort Worth: Texas Christian University Press.

HIRSCHMANN, Niloufer. 1976. "The World in a Paper Bag." *Kroeber Anthropological Papers* 47(976):44-70.

The Hubbell Papers. Documents, personal correspondence, ledgers and day books, 1885-1950. Special Collections Library, University of Arizona.

KANT, Immanual. 1951. *Critique of Judgment.* New York: Hafner Press.

LAMPHERE, Louise. 1976. "The Internal Colonization of the Navajo People." *Southwest Economy and Society* 1(1):6-14.

————. 1977. *To Run after Them: Cultural and Social Bases of Cooperation in a Navajo Community.* Tucson: University of Arizona Press.

LEACOCK, Eleanor, and Mona Etienne, eds. 1980. *Women and Colonization.* New York: Praeger.

McNITT, Frank. 1962. *The Indian Traders.* Norman: University of Oklahoma Press.

MAXWELL, Gilbert. 1963. *Navajo Rugs, Past, Present and Future.* Santa Fe Heritage Art.

MIES, Maria. 1982. *The Lacemakers of Narsapur.* London: Zed Press.

MOORE, J. B. 1987. *Collection of Catalogues Published at Crystal Trading Post, 1903 and 1911.* Alburquerque, NM: Avanyu Publishing.

NOCHLIN, Linda. 1988. *Women, Art and Power and Other Essays*. New York: Harper and Row.

PARKER, Rozika, and Griselda Pollock. 1981. *Old Mistresses: Women, Art and Ideology*. New York: Pantheon.

PEVSNER, Nikolaus. 1940. *Academies of Art, Past, Present and Future*. Cambridge: Cambridge University Press.

POLLOCK, Griselda. 1988. *Vision and Difference. Femininity, Feminism and the Histories of Art*. London: Routledge.

RANDOM House Encyclopedia. 1977. "Mathematics and Civilization."

REICHARD, Gladys. 1934. *Spider Woman*. New York: Macmillan. (Reprint ed. *Weaving — Navajo Blanket*. Dover Publications, 1974.)

———. 1936. *Navajo Shepherd and Weaver*. New York: J.J. Augustin. (Reprint ed. New Mexico: Rio Grande Press, 1968.)

———. 1939. *Dezba, Woman of the Desert*. New York: Macmillan. (Reprint ed. New Mexico: Rio Grande Press, 1971.)

RUFFING, Lorraine. 1978. "The Navajo Nation: Cultivating Underdevelopment." *Akwasasne Notes* 10:4.

RUSKIN, John. 1911. "Of Queen's Gardens." In *Sesame and Lilies: The Two Paths*. New York: E.P. Dutton.

SACKS, Karen. 1982. *Sisters and Wives. The Past and Future of Sexual Equality*. Urbana: University of Illinois Press.

SPICER, Edward H. 1962. *Cycles of Conquest: The Impact of Spain, Mexico, and the United States on the Indians of the Southwest 1533-1960*. Tucson: University of Arizona Press.

UNDERHILL, Ruth. 1956. *The Navajo*. Norman: University of Oklahoma Press.

UTLEY, Robert M. 1961. "The Reservation Trader in Navajo History." *El Palacio* 68:10-35.

VOGT, Evon. 1961. "The Navajo." In *Perspectives in American Indian Culture Change*, ed. E.H. Spicer. Chicago: University of Chicago Press, 278-336.

WEISS, Lawrence. 1984. *The Development of Capitalism in the Navajo Nation: A Political Economic History*. Studies in Marxism, vol. 15. Minneapolis: MAP Publications.

WELTFISH, Gene. 1967. "The Study of American Indian Crafts and Its Implication for Art Theory." *Indian Tribes of Aboriginal America, Selected Papers*, ed. Sol Tax. New York: Cooper Square Publishers, 200-09.

WHITE, Richard. 1983. *The Roots of Dependency: Subsistence, Environment and Social Change among the Choctaws, Pawnees, and Navajo*. Lincoln: University of Nebraska Press.

WITHERSPOON, Gary. 1975. *Navajo Kinship and Marriage*. Chicago: University of Chicago Press.

———. 1977. *Language and Art in the Navajo Universe*. Ann Arbor: University of Michigan Press.

———. 1981. "Self-esteem and Self-expression in Navajo Weaving." *Plateau* 52:28-32.

WITHERSPOON, Gary. 1987. *Navajo Weaving: Art in its Cultural Context.*
Monograph no. 37. Flagstaff: Museum of Northern Arizona Press.
WOODMAN, Nancy. 1980. "The Story of an Orphan." In *The South Corner of Time,* ed. Larry Evers. Tucson: Sun Tracks, 77-88.

CHAPTER 7

"A Little Free Time on Sunday"

WOMEN AND DOMESTIC

COMMODITY PRODUCTION[1]

Max J. Hedley

ANY CANADIANS ENGAGED IN FISHING, FARMING and trapping organize their commercial activities on a household basis. Whether outport fishers in Newfoundland, family farmers in Alberta or northern trappers, they depend on the labour and expertise of family members and the resources of the household to produce commodities for the market. An enduring attraction of this way of producing is that it seems to allow rural households to retain control over the work process and offers the hope that they may reap the fruits of their own labour. Of course this simplifies the reality, for the activities of domestic commodity producers are constrained by government regulations, indebtedness and contractual arrangements with processors as well as by national and global processes of accumulation. Moreover, these people must devise ways of coping with cost and price fluctuation, unpredictable variations in weather and illness and injury which at any moment may threaten their livelihood. Independence, then, is in part an illusion, for the interests of powerful social, political and economic groups and classes underlie both the formation and metamorphosis of rural lifeways. Yet domestic producers are never simply puppets moving in unison to the rhythms of others. Individually or collectively through political movements, they seek to impose their own order or interests on the course of events and create their lives out of the possibilities that they see.

It is the economic consequences of domestic producers' involvement in a global capitalist economy which have attracted most research. The literature is particularly concerned with the economic processes underlying the transformation of commodity production and rural life. This emphasis can be found in discussions about the organization and technology of production, the processes of specialization and differentiation, the creation of regional and national inequality, the fate of domestic producers as a class and the place of small-scale enterprises in an environmentally threatened world. Such studies have clarified our understanding of the nature and consequences of the economic subordination of small-scale producers and have contributed to a clearer perception of how rural households cope with the forces which threaten their survival.

A corollary of this emphasis is that the literature tends to bypass or render inconsequential activities which fall outside the commercial realm. Two significant results of this omission are of relevance here. In the first place, the practices of women in commodity-producing households have been largely ignored because they were primarily associated with the noncommercial realm. Secondly, failure to investigate noncommercial practices has obscured the extent and ways in which the interests of other social groups and classes have entered into the social construction, transformation and domination of household and community life in rural areas. At issue is not an abandonment of concern for economic forces, for they unavoidably constrain the lives of commodity producers, but a recognition that there are questions of gender and cultural domination which must be taken into account if we are to understand the lives of women and men in rural Canada.

The aim in this chapter is to further our awareness of the range and significance of noncommercial activities to the reproduction of commodity-producing households. After all, people see themselves involved in a way of life, not simply an economic endeavour. In raising this issue we are particularly concerned with enhancing our understanding of women's practices, for these tend to fall, though not necessarily exclusively, within the domestic realm. The growth of feminist research has led to a recognition of women's direct or indirect involvement in commodity production and their contribution to the reproduction of the household.[2] Nevertheless, there are many activities which are seldom discussed, yet are basic to the creation and reproduction of the way of life of rural households. A discussion of these activities will be based on the autobiographical account of Elizabeth Goudie's (1975) life in an early twentieth century trapping household in southern Labrador.

Before turning to a discussion of noncommercial activities, some conceptual issues will be raised. Our ability to fully understand the position of women and the impact of external interests on the lives of domestic producers requires a reappraisal of the ideas we hold about the household. Consequently, a brief outline of the image of the household found in the literature on domestic commodity production and a discussion of how it works to constrict our vision are provided. More specifically, I will argue that the image used in the literature on fishing, farming and trapping inhibits a full recognition of changes which have occurred in the social relations of domestic production, of the activities of women and of the new forms of domination and freedom which have emerged.

IDEAS/IMAGES OF THE HOUSEHOLD

Ideas about the household are incorporated into all attempts to understand domestic production in fishing, farming and trapping, though they are not always acknowledged or defined. This can be seen in those approaches which employ theoretical terms such as "independent," "simple," "petty" or "domestic" commodity production to reveal the importance of class or production relations in understanding the transformation of the rural world. The most explicit way that the household is incorporated into analysis occurs through its specification as a source of unpaid labour (recruited through marriage and kinship ties) and as a place of consumption. This is hardly surprising, for it is the reliance upon the labour and capital resources of the household which is seen to make domestic commodity production unique. In other words, the household, in a relatively unproblematic fashion, is viewed as little more than a unit of production and consumption. Failure to examine more carefully our ideas about the household facilitates the entry of assumptions into analysis which detract from our ability to understand the complexities of rural life.

One problem which emerges is a tendency to reify our ideas of the household: we consistently fail to remember that the "thing" we designate, the household as a unit of production and consumption, is socially and culturally constituted. A consequence of this, and one which undermines our understanding of the position of women, is a readiness to assume the presence of a non-exploitative harmony of interests within households (Hedley 1981, 1988; Phillips 1989). While stratification, reflected in differences in income and resources, may be noted, it is easy to overlook the presence of relations of inequality and possible exploitation within households. Moreover, the existence and consequences of conflicting interests between males and females, young and old, and the way these are influenced by the involvement of individuals in relationships beyond the household are obscured.

The assumption of a harmony of interests has not remained unchallenged. In particular, the influence of feminist scholarship has fostered a general recognition of gender differences and inequalities in rural households, though there is a temptation to substitute a vision of internal harmony with one of universal patriarchy (Friedmann 1986). In either case the task of unravelling the complex realities of household relations in specific social contexts remains incomplete. While recognizing the presence of conflicting interests and differences in power and authority, we also have to acknowledge that members of rural households share, at least at times, common goals and interests. However, the assumption of harmony obscures this by presupposing commonality without determining how this is forged, maintained or transformed.

A more elusive formulation through which preconceptions about the household are introduced into analysis occurs when a distinction is drawn between the logic of domestic and capitalist commodity production. Expressions of this are found where commodity-producing households are described as being oriented toward social reproduction or following a subsistence logic, in contrast to the profit-maximizing practices of capitalist enterprises. The presumed existence of a different logic is attractive because it appears to offer an explanation of the persistence, or resistance, of small producers and their ability to compete "effectively" when a recognition of the impact of processes of capitalist development (long hours, reduced consumption, etc.) proves insufficient. Expressed differently, the noncapitalist logic seems to account for the autonomy which allows domestic producers to resist the consequences of remorseless structural pressures. Of course we must recognize that the members of rural households are not simply oriented towards profit maximization, though they may be in part, but that they try to structure their activities in terms of their own interests. However, the very objectives that they pursue are forged within a context marked by the influence of other more powerful economic, political and social interests. In other words, the influence of other groups and classes unavoidably shapes both the character of local interests and the problems encountered in their realization. Assuming the presence of a noncapitalist logic introduces a form of dualism into our thinking. When this occurs, we lose sight of both the shifting web of relationships within which the lives of domestic producers are entwined and the way the interests of other social groups and classes leave their imprint on the social and cultural character of rural life.

RECOVERING DOMESTIC LABOUR

As mentioned earlier, the difficulty of comprehending the lives of domestic producers is compounded by an emphasis placed on the commercial activities of household members. It is to this issue that we now turn. The aim is to discuss the significance of the full range of noncommercial activities in which the members of commodity-producing households engage. This is necessary if we are to further our understanding of women's domestic practices and the ways external interests are incorporated into rural lifeways.

There is a growing literature on noncommercial domestic production which has been shaped by a variety of practical and political concerns. An interest in the experiences and practices of women is reflected in debates over such issues as the value of domestic labour and the distribution of the product of labour (Folbre 1982:318). There has also been a growing interest in (1) the range of household activities, (2) a critique of economic accounting policies, and (3) attempts to determine the value of domestic production in debates about the informal economy (Ross and Usher 1986), rural development (Brox 1972) and sustainable development (Tanner 1989). Concern with the hidden economy is frequently linked to practical political issues. For example, patterns of resource use by Native peoples have been identified in support of land claims; resettlement policies have been criticized for their failure to recognize the hidden value of domestic production; and preconceptions about the nature of domestic labour have been criticized where they devalue the activities of women and help perpetuate gender inequality. Interest in domestic production also appears in the debates about inequality and regional disparity. Concern is with the relationship of subsistence production to processes of accumulation through the provision of low cost goods and services or with the household's role in reproducing labour cheaply and providing a safety net for those who lose their position as wage labourers or experience declining incomes as commodity producers.

These studies reveal that a narrow focus on commercial activity has relegated domestic activity to the level of a peripheral concern. Practices in the domestic realm are too easily described as consumption or leisure, in contrast to the "real" work that is done in the realm of commodity production.[3] This separation is particularly noticeable with respect to urban households dependent on wage labour for an income. However, the same bias is present in our views of commodity-producing households, for in contemporary ideology the commercial activities of fishers, farmers and trappers are deemed to be most worthy of attention, while other practices, particularly those of women, are ignored (Porter 1985:116).

Activity not directly associated with commodity production is recognized in the literature on domestic production, though its significance is easily lost when an emphasis is placed on commercial production. Noncommercial activities are commonly referred to as subsistence production or, more recently, self-provisioning. Self-provisioning is generally defined in opposition to commercial production in that it is seen to involve production for direct use rather than market exchange. This distinction is reflected in the numerous attempts to establish a clear distinction between contemporary rural enterprises conducted as businesses and peasant households which are deemed to be primarily oriented toward subsistence production. Definitions of subsistence activity may be quite broad. Nevertheless, in practice a further narrowing occurs because attention tends to be directed toward those activities which are judged to contribute directly to the realization of material needs. These include, for example, the work entailed in constructing dwellings or boats, collecting and processing berries and other natural resources, managing a vegetable garden, making clothing, and many other practices which are oriented toward personal or family use rather than commercial exchange.

However, there is an implicit judgment associated with this categorization, for not all noncommercial activities are treated equally. Practices or products tend to be identified as belonging to the subsistence category if they do or could enter into circuits of commercial exchange. Brox's (1972) study of economic dualism in Newfoundland illustrates this point, though it should be noted that his concern is directed toward establishing policies which would allow for the expansion of commodity production. In his analysis of the "barriers to conversion" between domestic and commercial spheres of activity, significant practices in the domestic sphere are identified in terms of the availability of commercial equivalents. Access to an adequate income is seen as creating the conditions under which labour can be transferred from one sphere (out of subsistence) to the other (into commercial). The point I suggest here is that subsistence production is not only defined negatively — that which is not commercial — but it also excludes from consideration a wide range of practices which, from the perspective of the present, are not considered economic.

This economic bias inadvertently curtails the range of practices we take into account. While a broadening of our conceptions has occurred (Sinclair and Felt 1989), activities such as childcare, nursing sick or injured members of the household and cooking tend to be excluded or their significance diminished. Similarly, more cultural activities, such as those involved in the production of leisure, education or religious worship, also fall outside the framework of analysis. As a result, we lose sight of the significance for social reproduction of a wide range of domestic practices followed in the past, and we neglect to explore the ways in which they incorporated the experience of past domination. Moreover, we may fail to appreciate the extent to which contemporary cultural and material practices are realized through new forms of social relationships and embody new forms of autonomy and domination.

As we well know, many domestic activities primarily involve the labour of women. Because of this, it is necessary to clearly recognize the importance of gender bias, in conjunction with the aforementioned economic emphasis, in suppressing our appreciation of the range and significance of noncommercial activities. This suppression has meant that while the involvement of women in the "domestic" realm is readily mentioned or assumed, descriptions of their practices (skills, knowledge, organization of work), particularly in past accounts, tend to be narrowly construed or absent. For example, Firestone's (1967) "descriptive synthesis" of Savage Cove, a "folk community" in Newfoundland's Northern Peninsula, stresses the activities and organization of males. The involvement of women, other than a mention of such things as their "help" in processing fish and managing cows (1967:71), is barely noted, despite a willingness to identify their "subordination" in a "patriarchal" family (1967:74).[4] Thus we find an account of the real dangers and difficulties of men's work, such as pursuing seal on moving ice, but hear nothing of the dangers of childbirth, or coping with illness. Nor is there any mention of the importance of skills and knowledge required in domestic activities. Firestone was not alone in making such assertions or omissions, for his work was written at a time when they were the norm in the literature on fishing, farming and trapping.

It is only within the last decade or so that the position of women in commodity-producing households has come to receive more than passing attention (Davis 1983; Ghorayshi 1984; Kohl 1976; Murray 1979; Nadel-Klein and Davis 1988; Porter 1985, 1988; Rasmussen et al. 1976), and the significance of women's labour to processes of material, social, and cultural reproduction rendered more visible.[5] However, our knowledge is far from extensive. In order to provide a general idea of the range of activities involved in the reproduction of commodity-producing households, attention will focus on a trapping household in Labrador during the early decades of this century. This was a time when there was a considerable degree of local self-sufficiency. The example will make it easier to appreciate the extent to which members of rural households have transformed their activities and the relationships through which reproduction is now realized. I have already mentioned that in narrowly defining reproduction it is particularly the activities of women which are largely bypassed. It is with this in mind that the following discussion focuses on their practices.

"I RAISED NINE BABIES IN WINTERS LIKE THAT" THE DOMESTIC REALM

Elizabeth Goudie's account of her life in the Hamilton Inlet area of Labrador offers us a fleeting glimpse of the wide range of tasks and the type of skills and knowledge required for the reproduction of rural households during the first four decades of this century. Unlike settlers farther north who were involved in the exchange of fish (cod) and furs (Ames 1977; Brice-Bennett 1977; Brody 1977; Kennedy 1982), Elizabeth Goudie's household relied primarily on trapping, occasionally supplemented by casual labour, to generate an income. Moreover, with nearby areas already occupied, the family's trapline was about three hundred miles away in the Grand Falls (Churchill Falls) region.[6] Because of the time required to reach the trapping area, her husband was absent from the home for approximately six months a year. During this time she had to meet the

needs of her family primarily through her own efforts. The importance of domestic activities for the reproduction of the household is
illustrated in her comments about the consequences of poor fur
prices, seasonal failure, working a poor trapping area or the problems which arose if a husband was not good at trapping. Families
would experience difficulty: "Many times my aunt was half-starving
and poorly-clothed. Her husband didn't have a very good trapping
place and didn't know how to manage trapping well" (1975:47).
Like many of her counterparts in commodity producing households, Elizabeth was involved in a broad range of activities. These
included catching large quantities of fish for home consumption,
making boots and clothing, preparing pelts, baking bread, melting
blocks of snow for water, making soap and building cupboards.

References to activities such as these are readily acknowledged
in accounts of domestic commodity production in Canada, though
they are often inadequately discussed (Brox 1972; Dawson and
Younge 1940; deVries and Macnab-deVries 1987; Firestone 1967;
Johnson 1981; Nemec 1980; Zimmerly 1975). On the other hand,
it is more difficult to find accounts of the ways in which people
organized themselves to manage birth, death, childcare, accidents
and illness within the context of household and local relationships.
An insight into difficulties that had to be overcome is vividly
revealed in Elizabth Goudie's descriptions of the requirements
placed on her time, skills, knowledge, endurance and emotions.
Because she had to manage young children largely without assistance, the demands on her time could be particularly onerous. As
she put it, "I was never really able to get away from home at all, winter or summer, without my children. I nursed all my babies. I never
gave them the bottle." Ten months and then "meat and gravies and
fish" (Goudie, 1975: 30). If her children had not slept, she would
not have been able to complete the many tasks that were required
(1975:53). The work could be particularly difficult in winter: "We
would have to make about three fires and it would be an hour before
the house was warm enough to take the children out of bed. Every
night in winter when it was thirty or forty below zero outside, it was
below freezing inside the house. I often got up in the morning and
had to break the ice on top of my water bucket. I raised nine babies
in winters like that" (1975:55).

The difficulties of meeting the labour requirements of the household were further compounded by accidents or illness. With only limited services available, people had little choice other than to manage on the basis of their own resources, with some assistance from the members of other households. For Elizabeth Goudie, there were times when she coped alone with the illness of her husband, children or herself, while at other moments she would rely on the help of her husband and face the possibility of a decline in cash income or subsistence production. The decline of either placed even more strain on the resources of the household, since deficiencies had to be compensated for in other ways. Indicating the importance of the labour supply of the family, Goudie notes that it was only when children matured to the point that they could assume some of the more repetitive tasks that she and her husband experienced some permanent relief from an extremely demanding work regime (1975:105,106). There can be no doubt about the significance of the activities she described for the reproduction of the household:

The wife of a trapper played a great part in it because she had to live as a man five months of the year. She had to use a gun and she had to know how to set nets to catch fish and also how to judge the right distance from the shore to cut her fish holes.... That was the outdoors life. Indoors if you were a mother you had to know how to look after your children, you had to cook, make clothes for the family, sealskin boots, and often you had to act as a doctor or nurse.... To be a trapper's wife and keep up with all the chores you have to work from six in the morning to nine at night. I never had time to read a book. I would get a little free time on Sunday. (Goudie, 1975:162,163,43)

Elizabeth Goudie's experiences were unique. However, while recognizing the particularity of her own life history, it is also necessary to appreciate that the social conditions of domestic production were common to other trapping households in the region (Zimmerly 1975) and similar in many ways to those of trappers and fishers in more northern bays (Ames 1977; Brice-Bennett 1977; Brody 1977). Moreover, despite these unique qualities, it can be suggested that women in commodity-producing households throughout

Canada were no strangers to the range of activities she describes, nor to the fact that the skills, knowledge and capabilities of rural women were essential for material, social and cultural reproduction. There are, of course, practices that do not receive prominence in Goudie's account, which reflect differences in time and circumstances. These include the efforts that at times were spent in teaching children to read and write, providing a religious education (Elizabeth 1977; Zimmerely 1975) and producing the many social occasions which marked rural life (Murray 1979).

"THEY STILL WANT MORE"
CHANGING RELATIONS OF DOMESTIC PRODUCTION

It is neither reasonable nor desirable to expect a uniform picture of rural domestic practice to emerge from the discussion of a single trapping household. There were and there remain considerable differences in individual, local and regional circumstances. However, the purpose here is not to describe in detail the practices of commodity-producing households but to sensitize us to what is lost if we remain trapped in a de-gendered rural landscape. Goudie's description of her activities is valuable because it allows us to recognize and begin to recover the full range of women's activities and to understand their significance to the reproduction of a way of life. Yet this is not all. A failure to investigate women's activities, and noncommercial practices generally, prevents us from fully comprehending the processes and depth of rural transformation.

To briefly pursue the latter point, we can begin by observing that the members of Elizabeth Goudie's and many other households at the time depended heavily on locally available resources. Moreover, it was primarily through household and community (kin and neighbours) relations that labour was provided to support the reproduction of local society and culture. It can also be seen that the continuity of the material, social and cultural life of household members was intimately tied to success in both commodity and subsistence (broadly defined) production. The production of a commodity for exchange allowed households to derive some advantages from being part of an international division of labour, while inextricably linking their fate to international processes of accumulation. As Goudie's account shows, when access to commodities was denied, the whole work regime of the household, not just commodity production, could be adversely affected.

The practices of contemporary commodity-producing households and the relational context within which they are pursued are very different from those described in Goudie's account. Self-provisioning has declined, and its character has changed in that materials and tools entering the productive process are increasingly obtained through exchange. Even where reliance on the immediate environment to supply materials for domestic production has remained meaningful and materially important, the means and/or the organization of production are likely to have been transformed. In either case, changes in the range of tasks and the productivity of labour have been associated with a heightened dependence on access to a monetary income. A consequence of this, paralleling the situation in commodity production, is that a decline in income or rising costs of production may effectively preclude the members of rural households from applying their own labour to the exploitation of local resources.

Many of the tasks performed in the past, and the skills and knowledge associated with them, are now seldom or no longer part of the household's realm of activity. Others continue to sound familiar enough today, especially when categorized by such terms as cooking, childcare, washing and nursing. This should not be taken to mean that a process of de-skilling has occurred, a movement from a romantic past to a bleak present, though when domestic production is equated with consumption it is easily represented this way. However, it is important to appreciate the extent to which the character of these practices has changed. Not only has reliance on purchased commodities increased, but access to such services as education, health care, welfare and entertainment require that the members of rural households enter into relationships which, like the market, are largely beyond local control. In other words, the social context within which many of these activities are pursued has changed dramatically.

Domestic activities have become increasingly dependent on a wide range of commercial and service relationships with organizations other than local households. The ramifications of this transformation threaten to escape us when we reify the household and thereby ignore the shifting matrix of relationships in which its members are engaged. We too easily neglect to explore the implications of involvement in new social relationships for the changes occurring in particular interests of household members. For instance, young people contribute to the processes of transformation as they are influenced by formal education, enchanted by new commodities and incorporate new tastes and desires into their own vision of the "good life." The fashion of locality is shaped or replaced by the fashion of the marketplace, as the interests of other social groupings are incorporated into local social processes. People fail to develop, or reconstitute in new ways, a "taste" for the practices of the past. Goudie's observations about her children are indicative of such changes: "My first four seem to be happier than the last four with all they got. They have a lot and they still want more" (1975:160).[7] It is not only the changing interests of the young that is at issue. We must also note changes in the patterns of interest between husband and wife (individually or collectively pursued objectives), authority relations within household and locality, relationships with the members of other households and authoritative systems of discourse (sources of "legitimate" expressions of self-worth and identity) as well as changes in the ideological representation of work.

CONCLUSION

Emphasis on commercial production has obscured the activities of women and inhibited our ability to fully comprehend the social and cultural transformation of commodity-producing households. The brief description of Elizabeth Goudie's experience was meant to counteract this by drawing attention to the range and significance of women's activities. In addition, it allows us to see more clearly domestic reliance on a widening range of goods and services and the social relationships through which they are realized and to recognize that these relationships are not simply to be seen as benign, but as webs of appropriation which incorporate the practices of household members into the realization of the economic, political and moral interests of other social groups and classes. We can then ask how the purposes of other interests, such as organized religion, state bureaucracies and legal institutions, enter into the social constitution of commodity producing households (Cohen 1988; Taylor 1988). In other words, through the conceptions and activities that are brought to bear in the process of constructing their lives, the members of households inadvertently incorporate into their practices the interests of other, often more powerful, social groups. Domestic producers are "free," but it is a socially derived freedom in which ideas, tastes and practices are wrought from their own social experience.

We have identified some of the conceptual difficulties associated with the idea of the household. As with any broad concept, we are easily lulled into stressing a facticity which is not there and a continuity which threatens to unravel the moment we look away. We implicitly accept the view that something — the basic unit — is unchanging, though we are hard pressed to identify exactly what this is and remain in danger of accepting a false sense of continuity and difference. The extent and nature of the social and cultural transformations which have occurred is lost from view. In particular, we fail to recognize the complex ways in which the practices of domestic producers were created within, and continue to bear the mark of, global processes of accumulation (see Bernstein 1988:259).

Our understanding of the household must include a recognition that the term designates a realm of social practice which is permanently in flux and influenced by other interests. Without this, we may fall prey to our own reifications (saving that idealized thing we in fact do not understand) and uncritically accept idealized conceptions of the household which reflect the interests of other groups and classes in controlling social and moral life (a unit of bureaucratic control; an ideal of household relations which the institutions of church and state may seek to create, sustain and control). By recovering the "domestic" realm in all its evolving specificity, the lives of rural women and men can be better understood. Moreover, this would allow us to see the significance of the evolving relational context and to appreciate the ways in which the experience of domination is incorporated into domestic practice.

□

I would like to acknowledge the invaluable bibliographic assistance provided by Branka Malesevic and the generous financial support of the Social Sciences and Humanities Research Council and the Institute of Social and Economic Research, Memorial University.

NOTES

1.   The original version of this chapter was presented at the conference Politics, Culture and Markets: Rural Development in Peripheral Regions, June 1991, St. Francis Xavier University, Antigonish, Nova Scotia. It was then called "The 'Other' Logic: Culture and the Domestic Producer."

2.   Women's direct or indirect involvement may result as a matter of course where commercial activity is an established part of the division of labour (Porter 1985) or as a necessity when there is a shortage of male labour.

3.   This is not a distinction which people living in rural areas would necessarily accept. Hill observes that in Aquafort, Newfoundland, conflicting concepts of work coexist. The older generation uses the term more generally to incorporate subsistence activities, while for younger people it is equated with paid employment (1983:74).

4.   Porter (1985) convincingly points to the limitations of the portrait of women as being subordinate to men in an authoritarian outport tradition. She argues that the wives of domestic commodity producers "used their vital roles in initial settlement and in the fish-producing economy ... to confirm their control over at least their own spheres" (1985:122).

5.   It should not be assumed that the view found in the literature mirrors that found among rural males. Porter notes that Newfoundland males "unhesitatingly credit women with at least half the work of the family" (1985:117). This view was also found during my field research in Alberta (1979) when husbands, particularly in reference to the past, readily described the work of their wives as being fundamental to the survival of the farm and the foundation of community life.

6.   During the period Elizabeth Goudie described the place in question was called Grand Falls. As the following comment suggests, the change was not appreciated by many trappers: "To trappers it was their home and I would say their birthright. I have nothing against the name Churchill — he was a good man too — But no one asked us.... If Joe Smallwood had seen the trappers return from Grand River with their frostbitten faces, half starved and exhausted, he would have thought twice before he changed it" (1975:163).

7.   The first four children grew up prior to the transformation of the economy of the area which was associated with the establishment of an airbase at Goose Bay, southern Labrador.

BIBLIOGRAPHY

AMES, Randy. 1977. "Land Use in the Rigolet Region." In *Our Footprints are Everywhere: Inuit Land Use and Occupancy in Labrador,* ed. Carol Brice-Bennett. Nain: Labrador Inuit Association, 279-308.

BERNSTEIN, Henry. 1988. "Capitalism and Petty-Bourgeois Production: Class Relations and Divisions of Labour." *Journal of Peasant Studies* 15(2):258-71.

BRICE-BENNETT, Carol. 1977. "Land Use in the Nain and Hopedale Regions." In *Our Footprints are Everywhere: Inuit Land Use and Occupancy in Labrador,* ed. Carol Brice-Bennett. Nain: Labrador Inuit Association, 97-203.

BRODY, Hugh. 1977. "Permanence and Change among the Inuit and Settlers of Labrador." In *Our Footprints are Everywhere: Inuit Land Use and Occupancy in Labrador,* ed. Carol Brice-Bennett. Nain: Labrador Inuit Association, 311-47.

BROX, Ottar. 1972. *Newfoundland Fishermen in the Age of Industry: A Sociology of Economic Dualism.* Newfoundland Social and Economic Studies, no. 9. St. John's: Institute of Social and Economic Research, Memorial University of Newfoundland.

COHEN, Majorie G. 1988. *Women's Work, Markets, and Economic Development in Nineteenth-Century Ontario.* Toronto: University of Toronto Press.

DAHLIE, J. 1977. "Scandinavian Experiences on the Prairies, 1990-1920: The Frederiksens of Nokomis." In *The Settlement of the West,* ed. Howard Palmer. Calgary: Comprint Publishing Company.

DAVIS, Donna Lee. 1983. *Blood and Nerves: An Ethnographic Focus on Menopause.* Social and Economic Studies, no. 28. St. John's: Institute of Social and Economic Research, Memorial University of Newfoundland.

DAWSON, C. A., and Eva Younge. 1940. *Pioneering in the Prairie Provinces: The Social Side of the Settlement Process.* Toronto: Macmillan.

DEVRIES, Pieter, and Georgina MacNab-deVries. 1987. "'Taking Charge': Women in a Cape Breton Island Community." In *"Rock in a Stream": Living with the Political Economy of Underdevelopment in Cape Breton,* ed. C.P and J. deRoche. ISER Research and Policy Papers, no. 7. St. John's: Institute of Social and Economic Research, Memorial University of Newfoundland.

FIRESTONE, Melvin M. 1967. *Brothers and Rivals: Patrilocality in Savage Cove.* Newfoundland Social and Economic Studies, no. 5. St. John's, Newfoundland: Institute of Social and Economic Research, Memorial University of Newfoundland.

FOLBRE, Nancy. 1982. "Exploitation Comes Home: A Critique of the Marxian

Theory of Family Labour." *Cambridge Journal of Economics* 6:317-29.

FRIEDMANN, Harriet. 1986. "Patriarchy and Property: A Reply to Goodman and Redclift." *Sociologia Ruralis* 26(2):186-93.

GHORAYSHI, Parvin. 1984. "The Indispensable Nature of Wives' Work for the Farm Family Enterprise." *Canadian Review of Sociology and Anthropology* 26(4):571-95.

GOUDIE, Elizabeth. 1975. *Woman of Labrador.* Toronto: Peter Martin.

HEDLEY, M. 1981. "Relations of Production of the 'Family Farm': Canadian Prairies." *Journal of Peasant Studies* 9(1):71-85.

———. 1988. "The Peasant Within: Agrarian Life in New Zealand and Canada." *Canadian Review of Sociology and Anthropology* 15(1):67-83.

HILL, Robert H., et al. 1983. *The Meaning of Work and the Reality of Unemployment in the Newfoundland Context.* St John's: Community Services Council, Newfoundland and Labrador.

JOHNSON, L. 1981. "Independent Commodity Production: Mode of Production or Capitalist Class Formation." *Studies in Political Economy: A Socialist Review,* 6:93-112.

KENNEDY, John C. 1982. *Holding the Line: Ethnic Boundaries in a Northern Labrador Community.* Social and Economic Studies, no. 27, St. John's: Institute of Social and Economic Research, Memorial University of Newfoundland.

KOHL, S. 1976. *Working Together: Women and Family in Southwestern Saskatchewan.* Toronto: Holt Rinehart and Winston.

MURRAY, Hilda Chaulk. 1979. *More than 50%: Woman's Life in a Newfoundland Outport, 1900-1950.* Memorial University of Newfoundland Folklore and Language Publications Monograph Series, no. 2. St. John's: Breakwater Books.

NADEL-KLEIN, Jane, and Donna Lee Davis, eds. 1988. *To Work and To Weep: Women in Fishing Economies.* St John's: Institute of Social and Economic Research, Memorial University of Newfoundland.

NEMEC, Thomas F. 1980. *An Ethnohistorical and Ethnographic Study of the Cod Fishery at St. Shotts, Newfoundland.* Ph.D. thesis, University of Michigan.

PHILLIPS, Lynne. 1989. "Gender Dynamics and Rural Household Strategies." *Canadian Review of Sociology and Anthropology* 26(2):294-310.

PORTER, Marilyn. 1985. "'She Was Skipper of the Shore-Crew': Notes on the History of the Sexual Division of Labour in Newfoundland." *Labour* 15(Spring):105-23.

———. 1988. "Time, The Life Course and Work in Women's Lives." Paper presented to Sociology and History, the Annual Conference of the British Sociological Association, Edinburgh, March.

RASMUSSEN, L., L. Rasmussen, C. Savage, and A. Wheeler. 1976. *A Harvest Yet to Reap: A History of Prairie Women.* Toronto: Women's Press.

ROSS, David, and Peter Usher. 1986. *From the Roots Up: Economic Development as if Community Mattered.* The Canadian Council of Social Development

Series. Toronto: Lorimer.

SINCLAIR, Peter R., and Lawrence F. Felt. 1989. "Gender, Work and Household Reproduction: Married Men and Women in an Isolated Fishing Region." Paper presented at the annual meeting of the Rural Sociological Society, Seattle, Washington, August.

TANNER, Adrian. 1989. "More than Skin Deep: The Fur Trade and the Native Subsistence Economy." Unpublished Manuscript, Department of Anthropology. St. John's: Memorial University, Newfoundland.

TAYLOR, Jeffery M. 1988. *Dominant and Popular Ideologies in the Making of Rural Manitobans, 1890-1925.* Ph.D. Thesis, University of Manitoba.

ZIMMERLY, David William. 1975. *Cain's Land Revisited: Culture Change in Central Labrador, 1775-1972.* Newfoundland Social and Economic Studies, no. 16. St. John's: Institute of Social and Economic Research, Memorial University of Newfoundland.

CHAPTER 8

"Working at Home is Easy for Her"

INDUSTRIAL HOMEWORK IN CONTEMPORARY ONTARIO

Belinda Leach

THIS ESSAY[1] EMERGES FROM MY ATTEMPTS TO DEAL WITH issues arising from research with people who perform industrial homework[2] in two areas of southern Ontario, the greater London area and Metropolitan Toronto. I am concerned here with how industrial homework comes to be constructed around the fringes of capitalist work culture. To understand homework in the present period of late capitalism, we need to look at a number of complementary histories which together create the context for its existence. These include the emergence and apparent demise of putting out systems in the proto-industrial period in Europe (see for example Coleman 1983; Medick 1976), the work-related struggles that accompanied the development of factory industrialization in England[3] (see Hobsbawm 1984; Thompson 1963; and for feminist interpretations Humphries 1977; Hartmann 1982), and the more recent global economic and political trajectories which have resulted in calls for capital and workplace flexibility (see for example Pinfield and Atkinson 1988; Piore and Sabel 1984; Pollert 1988; Wood 1989). All these factors contribute to peoples' ideas about work and gender, to the kinds of work that are available and to who does what work—in other words, together they contribute to the production and reproduction of capitalist work culture.

I have set out here to explore the power of the concepts of "work" and "family" to see how they developed historically and how they are used to organize the worlds of industrial homeworkers and their families. Raymond Williams (1976) calls such words "keywords," and these particular concepts have been identified by feminists as crucial to our understanding of gender relations (see for example Rapp et al. 1979; Stichter and Parpart 1990). My aim is to determine the extent to which the conventional meanings of "work" and "family" represent a real world of work and the family for people struggling to make a living in present-day Ontario.

WORK AND FAMILY: THE CULTURAL CONSTRUCTION OF SEPARATE SPHERES

The study of industrial work has tended to privilege certain kinds of labour, particularly male, blue-collar factory work, while leaving other kinds of work, notably that of women and those people performing various kinds of casual work, invisible to sociological treatment (Burawoy 1985; Goldthorpe et al. 1968; compare with feminist approaches, e.g. Pollert 1981; Westwood 1984). All of this has contributed to shaping the discourse concerning what is and what is not work. As an example, some recent reviews of research on economic activity at the local level (Miller 1988) have suggested that a feature of the contemporary period of economic restructuring is a blurring of the separation between home and work. Yet industrial homework, as well as other forms of home-based casual work, is a perfect example of work where such a separation is not meaningful. Since we know that industrial homework has been persistent in some industries, such as the garment industry, and has been introduced into newer ones, such as electronics, for many people the separation between home and work has not been a part of their lived experience. Yet the way this observation is framed demonstrates how the ideological separation of home and work pervades scholarly thinking in much the same way as it is reflected in a popular discourse which distinguishes between home and work in a mutually exclusive fashion.

Within late twentieth century capitalist culture the separation of home and work appears to be a central principle of the organization of production and helps to provide for people a set of meanings which guide their lives. Accordingly, the production of commodities "should" take place in a sphere distinct from the household, where only reproductive activities take place. Yet industrial homework requires that home and work come together. This raises a number of questions. For example, how are the relations of production in industrial homework organized to permit the convergence of the two spheres, and how does this relate to cultural and ideological constructions of what work is?

The concepts "work" and "family" represent ideologies and cultural practices which interact to support and reinforce the social relations of industrial homework. "Family" connotes the home, prescriptions around gender roles, including a gendered division of labour, and the identification of women with the domestic sphere. The nature of work under capitalism involves ideas about where it takes place, who does it, and what is and is not real work. The two concepts operate together to produce popular ideas about what women's work is and what men's work is. Ideas about "family" influence work patterns in ways people take for granted, while ideas about "work" constrain the way members of families operate to survive.

In a way, the categories "family" and "work" represent a familiar opposition within capitalist culture, and for the industrial homeworkers I worked with, they conjure up sets of meanings which seem to be clear to them. The ideology of family is a crucial component of capitalist society (Harris 1981; Rapp et al. 1979). The idea of a blood or marriage bond is used to include people in a privileged category, providing an immediate frame of meaning around which to organize people's lives. Ideologies concerning the concept of family are extremely powerful and compelling, partly because of the relations of affection they subsume. Yet the idea of family is used to make pragmatic decisions as well, such as how the labour of individuals will be used.

Ideas about work and family need to be viewed as subject to ideological and social construction and manipulation, which then permit change over time and from place to place. Recent work by feminists has sought to dispel stereotypical notions of "the" working-class family (Stacey 1990), and instead to stress that the reality of kinship and gender practices span a wide variety of configurations, roles and strategies (Ginsburg and Tsing 1990). As well, where immigrant families are concerned, as they are here, we must be cautious about generalizing from individual experience to a shared set of cultural practices.

For one thing, the experience of immigration disrupts common practice. Women with children may have to seek childcare which in the home country would have been provided by members of an extended family, while an adult son or daughter's responsibility to an aging parent may take the form of sending money (remittances) rather than physically caring for them. Consequently, the demographics of immigration, who migrates and at what age, are crucial to the economic strategies pursued in the new setting. While members of an immigrant group may articulate an ethnic ideology using recurring symbols, symbols which frequently concern the work of women in the home around food and family, these by no means assure a common set of cultural practices (di Leonardo 1984:113-228). While in this essay I am primarily concerned with the development of ideologies of work and gender which underlie the construction of industrial homework, clearly ideas about home culture also shape the experiences of immigrant casual workers.

The historical development of the ideological separation of home and work is important since it underpins the subsequent gendered division of labour under capitalism. The idea of a man working to support his family emerged in England in the nineteenth century (Williams 1976:133), while at the same time a woman's primary responsibility to family centred on maintaining the home and rearing children (Hall 1980). Through a series of struggles in the eighteenth and nineteenth centuries, the idea of family was called on and came to shape notions of appropriate work, affecting people most notably on the basis of gender and age. Subsequently, a number of concepts key to the operation of capitalism were quite dramatically reshaped and redefined. Old jobs and old technologies disappeared and new ones came into being, but new ones did not simply replace old ones. Rather their emergence changed forever the way people thought about work. Concepts like labour, home, women's work, childhood and skill all had their meanings transformed over this period, and new ones like unemployment, the family wage and the factory, were introduced into the language.

A new understanding of the concept of labour emerged. Before industrialization the term labour connoted ideas of toil, of all kinds of manual work as well as a special meaning related to childbirth, but as the factory gained dominance, labour came to refer to the work of those pressed into the service of capitalists. The emergence of a specialized meaning to the word labour is a significant one. For one thing, the distinction that capitalists had insisted upon, between work in the factory undertaken by labour on the one hand and activities outside of that sphere on the other, was quickly taken up by the labourers themselves and used politically to set limits upon how far the capitalists could encroach upon the worker's time which had not been paid for. What had been employed originally as a mechanism for disciplining an apparently unruly workforce was then turned back upon those who had introduced it. This served to reinforce the distinction between labour and capital and helped to crystallize nascent class consciousness. Yet it was also a term of "political exclusion" (Stedman Jones 1983:104). Setting up labour as a specific category made quite clear who did not belong to that category. And this was more than simply a distinction between capital and labour. It was also a distinction between those who sold their labour at the factory and those who did not. The importance of labour as a category lies in recognizing who was excluded. Among those were the agricultural worker, the skilled craft worker, the worker inside the household and casual workers. Despite the continued existence of these other forms of work throughout the industrial period, "labour" with its new, narrow meaning, became a privileged category which attracted attention to itself and away from the other kinds of work.

As the nineteenth century came to a close the relationship of men and of women to work had taken on different meanings. For men, identity and dignity emerged from their work relations, while for women they were to be found elsewhere, not at the workplace. The exclusion of women from the capitalist labour process took place more at the level of ideology than in terms of everyday practice. Yet this ideology precluded them from finding identity and dignity there. A woman's most important work, and the source of her identity, was to be found in the family, but there too she could find a strand in the labour process to occupy her — homework.

During the period immediately preceding industrialization, homework acquired popularity and was used extensively in rural areas of Europe. Changes in rural land use and ownership diminished opportunities for agricultural work, so people took in work to provide them with additional income. The introduction of technology, which speeded up processes formerly performed by hand, made production costs cheaper and led to a general decline of domestic industry. The factory system also facilitated control over the expanding labour force, which had been difficult to control while it was dispersed. However the transition to factory production did not occur in all industries, and in a number of areas and industries homework persisted well past the time when factories were becoming fashionable. In the advanced and peripheral capitalist economies, industrial homework has persisted in some industries, most notably the clothing and footwear industries. It has emerged recently in newer industries, such as electronics, and in the Third World for the production of a wide range of items.

I turn now to two case studies of households undertaking industrial homework. By observing the work strategies of these households carefully, we can see how certain kinds of work diverge from "proper work," as it had become defined through the industrial revolution, and how people seek to find for themselves a place in the work culture of southern Ontario.

HA AND VINH'S HOUSEHOLD

Ha and Vinh migrated to Toronto from Vietnam in 1979 with their three children. Although my first contact was made with Ha, Vinh was present at all our meetings, and he always took the lead in conversations, speaking "for" Ha as I asked questions. Both of them claimed that Ha spoke little English, but she seemed to understand the discussion. Both had worked as pharmacists in Vietnam. Once in Canada Ha began sewing for a large American-owned clothing company because, as Vinh put it, "She could sew from a little girl." Vinh studied for Canadian accreditation to practise pharmacy, but he gave it up because he said he felt compelled to get into the workforce sooner "because I have to support my family." In 1988 they owed about $15,000 on the family home and owned two cars, but they said they spent a lot of money on their children for things like piano and computer lessons. For a time they both worked in factories, Vinh as an electronics technician, while Ha sewed. They worked different shifts so that they could look after the children, and relied on a neighbour to watch the children during periods when they were both unavailable. After a couple of years Vinh's father joined them from Vietnam. In 1980 Ha began doing industrial homework as well as her factory job. There was a good supply of work for her, and in 1982 she gave up her factory job to concentrate on home sewing. In 1986 Vinh followed suit, Ha providing some sewing instruction, "But I taught myself, too." Vinh explained how they brought all the family labour to the task:

The whole family sews, the children help, my father, he doesn't have anything else to do. There are a lot of odd jobs with home sewing, we need them.

With both Ha and Vinh working eight to ten hour days, seven days a week, and with the help of the other family members, they could make about $400 a week. Since Ha was the experienced sewer, she always carried out the more skilled parts of the work, like the collars and cuffs on shirts.

Over the next couple of years the company for which they sewed altered its design concept. According to Vinh:

[The piecerate is] exactly the same, but the designs are more and more difficult, so you make less money. So a lot of people quit, they don't want to work because they make less money than they can make in the factory. It's exactly the same [work], but if you work in the factory you get benefits, but at home we don't get anything.

By 1988 their weekly income from sewing had dropped to about $300, and Ha went back to a job outside the home, working the night shift at a meat processing factory, where she could get important benefits such as health insurance premium contributions, but she still carried out the more difficult sewing tasks. As Vinh says:

A couple of hours a day. And sometimes when she has spare time, because there are parts I can't do.

GRACE'S HOUSEHOLD

Grace immigrated in the early 1970s. In Italy, she had worked in a dry cleaning shop, and she did the same kind of work in Toronto. When she had children she stopped working for pay and started again when her youngest child was seven. Then she took up sewing leather nurses' shoes at home. She began sewing about 100 pairs of shoes a week, but it became increasingly demanding and time-consuming work:

Sometimes one pair would take maybe 10 minutes, maybe more, but some took a lot more. I made maybe $3 an hour, but it's no good to work so much. My hands tired with so much work.

She spent sixty to seventy hours per week sewing, helped by her daughter, and was constantly pressured by the company to take more and more shoes each week. Everything had to be ready to return to the factory on a Friday morning:

I wake up at 5 o'clock in the morning, and work, then finish at 7:30, call the kids, make something for them to go to school, and start the shoes again at 9. I fix something in the house [domestic labour], but not every day because I don't have time.... If I fix the house I don't fix the shoes ... I finish at 11:30 because my kids come home for lunch. Then at 1:00 I start again the shoes, and finish at 5:00, then cook for the family, they eat, then at 7:30 or 8:00, when they have finished I start the shoes again, and finish at 10:00 or 11:00.

I work a little bit Sunday, one hour or two hours. I work hard on Saturday. If I work Sunday 2 or 3 hours, then the week stay okay, I don't have to work to 11 every night. If I don't work Sunday, trouble in the week.

If other responsibilities intruded on her work time, she would often stay up all night on Thursday to finish. At the same time she looked after a neighbour's child during the day. She explained that she finally gave up the shoe work because her husband felt she was making too little money from it. She then found work cooking at an Italian banquet room where she worked on Saturdays throughout the year, and on Sundays and Mondays as well in the busy wedding season in May and June. Her hourly rate of $8 was considerably more than the $2 or $3 an hour she made from industrial homework, but she was usually away from home from 9 on Saturday morning until the early hours of Sunday. Her daughter sometimes worked there with her.

Grace's husband worked as a cabinet maker for a small contractor. He had a close friendship with his boss, and Grace was expected to prepare canned tomatoes and preserves for the boss's wife. She disliked this woman and had told her husband she would do this no more. In late summer Grace always prepared vegetables for preserves for the family. Either she or her husband went to pick them, then she would get up one morning at about 4:00 AM, and with her daughter's help, she would prepare twenty bushels of tomatoes for bottling. She also preserved other vegetables, and grew her own garden for the family's day-to-day needs through the summer.

INDUSTRIAL HOMEWORK: IN THE CONCEPTUAL SPACE BETWEEN WORK AND HOME

These two case studies show that a sexual division of labour where men go out to work, while women stay home and do not "work," does not correspond with the lives of the industrial homeworkers. While both the women had worked outside the home at some time, the responsibility for domestic labour[4] hangs heavy on their minds, and they measure other activities beside it. Ideology reinforces the primacy of the roles of wife and mother in the family, while the role of "worker" is given secondary status. As the daughter of another elderly industrial homeworker expressed it:

My mom doesn't want to work hard, she just wants to relax. Working at home is easy for her, because she can do anything she wants, any time. It's not difficult to get jobs, but she doesn't want to because she wants to take care of us.

There is a degree of ambiguity in the way the daughter speaks of her mother's work. When she says, "Working at home is easy," she could as easily be referring to domestic labour as to industrial homework. It is this ambiguity at the boundary between paid and unpaid work which permits both to take place in the same place and during the same time period. Women do not necessarily perform all the domestic labour, but they are responsible for ensuring that it is done. By his own assessment, Vinh performed most of the domestic labour in their household, and Ha agreed that he did more than she because he spent his days at home. He said he was a better cook than she was, but also expressed the general idea that some tasks such as cooking were usually better carried out by women. Although such a discrepancy between general ideas and actual practice in the household gives rise to tensions, it does not necessarily alter ways of thinking. Hence, it was more likely to be daughters who were called on to help with domestic labour, and not sons, in Ha and Vinh's household as well as in many others I knew.

The early socialization of girls into domestic labour helps to reproduce the social relations which assign such labour to women, freeing men from the responsibility for ensuring that domestic labour is done. Being responsible for domestic labour does not exclude women from taking paid work of some kind, but the kinds of paid work they do are constrained by the ideology which gives primacy to their roles as housewives who do not work in the paid labour force. Thus for Grace, responsible for performing all the domestic tasks, paid work was limited to certain informal work, while Ha, who no longer performed most of the domestic labour, could take a full-time factory job. Working at home permits some flexibility regarding time, and there is the perception of having more control over it (Sanchis 1984). Yet Vinh and Grace make it quite clear that their hours of work are very long.

In the absence of a traditional division of labour, there is still a distinctive difference between the way male labour and female labour is mobilized, which relates to the way the concepts of family and work are constructed. Vinh was not the only man I encountered who had performed industrial homework, but he was the only one who continued to do it, and who carried out most of the domestic labour. In Grace's household the gendered division of labour fulfilled the expectation of a man who worked outside the home and a woman whose work was home based, but clearly she worked a lot. All the paid work activities of the women, formal (in the full-time labour force outside the home) and informal ("casual" forms of homework), were intensified domestic labour (e.g., food processing and sewing), underlining the way certain skills are "naturally" acquired.

In both these households every member played some part in the work strategy, and everyone was expected to work to make money. Yet the divisions of labour within the households are quite different. In Ha and Vinh's case the division of labour had changed as they moved away from formal work outside the home to entirely home-based work, and then returned to some formal work outside the home, carried out by the woman. In both households younger people were expected to work as well, and even where a premium was placed on their education, as in Ha and Vinh's household, they were expected to participate in an unpaid capacity with the industrial work being performed at home. In many of the households I knew, however, teenaged children were expected to contribute to the household financially by getting a paid part-time job. There was an unquestioned expectation that all family members would contribute to the informal work of the household in whatever way they could. In Ha and Vinh's household, the children and grandfather helped, and Ha took on skilled tasks relating to the industrial homework as well as holding a formal job. Grace's daughter helped to sew shoes and later worked in the banquet hall. This amounted to a significant contribution of work in most of these households, yet it is a form of work in and for the family which analysts often overlook.

Those adults most heavily engaged in casual work are responsible also for the major part of domestic labour performed in the home, and this applied as much to Vinh, the male industrial homeworker, as to the women homeworkers. But although Vinh performed domestic labour, I would argue that the ultimate *responsibility* for these tasks remained with Ha, and the clue to this is in the contradiction between Vinh's ideas about domestic labour and the day-to-day practice in his own household. When women do paid work as well as domestic labour, they themselves, their families and the people they work for identify them as housewives first. When women take paid work, it is an extension of their domestic work, both in terms of their role and in terms of the kinds of work they turn to (in other words, their jobs are related to domestic activities, such as sewing, cooking and caring for children). Their task is to improve the financial situation of the household, not to assume an occupational status of their own.

When men take on industrial homework and domestic labour it is, I would argue, an indication of their greater power to make personal choices. Vinh said he liked to stay at home "because I can go out for coffee with my friends," a sentiment I never heard expressed by any of the women industrial homeworkers. Gender ideology is clearly a very powerful component here. Although familial ideologies are brought forward to provide the underlying rationale for the work people do, ideas about working for the family are themselves underlain by ideologies about gender and work.

While industrial homework may occupy a significant amount of time and may indeed constitute an important source of income, it fails to achieve the status of real "work" on a number of counts. First, it is usually carried out by the housewife who is not considered to be a "worker"; second, it is not physically situated in a place specifically set aside for its practice; and third it is frequently one of a number of activities being carried out apparently simultaneously and from which it is often practically indistinguishable. All these features make the work women do flexible, and flexibility is thus a practical manifestation of the way women's work is ideologically constructed. This is an especially important issue in the present economic context where, as stable, secure, full-time jobs disappear, flexible work strategies (usually meaning part-time, irregular or contract jobs) are being promoted from many directions. While this is recognized as a shift in the kind of expectations men have of work, it is taken for granted that women's labour can be utilized in this way, in much the same fashion as it was in the nineteenth century, where the labour of women was profitable because it could be used in ways "which were traditionally forbidden and for which they had no well-developed expectations" (Reddy 1987:163).

In this chapter I have tried to show how struggles around the labour process during the Industrial Revolution involved the allocation of men and women to certain positions in that labour process. This then formed the basis for a sexual division of labour under capitalism based on the separation of home and work, where men and women have certain and different expectations regarding the kind of work they will perform during their lives. These include ideological determinants of what work is and what it is not, who "works" and who doesn't, what a man is and does and what a woman is and does. These expectations order the family and define the social possibilities for men and women (Kessler-Harris and Sacks 1987:71). Women ought to be housewives who do not "work," while men are the ones who should "work." Yet economic, social and political forces shaping the everyday struggle to make ends meet make these roles difficult to fulfil in practice. The cultural construction of the key categories of work and family is in tension with their actual practice. On a daily basis people have to deal with contradictions for which they are ideologically unprepared, and this leads to renegotiation on a daily basis. Women's "work" is disguised as domestic labour, and not "labour" in the sense of a commodity which is bought and sold. Being a housewife encompasses a wide range of activities which are not simply reproduction, but include productive work as well. In the work culture of southern Ontario, industrial homework exists then in the conceptual interstices between home and work.

In the late 1970s feminist scholars took the idea of "the family" (closely linked, as we have seen, to the idea of home) and made it a problem for analysis, emphasizing people's different experiences within and between families on the basis of gender, age and class. In a similar way, feminists have reconsidered the idea of "work," insisting upon examining a wider range of tasks than the male, blue-collar jobs traditionally the focus of work studies. This has opened up to scholarly scrutiny forms of work, like industrial homework, performed mainly by women, which had been largely neglected. As we move toward the twenty-first century the only kind of work available to more and more people is "poor work" (Brown and Scase 1991), meaning work that pays below a living wage. Yet what such work means to peoples' everyday lives can easily remain a private matter. However cognizant of ideology they may be, members of households negotiate cultural practices within the limitations of difficult living conditions. Feminist ethnographic approaches to examining these kinds of work make the everyday reality of subjective experiences essential for analysis. As casual forms of work like industrial homework become more common, and certainly more visible in the 1990s, feminist approaches to its study will be necessary to sustain an analysis which both accounts for personal experience and promotes political change.

NOTES

1.   An earlier version of this paper was presented at the meetings of the Canadian Anthropological Society, London, Ontario in May 1991. The research reported here was carried out for a doctoral degree in social anthropology at the University of Toronto and was financially supported by the Social Sciences and Humanities Research Council of Canada. Field research was carried out between 1987 and 1989 and included interviews with homeworkers, subcontractors, company management, union representatives and others, as well as the analysis of company documents.

2.   By industrial homework I mean work that is carried out in the home, which is supplied by a work distributor who is also responsible for the disposal of the product, and which is paid for by the piece. For important contributions to the literature on homework see Johnson 1992 and Lipsig Mumme 1983 for Canada; Allen and Wolkowitz 1987 for England; Benería and Roldán 1987 for Mexico; Benton 1990 for Spain; Boris and Daniels 1989 for the United States.

3.   It may appear to be rather a large leap to make the connection between industrializing England in the nineteenth century and Ontario in the late 1980s. I would argue, however, that industrial England is part of the historical culture of Ontario and that along with the penetration of capitalism into "peripheral" regions such as Canada went ideas about work and gender which developed in early industrial England. As far as this study is concerned, significant among these ideas was an ideology of male breadwinner and female dependant. The English pattern of industrialization was then assumed to have followed, although empirically the sexual division of labour may not have mirrored the ideology. For a discussion of the discrepancy between ideas about industrialization and actual practices in Ontario see Cohen 1988.

4.   I define domestic labour as unpaid reproductive work undertaken in the home. As I point out later in the essay, the division between industrial homework and domestic labour is not always a clear one, especially since other members of the family may help in the industrial homework but not be paid.

BIBLIOGRAPHY

ALLEN, Sheila, and Carol Wolkowitz. 1987. *Homeworking: Myths and Realities.* Basingstoke: Macmillan.

BENERÍA, L., and M. Roldán. 1987. *The Crossroads of Class and Gender.* Chicago: University of Chicago Press.

BENTON, Lauren A. 1990. *Invisible Factories.* Buffalo: SUNY Press.

BORIS, Eileen, and Cynthia R. Daniels, eds. 1989. *Homework: Historical and Contemporary Perspectives on Paid Labor at Home.* Urbana: University of Illinois Press.

BROWN, P., and R. Scase, eds. 1991. *Poor Work: Disadvantage and the Division of Labour.* Milton Keynes: Open University Press.

BURAWOY, M. 1985. *The Politics of Production.* London: Verso.

COHEN, M.G. 1988. *Women's Work, Markets and Economic Development in Nineteenth-Century Ontario.* Toronto: University of Toronto Press.

COLEMAN, D.C. 1983. "Protoindustrialization: A Concept too Many." *Economic History Review.* 2nd Series 36:435-48.

DI LEONARDO, M. 1984. *The Varieties of Ethnic Experience: Kinship, Class and Gender among California Italian Americans.* Ithaca: Cornell University Press.

GINSBURG, F., and Tsing, A.L., eds. 1990. *Uncertain Terms: Negotiating Gender in American Culture.* Boston: Beacon.

GOLDTHORPE, J.H., D. Lockwood, F. Bechhofer, and J. Platt. 1968. *The Affluent Worker: Industrial Attitudes and Behaviour.* Cambridge: Cambridge University Press.

HALL, C. 1980. "The History of the Housewife." In *The Politics of Housework,* ed. E. Malos. London: Allison and Busby, 44-71.

HARRIS, O. 1981. "Households as Natural Units." In *Of Marriage and the Market,* ed. K. Young, C. Wolkowitz and R. McCullagh. London: CSE Books, 49-68.

HARTMANN, Heidi I. 1982. "Capitalism, Patriarchy and Job Segregation by Sex." In *Classes, Power and Conflict,* ed. A. Giddens and D. Held. Berkeley: University of California Press, 446-69.

HOBSBAWM, E. 1984. *Workers: Worlds of Labour.* New York: Pantheon.

HUMPHRIES, J. 1977. "Class Struggle and the Persistence of the Working-class Family." *Cambridge Journal of Economics* 1:241-58.

JOHNSON, L.C. 1982. *The Seam Allowance: Industrial Home Sewing in Canada.* Toronto: Women's Press.

KESSLER-HARRIS, A., and Karen Brodkin Sacks. 1987. "The Demise of Domesticity in America." In *Women, Households and the Economy,* ed. L. Benería and C. Stimpson. New Brunswick NJ: Rutgers University Press.

LIPSIG MUMME, Carla. 1983. "The Renaissance of Homeworking in Developed Economies." *Relations industrielles* 38(3):545-67.

MEDICK, H. 1976. "The Proto-industrial Family Economy: The Structural Function of Household and Family during the Transition from Peasant Society to Industrial Capitalism." *Social History* 3:291-315.

MILLER, S.M. 1988. Foreword. In *The New Era of Home-based Work: Directions and Policies,* ed. K. Christensen. Boulder: Westview Press.

PINFIELD, L.T., and J.S. Atkinson. 1988. "The Flexible Firm." *Canadian Business Review* 15(4):17-19.

PIORE, M.J., and C.F. Sabel. 1984. *The Second Industrial Divide: Possibilities of Prosperity.* New York: Basic Books.

POLLERT, A. 1981. *Girls, Wives, Factory Lives.* London: MacMillan.

———. 1988. "The Flexible Firm: Fact or Fiction?" *Work, Employment and Society* 2(3):281-316.

RAPP, R., E. Ross, and R. Bridenthal. 1979. "Examining Family History." *Feminist Studies.* 5(1):174-200.

REDDY, W.A. 1987. *Money and Liberty in Modern Europe.* Cambridge: Cambridge University Press.

SANCHIS, E. 1984. *El trabajo a domicilio en el pais Valenciano.* Madrid: Ministero de Cultura: Instituo de la Mujer.

STACEY, J. 1990. *Brave New Families.* New York: Basic Books.

STEDMAN Jones, G. 1983. *Languages of Class.* Cambridge: Cambridge University Press.

STICHTER, S., and J. Parpart. 1990. *Women, Employment and the Family in the International Division of Labour.* Basingstoke: Macmillan.

THOMPSON, E.P. 1963. *The Making of the English Working Class.* Harmondsworth: Penguin.

WESTWOOD, Sallie. 1984. *All Day Every Day.* London: Pluto.

WILLIAMS, R. 1976. *Keywords: A Vocabulary of Culture and Society.* London: Fontana.

WOOD, S. 1989. "The Transformation of Work?" In *The Transformation of Work? Skill, Flexibility and the Labour Process,* ed. S. Wood. London: Unwin Hyman.

CHAPTER 9

"I Know Now that You Can Change Things"

NARRATIVES OF CANADIAN BANK WORKERS AS UNION ACTIVISTS

Patricia Baker

We didn't even know how many would go out. We had no idea amongst our own friends if they would go or not. No one knew until ten to twelve, when Peggy got up and said we were ... taking off. And everybody went, and we were so shocked. There were so many people in one department where we were going to have our sit-in that you couldn't move ... and I thought, holy shit, after all this it's so nice to see everybody finally get out of those chairs ... I was so happy. That was one hell of a strike, I tell you ...

Jackie, bank worker and union activist. February 3, 1989

WHY — DESPITE THEIR "OBJECTIVE" CIRCUMSTANCES of poor working conditions, low wages, limited opportunities for advancement and job security, diminished job quality, and job loss due to technological change — have the majority of women bank workers across Canada not successfully unionized?[1] Bank workers have been the targets of at least a dozen unions which have, with varying degrees of interest and intensity, attempted to organize bank branches and larger bank offices in rural and urban areas and in virtually every province in Canada during the past fifteen years. In the short term, these efforts have in some cases been successful.[2] In the longer term, however, the extent of union membership in the Canadian financial industry as a whole (including banks, credit unions, caisses populaires, etc.) has been extremely limited, involving in 1988, for example, no more than 4 percent of all financial workers (Statistics Canada, 1990:40).

Academics, including myself, have tended to focus on the structural and ideological constraints which limit women bank workers' interest in and ability to unionize.[3] What I have come to realize in my current research is that we can also learn a great deal about the potential for bank unionization from bank workers' direct involvement in union activity. In this paper I argue that we gain important insights into bank workers' positive unionization experiences, and not simply the limitations they face, by viewing union activity from the perspectives of unionized bank workers themselves. The bases of my argument are the narratives of six women bank workers, in which they discuss and evaluate both their experiences of union activism and leadership and the consequences of these experiences for their lives.

Several themes emerge from the stories these women tell. First and foremost is the fact that, although the experiences and circumstances of these women are diverse, union activism offered them collective strength that they had previously not known, individual self-confidence, the resources to improve their lives beyond the workplace and a sense of the community networks within which they live and work. Further, they considered the extent to which their experiences of unionism are filtered through the matrix of family relationships and whether consequently their possibilities for empowerment are nurtured or stifled. In this article I argue, following the work of Karen Sacks (1989), that women bank workers' narratives illuminate for us a variety of ways in which relations of community and family are central to women's empowerment through union activism.

WOMEN BANK WORKERS AND THEIR UNIONS

Women's stories of resistance and collective action in the paid work-place have been acknowledged in recent academic work.[4] Specifically, Sacks (1989), in her research among hospital workers attempting to unionize at Duke Medical Centre in the United States, found that learning the life histories of a number of activist women gave her insight into the relationships among race, gender and family, and work and unionization. Like me, Sacks was puzzled at the variable success and activism of women involved in the union drive at Duke. She found that women's life histories were important to her understanding of these issues, specifically because they could reveal how the interpersonal processes of politicization and activism develop and are nurtured. Sacks demonstrated that women's inter-personal experiences of activism are linked to the political and eco-nomic conditions within which such activism flourishes or stagnates. Further, she argued that life histories can expose the links between these levels — between individual experience and broader social, political and economic contexts that condition, and are con-ditioned by, that experience. These are precisely the sorts of issues which I believe are pertinent to our understanding of the unioniza-tion of Canadian bank workers.

Bank worker unionization in Canada has been an uneven process, both temporally (there have been "spurts" of organizing activity over the past fifteen years or so) and geographically. In recent years there have been prominent episodes of bank worker unionization in two Canadian communities: Toronto and Antigonish (Nova Scotia).[5] In each community not only have bank workers successfully organized, they have also gone on strike.

Between 1984 and 1986 in Toronto, the Visa Centre, the Mail Room, and the Mortgage Servicing Department of the Canadian Imperial Bank of Commerce (CIBC) were organized by the Union of Bank Employees (UBE — a directly chartered local of the Canadian Labour Congress). The Mortgage Servicing Department only remained unionized from 1986 to 1987. In 1985-86, the Visa Centre and Mail Room took part in a well-publicized strike, which resulted in the imposition of first contracts in each workplace. In

1987-88, eleven women workers at the Antigonish branch of the CIBC became involved in another high-profile strike (having been organized in 1986 with the UBE). Since 1988 I have been conducting field research on the unionization and strike process in each community. The narratives presented here come from interviews with six women who had participated in union activity — four at the Visa Centre in Toronto, one at the Mortgage Servicing Department in Toronto, and one at the CIBC branch in Antigonish.

Women at the Visa Centre

The four women I came to know at the Visa Centre were all long-time employees of the bank, having worked there at least ten years. None had ever been involved with a union before, although Jackie[6] was familiar with unions because her husband had been involved in one for many years. It was Jackie who, in response to increasing work loads, her harassment by management and a deterioration in her merit reports, had first enquired about unionization with the Canadian Labour Congress (CLC). Peggy, Lisa and Mary became involved shortly afterward, joining a small group of Visa workers and a CLC staff representative who spent months preparing to launch the very successful organizing drive. Once the Centre had been certified, these four women and one man became members of Visa's first bargaining committee and began negotiations with the CIBC for a first contract.

The Visa strike was an immediate response to the CIBC's intransigence in negotiations. Because the Visa Centre was the largest group of bank employees (about 250) to join a union since the CLC began its bank organizing drive in 1977, its strike was seen as a key test of the labour movement's ability to make inroads into the financial industry.

The strike was well orchestrated, tactically creative and consequently quite effective. It became the subject of national media coverage and public and trade union support (see Baker 1989b). The strike ended after six and a half months, when the Canada Labour Relations Board imposed a first contract at the Visa Centre and Mail Room, in response to its determination that the Bank of Commerce had remained anti-union in its bargaining.[7] The strike was an important event for many Visa workers, and especially so for Jackie, Peggy, Lisa and Mary, who were actively involved in running the strike office and setting up picket lines, organizing a wide variety of strike activities, speaking to union groups and the media, and becoming more informed about unions and the CLC through courses and steward training. The strike was a long one and its outcome far from certain, particularly in the face of constant management intimidation and surveillance. These four women were instrumental to the success of the strike. Not only were they involved in the negotiations with the bank, but they also emerged as leaders and public spokespeople during the strike.

In January of 1989 I asked them about their experiences and observations of the strike. According to Mary, a divorced woman without children who had worked at the Visa Centre for eleven years:

The five of us [on the bargaining committee], we were pretty strong in the fact that we would stand up to management, and we had to keep doing that because then other people would ... follow us.... We constantly had to be leading, and ... setting an example, pushing, trying to keep the spirit up [even through all the harassment that came up after the strike].

Peggy, who had worked at Visa for over ten years and whose husband was a union member, discussed the problems of developing leadership skills with Lisa, her co-worker and friend, who was unmarried and also a long-time Visa employee:

Peggy: Basically, too, we [the bargaining committee] ran the strike on our own, a lot ... we learned very fast ...
Lisa: We had no choice ...
Peggy: We'd never done courses on how to do collective bargaining. We learned extremely quickly. We never knew what mediation or conciliation were.... We put our own collective agreement together, with the guys' [the CLC and Auto Workers] help ... many, many late nights ...
Lisa: We were thrown in.... You either sank or you swam.... None of us were prepared to sink.... We got a very good education ... out of this experience.

Peggy: We educated a lot of people too ...[We] put on a lot of seminars ... collective bargaining ... public speaking ...

Lisa: I think for Peggy and I, it made us more aware.... We never knew that we had certain skills that we now possess.... We learned to write speeches on the spur of the moment.... We had to do things that we never did before.

The stresses of leadership and of a high profile within the union took its toll on them. Of these four women on the first bargaining committee, three were no longer working at the bank at the time of my interviews with them, having quit due to ongoing harassment from management and their consequent limited job opportunities with the bank.[8] Mary, the one remaining, took a break from formal union activism:

After the strike ... personally, I was very drained ... I got very drained physically, and I was very tired out also emotionally. After about the first year of being back in, I pulled away a lot from the leadership, but I was always there, people would still always come and ask my opinion, and I was always pushing discussion ...with different groups of my friends ... I'd never backed off on ... my ... feelings about unionism.... I backed away a little bit from the leadership and the politics for a while. And now I can look back on it and think ... emotionally and physically I needed to back away for a little while, because it was very stressful and draining.... You were always fighting the bank, you were always fighting to keep people involved and committed and interested ... [particularly afterwards, with the intimidation and harassment from the bank].

In the years since the first contract, the Visa Centre has remained unionized. Those years have not been trouble-free, however. Bank management remains hostile to the union, and there have been several unsuccessful attempts to decertify the Visa Centre (see Baker 1989b).[9]

Since the original leaders have either quit the bank, pulled back from union activism or been promoted,[10] active new leadership must emerge to prevent decertification and to maintain the union by rallying the membership at critical times. Reflecting on the task that faces those who take on leadership positions at Visa, Lisa (who had quit the bank in December, 1988) said:

If they can maintain a good rapport with the people ... they have to get away from ... a "them and us" situation.... They have to look at the new hires that have come in there, because there's an awful lot of them, and just don't think about our numbers being depleted, but these people can be an asset to us. If they do that, they won't have any problems with a decert[ification].... They've got to establish a working relationship with the people in there.

The Union at the Mortgage Servicing Department

Maria had worked at the Mortgage Department since 1985, having started work at the bank a year after her university graduation in 1984. She lived with her parents throughout university and continued to do so while she worked at the bank. She attended one of the union meetings held at Visa; as a result, she joined an organizing committee of about ten people at Mortgage, who were inspired by the events at Visa and who were anxious to improve the conditions of their workplace — including arbitrary supervision, promotion by favouritism, inconsistent merit reports, low wages and heavy work loads.

While like the women who worked at Visa, Maria had had no direct personal experience with unions, she told me that she had grown up and continued to live in an environment sympathetic to unionism:

We grew up in a socialist environment. So my parents have always been ... workers. And my mother used to work at Tip Top Tailors, and she was ... involved in strikes before, and unions, and, I mean, growing up I heard of all this, and this wasn't anything abnormal for me. Even when I was growing up — I wasn't born here, I was born in Italy — even when I was growing up in Italy, strikes were an everyday thing, I mean, if there was a strike going on, we wouldn't go to school, because of the strike, and so it wasn't anything ... out of the ordinary for me ... I've always believed in fighting for your rights.

According to Maria, her background clearly had an impact on her extensive involvement in the unionizing process at Mortgage.

Despite its promising beginnings and the hard work and enthusiasm of women like Maria, in the long term the process of unionization at Mortgage was unsuccessful. Worker mobilization was not as thorough as at Visa, and bank management effectively stalled the certification process with complex legal manoeuvres. Consequently, while the Mortgage Servicing Department was certified in 1986, it was decertified the following year (see Baker 1989b, 1991). When I first met Maria, in October of 1988, the Mortgage Servicing Department had long been decertified. Nevertheless, Maria herself remained active in the union. Not only was she involved in planning a renewed attempt to unionize Mortgage (an attempt which has not yet materialized), but she also worked with the CLC representative responsible for the UBE in the Toronto area as a volunteer bank organizer, trying to organize other bank workplaces.

As with the Visa women, the process of unionization was a transformative one for Maria, but in a different way. It altered her relationship to her workplace and had an impact on her plans for her own future:

That's what it's serving as right now, that's the purpose of me staying at the bank right now. To be quite honest with you, if I wasn't involved within the Union of Bank Employees, I would've been gone ... from the bank. I mean, it's not a place for me. Not because I feel I'm some terrific person, no. But, it's not a place for me. I don't want to be a bank worker. I don't want to be an office worker ... and in fact, at the time when I was ... ready to leave [the bank], I got involved [in the union].

These comments were prophetic of subsequent events in Maria's life. In a letter I received from her in September 1990, Maria told me of some important changes that had taken place for her:

Back in October/89 I had a car accident, it's not as bad as it sounds. The time away from the bank, gave me time to think about my future and the career I was interested in pursuing. I eventually returned to the bank after about a month and a half but during the time I was off, I had the

opportunity to look for other work ... I have resigned from CIBC and
started working with [another union, local X] back in May. I'm very
happy and excited about the work I'm doing, because as I said before the
time away from the bank made me think about my priorities, and by re-
examining myself I discovered that I wanted to devote my life to helping
working people.

Union Organizing in Antigonish

The working conditions which prompted unionization and the
strike in Antigonish (a town of about 5500 in eastern Nova Scotia)
were similar to those at the Visa Centre: low wages, management
favouritism in promotions and management arbitrariness, particularly with respect to merit evaluations. And as at Visa, specific
circumstances made deteriorating working conditions intolerable.
Branch management hired a person from another bank for a job for
which employees within the branch were qualified, but which was
not offered to them. At that point, in 1986, one employee at the
branch — Marilyn, the woman I interviewed — contacted a local
CLC organizer, and the drive to organize the branch began.

As was the case with Jackie, Peggy, Lisa, Mary and Maria,
Marilyn had had no experience with unions. She was born and
raised in Antigonish; she left the community to attend university,
but because she wanted to live in Antigonish (where she now lives,
with her sister), she returned there to find employment. The number of jobs available in Antigonish were limited; she took the job at
the bank about eleven years ago because it was considered to be a
reasonably good and well-paying job for a woman to have. However,
once working conditions had reached the point where she felt something had to be done, she contacted a friend, who put her in touch
with the local CLC organizer. He helped Marilyn and her co-workers to unionize, negotiate and strike. Marilyn became branch steward, and has been involved in all branch negotiations.

The strike at the Antigonish branch came during the second
round of negotiations (the first contract having established the
union in the branch). Like the Visa strike, the Antigonish strike
became a focus of local and national support. From November of
1987 to February of 1988, eleven (of a possible thirteen) women

bank workers walked a picket line to obtain what they and their supporters locally and nationally saw as a fair and reasonable settlement — a 15 percent wage increase that would give them parity with tellers at other banks in the province.

The Antigonish bank workers were attempting to do what other UBE branches (and the Visa Centre) had failed to do: make substantial monetary gains and thus prove that a union could provide bank workers with specific and real benefits. Although the women were intimidated by the prospect of being on strike and were uncertain of its outcome, they were encouraged by community support that began on the first day of the strike. This support came from several sources: a strike support group, the local university, the Catholic Church, trade unions, local businesses and community groups, the hospital workers, local media, women's groups, political parties and bank customers (see Baker 1989a).

National support for the strikers was prompted by Marilyn's appearance at the Bank of Commerce annual general meeting in Toronto in January 1988, at which she challenged bank management to come back to the bargaining table (talks had ended in September 1987). In response to this heightened, and now public, pressure, the bank agreed to resume negotiations in February 1988. The strike ended in late February when the strikers voted by a narrow margin to accept a wage increase substantially lower than their original demand — an increase of 7.3 percent over nineteen months, with a cash signing bonus.

This decision was a controversial one. According to various sources and contradicting official CLC claims, representatives from the CLC had coerced the women into accepting the settlement against their better judgment (see Baker 1989a, 1989c). However, despite the disappointments of the settlement, the strike had a positive impact on the women's perceptions of themselves and their jobs. Since the strike, several have become more assertive and willing to file grievances when complaints arise. With the experience of the strike and the support of the community they have come to realize their worth as people and as workers. By mobilizing themselves and winning a broad base of community, labour and national support, these women experienced, perhaps for the first time, the extent of their power in collective action.

Marilyn, who played an instrumental role in the success of the union in the branch, and who has served as steward and as one of the branch negotiators in each of its four rounds of negotiations, observed:

I'm not as afraid any more.... When I was in university if I had a course that had a seminar in it, I'd drop it ... so now I know you can do it if you really believe in what you're doing.... If it has to be done, it can be done ... I'm much more political [now].... Being on strike and being in a union I can see the labour laws ... weren't set up for workers ...

I know now ... I'd like to do this sort of work [working with unions. I was wandering around before, I'd] never found something that was really interesting for me to do... [It's taking up most of my time,] I don't really have a social life any more ... [but] that's what I want to do, and I really like it ... I know now that you can change things ...

[Forming a union and going on strike made me realize that] ... if you think it's important enough, then go for it, and fight for it ...

I think, one of the things that, not so much from belonging to a union as such, but being on strike ... is we're much more tolerant of ... people.... The people that supported us during the strike sometimes were the worst customers we had.... You judge people on what their beliefs are.... They may still be cranky ... but you respect them for what they believe in.... I find that that has made a big difference ...

[As a result of forming a union and going on strike, the women in the branch] feel more towards women now, they can see women should be sticking together more.... They've recognized the fact that yes, the bank was discriminating against us because we were women ...

I think people see you differently [as a result of the strike].... Well, I think now they see you!.... People in town ... still ask ... they know when our negotiations are going on ... they ask how they're going ... are you going to be out again ...

The town ... took it [the strike] on as their own ... they feel a part of it....
[I think that] Antigonish is kind of proud of itself that it was the town
that took them [the Bank of Commerce] on. (interview, February 1991)

The branch remains organized, largely because of the positive
relationships that developed, as Marilyn described them, among the
workers and with the community.

ANALYSIS AND CONCLUSIONS

While all six women shared the experience of unionization — an
experience uncommon for the vast majority of bank workers — its
impact on their lives, and their impact on it, varied a great deal, for
a number of reasons. Perhaps the most obvious point to be made is
that, although their participation was key to the transformation not
only of their own but of their co-workers' conditions of work, for
each woman it was also a profound personal experience. Union
activism was not simply an experience impinging on their lives from
outside; it became a part of their lives and of their identities as
women and as workers.

The longer-term consequences of these experiences were different among these women. As mentioned earlier, of the four women
at Visa, three no longer work for the bank. Peggy saw no future for
herself at Visa and left the bank because of her union activity. She
went to work at a centre for education and skills training in Toronto
where she continued to be involved in union politics in her new
workplace, and in the bargaining committee in particular. Lisa was
looking for a new job when I last spoke to her in 1989, having quit
the bank the month before because of management harassment and
limited job opportunities. Jackie also left the bank because of limited opportunities, and at the time I interviewed her was working
for an employment agency. She told me that she loved the freedom
and variety of working for different employers. Mary remained with
Visa, but had pulled back from her unionizing activity; when I
interviewed her, however, she was beginning to get actively involved
again, and had stood for recording secretary of the union local.

While it was clear from my conversations with the women at
Visa that they had learned a great deal about themselves, their co-

workers, unions and the bank from their union activity, it also appears that for some, at least, the knowledge was not union- or bank-specific. That is, they recognized the limitations facing them in staying with the bank; their union experiences not only gave them a whole new range of skills and expertise, but also the confidence to move on to better, more satisfying employment. As Lisa commented to me:

The bank is not ... the be [all] or end all.... There is life after the Bank of Commerce.

Maria also discovered "life after the Bank of Commerce." In her case, however, her union activity had a specific impact on her life. Ironically, though the union was far less successful at Mortgage than at Visa, Maria herself remains committed to union activism and organizing. The direction her life has taken is directly attributable to her union experiences, and she now perceives union activism as a central component of her life and her identity.

Marilyn's experiences have produced yet another set of outcomes for her. Not only has her involvement in unionism changed her life but she has had, and plans to continue having, a major role to play in the union at the Antigonish branch. She is less clear about what the future might hold for her than Maria appears to be, but feels a strong sense of responsibility to the branch, her co-workers, and the union:

I'd like to see our union issue settled ... a good strong union. I think then I would look elsewhere ... I wouldn't leave right now.... I think I started something and I should see it through.... I wouldn't ever want to leave and see it fail.

In order to gain an understanding of the variability and similarity of these bank workers' experiences and circumstances, and based on my interviews with Jackie, Lisa, Peggy, Mary, Maria and Marilyn, I have found two avenues important to explore: the role of community networks and the nature of women's family roles.

First let us examine the relationship of community networks to successful unionism, to the nature and extent of support for women's union activism and to the possible choices and social networks available to women in their paid and unpaid work lives. Toronto and Antigonish clearly are very different communities in size, history, geographic situation and political and economic location in Canada. As I mentioned earlier, and as I have discussed in more detail elsewhere (see Baker 1989a), the Antigonish strike and the bank workers' union activities had a considerable, enduring and largely positive impact on the community of Antigonish. To a large extent, Marilyn's union activism and the success of unionism within the community were accepted and supported because Marilyn was a native of Antigonish with well-established roots in the community. This factor is particularly interesting given not only Marilyn's original lack of familiarity with unions, but the fact that Antigonish itself has very little in the way of union traditions within which to situate bank workers' union activity (see Baker 1989a).

The role of community is very different in a city like Toronto, which incorporates different ethnic communities and municipal jurisdictions. The impact of the Visa strike in such an environment was largely due to its success as a "media event" (a success created by the hard work of the women active in the union, of labour representatives from the CLC and the Canadian Auto Workers), and to the fact of Visa's uniqueness as the largest bank unit organized by the CLC. I have explored elsewhere in greater detail (see Baker 1989b) reasons why I feel that Visa was so successful, including the course and timing of the organizing drive and certification, the Visa strike itself, successful mobilization of union membership and support by union activists, and support from the labour movement. Clearly any notion of "community" in this case is very different from Marilyn's experiences in Antigonish.

Paradoxically, while situated very similarly to Visa in terms of location, size and working conditions, the unionization of the Mortgage Servicing Department was never as successful as Visa. In fact, I have argued elsewhere (Baker 1989b) that the success of the one was linked to the failure of the other. The organizing drive at Mortgage was not independent of the Visa drive, nor did the union have the kind of worker support or organizational infrastructure at Mortgage that it did at Visa. Mortgage had no strike to galvanize and draw workers together. The relationship between leadership and membership at Mortgage was not so reciprocally positive as at Visa. Willing and energetic leaders like Maria were unable to communicate their own commitment to the union because there was little in the material experiences of Mortgage workers with regard to the union to reinforce that enthusiasm. And finally, while the CLC was prepared to go to great lengths to ensure that the Visa Centre was organized and that it gained a wide range of union and popular support, it did not provide the Mortgage Servicing Department with similar extensive support.

Thus the six women activists were operating within very different internal and external structural conditions. As a result, as individuals their impacts, both within their particular workplace and in other social and work contexts — and the impact of union activity on them — have been quite different.

Second, it is clear from the women's narratives that in each situation unionization depended directly on the appearance of individual women as leaders. These leaders not only responded to the process of unionization or the anticipation of a strike; they were in large part responsible for generating interest in the union and support for the strikes. Analysis of the conditions under which some women emerge as leaders requires us to explore their family relationships, because, as Karen Sacks (1989) has noted, one prevailing view within labour unions and on the left is that women's participation in unions and more specifically in union leadership positions are compromised by their ongoing domestic responsibilities and family focus. However, as Sacks also suggests, recent studies by labour historians of women's union militancy indicate that family and kinship ties among women and among women and men may in fact promote activism.

In order to better understand the role of women's family relationships in their union activism, I asked each woman about her family. As mentioned earlier, three were single, but each lived with family members — Lisa with her mother, Maria with her parents and Marilyn with her sister. Mary was divorced (with no children), and Peggy and Jackie were married at the time of my interviews with them. Both husbands were union members themselves and remained supportive of their wives throughout the Visa strike. Jackie had a twenty-year-old son, and Peggy had two children, fourteen and sixteen. In these respects, their different family circumstances appeared less restricting than for many women in their workplaces, who had unsympathetic husbands and small children to care for. When I asked Marilyn about her role as a leader, she acknowledged that women's domestic circumstances were an important factor in their ability to become and remain active in their union:

I've never considered myself a leader.... I don't really care to be, I could work very well in the background. But I think it's just ... circumstances were right in my case.... I was older, I've been there a long time.... To be older and still to be single and not have any children.... I was somewhat the same age as the ones older than me, I just don't have the family responsibilities.... They didn't look at me ... as a smart aleck young kid trying to tell them ... what to do.... I had the time to do it.... There are women there probably who are just as capable as I am, but they just don't have the time.... If it ... meant that I had to go to a meeting to meet somebody or call somebody or leave town ... and it meant that I didn't put supper on that night, nobody cared.... I didn't get static from a husband or kids if I was away a lot, or this was taking up a lot of my time.... Because we're new ... [and because] the CLC doesn't seem to be doing much to educate us ... I take it upon myself to go to all kinds of things that normally if I had a family I wouldn't really be able to do.

Clearly, family connections are an important consideration in our understanding of women's activism. But the matter is more complex than this. As these women's narratives suggest, there is an intricate set of relationships between familial history, women's present circumstances, community connections, workplace conditions, and women's awareness of, interest in and capacity to engage in union activism.

The narratives presented here offer us two final conclusions. First, women bank workers' narratives tell us directly about the obstacles they face in attempting to improve their working conditions; these stories also help us understand how structural conditions which affect work places, communities and indeed different regions of Canada are directly experienced by women in their work places, homes and communities. Second, as we learn about the realities of women's working lives by listening to their stories, the stereotypes of the disinterested, passive or frightened woman worker disappear. We learn that women do act to change and improve their own and others' lives. By listening to women's stories, we learn about women and their daily struggles — in short, we reveal the reality of women's empowerment.

□

I would like to thank the Social Sciences and Humanities Research Council of Canada for its financial assistance through a Postdoctoral Fellowship in 1988-89, which provided me with the resources to do the research for this article. I would also like to thank Lynne Phillips and Sally Cole for their insightful and supportive comments and criticisms; the responsibility for the final product is, of course, my own.

NOTES

1. This paper is part of a larger research project which includes the collection of interviews and women's life histories to investigate the development and consequences of union activism and leadership among women who are active in bank unions.

2. See, for example, the successes of the Service, Office Retail Workers Union of Canada (SORWUC) in the late 1970s in British Columbia and Saskatchewan (The Bank Book Collective 1979); the certification (with the CSN), as a single unit, of employees at all branches of the National Bank of Canada in Rimouski, Quebec (see the Canada Labour Relations Board 1985; Warskett 1988); the unionization of the Visa Centre (1984) and the Mortgage Servicing Department (1986) of the Canadian Imperial Bank of Commerce (CIBC) in Toronto (Baker 1989b); the unionization and strike at the Antigonish, Nova Scotia branch of the CIBC (see Baker 1989a; Gilson, Spencer and Granville 1989).

3. For a detailed examination of these factors, including the changing structure of the Canadian financial system, bank managements' consistent anti-unionism, the structure of federal labour law in Canada, inter-union rivalries, and men's attitudes about and responses to women's union participation, see Baker 1991, 1989a, 1989b, 1989c; The Bank Book Collective 1979; Beckett 1984; Beynon and Blackburn 1984; Brown 1984;

Costello 1988; FitzGerald 1981; Lennon 1980; Lowe 1978, 1980; Purcell 1984; and Warskett 1987, 1988.

More generally it has been argued that while women may be willing to take part in active struggles to change their conditions of work, for a variety of reasons it has been and remains difficult for women to engage in sustained participation in unions. Certainly the nature of the work of many women does make it difficult for them to become consistently and actively involved in their unions. With their double burdens of paid work and domestic labour, many women do not have the time or energy to participate in union negotiations, meetings or conferences, particularly when these are held on evenings or weekends. Nevertheless, despite these obstacles women have been and continue to be active in their unions.

4. The collection of life histories has been an important method of research in a variety of disciplines, including anthropology, history, literary studies and sociology (see, for example, Allen and Montell 1981; Anderson et al. 1990; Geiger 1986; Grele 1975; Henige 1982; Langness and Frank 1981; The Personal Narratives Group 1989; Plummer 1983; Shostak 1981).

5. In the late 1970s Vancouver, the Lower Mainland of British Columbia and the islands off the coast of British Columbia were the focus of organizing activity involving the Service, Office, Retail Workers Union of Canada (SORWUC) (see The Bank Book Collective 1979).

6. All names used here are pseudonyms.

7. There has been considerable debate concerning whether this contract was the victory for the interests of bank workers that it was anticipated to be. On the one hand it included a number of issues for which the workers had been negotiating; on the other it retained certain management prerogatives (including the right to give workers merit pay), there were no improvements in benefit plans and there were no across-the-board wage increases (see the Canada Labour Relations Board 1986). Perhaps the most important material gain made by the Visa workers as a consequence of the strike was the establishment of a union in their workplace.

8. Two of these three, Peggy and Lisa, had taken on other leadership positions after the strike: Peggy was the first chairperson of the Visa unit in Local 2104 of UBE (the local for all organized bank units in Ontario) from 1984 until she left the bank in 1987; after she left, Lisa was elected to that position. In addition, Peggy was Secretary-Treasurer of Local 2104 from 1986 to 1988. Lisa was re-elected to the bargaining committee, and was the President of Local 2104 from 1986 until her resignation from the bank in late 1988.

9. In December 1989 the CLC gave jurisdiction over bank workers in Ontario to the United Steelworkers of America. The Visa workers are now members of the United Steelworkers Local 2104B. In Nova Scotia, the only unionized bank branch in the province to vote against joining the Steelworkers was the branch in Antigonish. It is too early to say what the long-term implications of this shift in jurisdiction will be for unionized bank workers.

10. The one man on the bargaining committee was promoted.

BIBLIOGRAPHY

ALLEN, Barbara, and William Lynwood Montell. 1981. *From Memory to History. Using Oral Sources in Local Historical Research.* Nashville, TN: The American Association for State and Local History.

ANDERSON, Kathryn, Susan Armitage, Dana Jack, and Judith Wittner. 1990. "Beginning Where We Are. Feminist Methodology in Oral History." In *Feminist Research Methods. Exemplary Readings in the Social Sciences,* ed. Joyce McCarl Nielsen. Boulder, CO: Westview Press, 94-112.

BAKER, Patricia. 1989a. "Union and Community: The Case of the Bank Workers in Antigonish." Paper presented at the CESCE Annual Meetings, University of Ottawa, May 20-23.

———. 1989b. "Organizing and Staying Organized: Issues for Bank Workers." Paper presented at the Canadian Sociology and Anthropology Association 24th Annual Meeting, Laval University, June 3-6.

———. 1989c. "Unionizing Canadian Bank Workers: Time for a Change?" Paper presented at the International Colloquium: Gender and Class, University of Antwerp, Antwerp, Belgium, September 18-20.

———. 1991. "Some Unions are More Equal than Others: A Response to Rosemary Warskett's 'Bank Worker Unionization and the Law'." *Studies in Political Economy* 34(Spring):219-33.

The Bank Book Collective. 1979. *An Account to Settle. The Story of the United Bank Workers (SORWUC).* Vancouver: Press Gang Publishers.

BECKETT, Elizabeth. 1984. *Unions and Bank Workers: Will the Twain Ever Meet?* Prepared for The Women's Bureau, Labour Canada. Ottawa: Minister of Supply and Services Canada.

BEYNON, Huw and Robert Blackburn. 1984. "Unions: The Men's Affair?" In *Women and the Public Sphere. A Critique of Sociology and Politics,* ed. Janet Siltanen and Michelle Stanworth. London: Hutchinson, 75-88

BROWN, Richard. 1984. "Women as Employees: Social Consciousness and Collective Action." In *Women and the Public Sphere. A Critique of Sociology and Politics,* ed. Janet Siltanen and Michelle Stanworth. London: Hutchinson, 68-74.

CANADA Labour Relations Board. 1985. La Banque Nationale du Canada, Rimouski, Quebec. Decisions Information Board File 555-1685, Decision No. 542.

———. 1986. Collective Agreements Settled by the Canada Labour Relations Board Between the Chargex Centre and the Mail Room and Reproduction Services, and the Union of Bank Employees, Local 2104, January 27. Toronto.

COSTELLO, Cynthia B. 1988. "Women Workers and Collective Action: A Case Study from the Insurance Industry." In *Women and the Politics of Empowerment,* ed. Ann Bookman and Sandra Morgen. Philadelphia: Temple University Press, 116-35.

FITZGERALD, Maureen. 1981. "Whither the feminist unions? SORWUC, AUCE and the CLC." *Resources for Feminist Research* 10(2):19-21.

GEIGER, Susan N.G. 1986. "Women's Life Histories: Method and Content." *Signs* 11(2):334-51.

GILSON, C.H.J., I.S. Spencer, and S. Granville. 1989. "The Impact of a Strike on the Attitudes and Behaviour of a Rural Community." *Relations Industrielles* 4(4):785-803.

GRELE, Ronald J., ed. 1975. *Envelopes of Sound.* Chicago: Precedent Publishing.

HENIGE, David. 1982. *Oral Historiography.* Essex: Longman Group.

LANGNESS, L.L., and Gelya Frank. 1981. *Lives. An Anthropological Approach to Biography.* Novato, CA: Chandler and Sharp.

LENNON, Elizabeth J. Shilton. 1980. "Organizing the Unorganized: Unionization in the Chartered Banks of Canada." *Osgoode Hall Law Journal* 18(2):177-237.

LOWE, Graham S. 1978. *The Canadian Union of Bank Employees: A Case Study.* Toronto: Centre for Industrial Relations, University of Toronto.

———. 1980. *Bank Unionization in Canada: A Preliminary Analysis.* Toronto: Centre for Industrial Relations, University of Toronto.

THE Personal Narratives Group, ed. 1989. *Interpreting Women's Lives. Feminist Theory and Personal Narratives.* Bloomington: Indiana University Press.

PLUMMER, Ken. 1983. *Documents of Life. An Introduction to the Problems and Literature of a Humanistic Method.* London: George Allen and Unwin.

PURCELL, Kate. 1984. "Militancy and Acquiescence among Women Workers." In *Women and the Public Sphere. A Critique of Sociology and Politics,* ed. Janet Siltanen and Michelle Stanworth. London: Hutchinson, 54-67.

SACKS, Karen. 1989. "What's a Life Story Got to Do With It?" In *Interpreting Women's Lives. Feminist Theory and Personal Narratives,* ed. The Personal Narratives Group. Bloomington: Indiana University Press, 85-95.

SHOSTAK, Marjorie. 1981. *Nisa: The Life and Words of a !Kung Woman.* Cambridge, MA: Harvard University Press.

Statistics Canada. 1990. *Industrial Organization and Finance Division Labour Unions Section. Annual Report of the Minister of Industry, Science and Technology under the Corporations and Labour Unions Returns Act (CALURA). Part II. Labour Unions.* 1988. Ottawa: Supply and Services Canada.

WARSKETT, Rosemary. 1987. "Legitimate and Illegitimate Unionism: The Case of SORWUC and Bankworker Unionization." Paper presented to the Political Economy sessions of the Canadian Political Science Association, Hamilton, Ontario, June.

———. 1988. "Bank Worker Unionization and the Law." *Studies in Political Economy* 25(Spring):41-73.

PART III

Experiments in Ethnography

I N THIS SECTION AUTHORS EXPERIMENT WITH ethnography that is multivocal and, in one case, multiauthored in efforts to represent the diverse, often contradicting and conflicting possible interpretations of women's social realities and experience. In "Is Feminist Ethnography 'New' Ethnography?" Sally Cole situates the essays in the context of current debates within anthropology about ethnography. The opening words of the

Portuguese fisherwoman, Maria, who tells Sally, the researcher, "I am not an object, I am a person," set the tone for a discussion of feminist anthropology's concern that ethnography seek to represent women's lived experience rather than seeking to construct coherent and integrated ethnographic "wholes" that often homogenize, if not obliterate female subjects. Sally Cole discusses differences as well as the apparent yet often unrecognized parallels between these goals — of what she characterizes as feminist ethnography — and the goals of the so-called "new" ethnography influenced by postmodernist critiques of anthropology. She notes often similar textual strategies but locates sources of difference in feminist anthropologists' political commitment to scientific theorizing of inequality and oppression.

Artist and anthropologist, Rae Anderson, in "Engendering the Mask: Three Voices," presents three voices on women and masking: photos of images of Anderson's visual art are one voice; Anderson's reflexive account of her experience as a twentieth century feminist mask maker (including receiving reviews of her work as "tasteless" or "offending sensibilities") is a second voice; and, the third voice is Anderson, the anthropologist, exploring the existing ethnographic literature on masks and "primitive" art in which women are largely absent. In an approach reminiscent of recent questioning and engendering of interpretations of the archaeological record (Gero and Conkey 1992), Anderson deconstructs conventional ethnographic reporting of maskmaking and the production of visual art. She exposes the androcentric bias in interpretations that assume that women do not make masks because only men are positioned to make authoritative images or because women work in "soft" (and perishable) materials (like clay and cloth) whereas men work in "hard" (and enduring) materials like wood and stone — the materials of masks. She argues instead that the making, wearing and/or viewing of masks has to do with larger questions of who has access to ritual knowledge and that ritual knowledge accompanies a diversity of roles in human societies, roles which may in some ethnographic instances be associated with men and in others with women. Multi-voiced ethnography that results from simultaneous presentation of different views on one subject — in this case, women and masking — is one strand in contemporary feminist ethnographic research (see also Margery Wolf 1992).

In "New Voices on Fieldwork" Clara Benazera, Marie-Hélène Bérard, Elizabeth Houde and Renée Ménard, graduate students returning from the field in Burkina Faso, Costa Rica and Colombia, question the appropriateness of academic feminism for "describing the day-to-day reality of women" and go on to ask whether "the mere fact of being interested in women and wishing to convey their reality as accurately as possible made us feminist anthropologists." They challenge existing notions of methodology in both anthropology and feminism that do not prepare students to interact ethically with the reality of women's lives. Specifically, their experiences in the field lead them to challenge both feminist theoretical frameworks (that highlight universal subordination and oppression of women) and the recent pre-eminence given by postmodernists in the discipline to textual style. These authors urge that a greater concern for how women organize, manage and give meaning to their lives will yield texts that respect their subjects. They further urge a reaffirmation of feminist commitment and of the social responsibility of the researcher and refuse to accept what they see as a *fin-de-siècle* defeatism about the possibilities of ethnography.

Judith Abwunza's "Outrageous Voices" are three: the voices of the rural Kenyan women she worked with who do not see themselves represented in anthropological writing on Kenya; the educated African feminists who contest Western feminists' interpretations and power; and the feminist graduate student (herself) who experiences silencing and disciplining in the academy. Abwunza echoes Henrietta Moore who defined the challenge of feminist ethnography as to navigate the "political and theoretical complexities of trying to speak *about* women, while avoiding any tendency to speak *for* them" (1988:191-2). For Abwunza the key lies in seeking women's personal narratives as "primary data." It is, she says, through listening to women's words and taking seriously women's statements about their needs based on their own experience that feminist anthropologists may hope to ameliorate what Abwunza describes as a "matriarchal attitude" or what Deborah Gordon (1993) calls "matronization." Working in the politicized context of research on African economic development, however, Abwunza is not sanguine about the possibilities of achieving a "conversation between cultures."

Trish Wilson's essay, "Reading The 'Montreal Massacre': Idiosyncratic Insanity or the Misreading of Cultural Cues?" is a textual analysis of what Canadian and Quebec media described as the "Montreal Massacre." Wilson deconstructs media stereotypes that view male violence as individual, idiosyncratic and even insane. She argues, instead, that the cultural rationality of male violence against women in advanced capitalism is sanctioned and institutionalized by hierarchical social institutions, including the media. The essay pivots on the tension between the heard voice of the male murderer whose violent act was a way of speaking and the heard voices of media analysts, on the one hand, and the silenced voices of the fourteen women victims and of feminist critiques of the media on the other.

BIBLIOGRAPHY

GERO, J.M., and M.W. Conkey. 1991. *Engendering Archaeology: Women and Prehistory.* Oxford: Basil Blackwell.

GORDON, Deborah. 1993. "Among Women: Gender and Ethnographic Authority of the Southwest, 1930-1980." In *Hidden Scholars,* ed. Nancy Parezo. Albuquerque: University of New Mexico Press, 129-45.

MOORE, Henrietta. 1988. *Feminism and Anthropology.* Minneapolis: University of Minnesota Press.

WOLF, Margery. 1992. *A Thrice-told Tale. Feminism, Postmodernism and Ethnographic Responsibility.* Stanford: Stanford University Press.

CHAPTER 10

Taming the Shrew in Anthropology:

IS FEMINIST ETHNOGRAPHY "NEW" ETHNOGRAPHY?

Sally Cole

A PORTUGUESE FISHERWOMAN'S STORY: MARIA

You see, I was at the same time housewife and fisherman.

T HERE IS NOTHING REMARKABLE ABOUT MY LIFE. I AM A *poor woman. I did what I had to do. I worked hard — all the women here did. I have worked very hard all my life.*
    I was born in 1926, the third of four children. We had no father. I was raised in Vila Chã by my mother who worked as a jornaleira *[an agricultural day labourer], harvested seaweed, and sold fish in order to feed us. But often there was no food and we had to beg from our neighbours.*
    In my childhood girls used to collect seaweed both from the beach in a hand net and from boats using a rake. It was also common for them to accompany relatives fishing. When only ten years old I began to accompany neighbours when they went fishing. When I was fourteen I took out my licence and I continued to fish as a crew member on boats owned by neighbours. These men are all dead now but it was they who taught me this work.

I married when I was only twenty years old and I think this is too young. My husband was a fisherman from a neighbouring parish. He came to live with me and my mother and my grandmother and took up fishing in Vila Chã. I continued fishing whenever I could, and after my daughters were born I left them in my mother's care so that I could go out on the sea. I also worked on the seaweed harvest, often going out alone in the boat to collect seaweed.

From the beginning my husband was selfish [egoista]. He never helped me with my work but would instead go off to attend to his own affairs. I married too young. We had two daughters, and when I was pregnant with the third, my husband emigrated to Brazil. He was gone for almost four years during which time I heard nothing from him and he sent no money. I decided to go to Brazil to find him. In 1955 I went by ship with my sister-in-law who was going to join her husband, my brother, in Brazil. I found my husband involved in a life of women and drink, and after a few months I returned home alone. I wanted to make my life in Vila Chã and I missed my daughters. I took up fishing full time and harvested seaweed when I wasn't fishing, and in this way I supported my mother and my children. In 1961 I bought a boat of my own and took out my skipper's licence.

I like my profession, but I fished because I was forced to. My marriage became difficult. My husband went away to Brazil leaving me in the street with three children, and I had to face life on my own. Fishing was not as productive then as it is now and the life of a fisherwoman was a hard one. But I had to turn to what I knew. First I fished in a boat belonging to another fisherman and then for eighteen years I owned and fished in my own boat, the Três Marias. *About fourteen years ago I managed to buy this small house which, little by little, I have fixed up and this is where I live now.*

Although in recent years I have been the only woman skipper, there have been no difficulties for me at all because I know my profession very well — as well as any of my comrades. Men used to like to fish with me because they knew I was strong. C., a member of my crew, used to say that I was stronger than he. Fishing holds no secrets for me, and, besides, I think that women have the right to face life beside men. What suits men, suits women. I am respected by everyone, men and women. I have many friends, and when the weather prohibits fishing we all stay here on the beach working on the nets and enjoying conversation. I have always enjoyed my work on the sea. I was never one who liked to stay at home.

When my daughters were small I used to be at sea day and night — whenever there was fish. They stayed at home with my mother. Later, when they were older and I was fishing, my daughters assisted my mother harvesting seaweed, and in this way they contributed to the maintenance of the household. As soon as I returned from fishing I would start the housework. You see, I was at the same time house-wife and fisherman.

I retired in 1979. I sold my boat and I gave my fishing gear to my son-in-law. I sold my boat to a fisherman in Matosinhos because I could not bear to see it anymore here on the beach. In 1982 I bought a piece of land, and two of my daughters are building a duplex on it now. My youngest daughter lives with me in my house along with her husband and three children. I have helped all of my daughters to establish their households. I have been very good to them. And now that I am old and my heart is not good, they are looking after me. When I returned from Brazil, leaving my husband there, I could have found another man to live with. I could have lived with another man. But I never wanted to do that because, if things didn't work out with us, I worried that he would take it out on my daughters because they were nothing to him. I preferred to have my daughters.

Recently my husband has begun writing to me from Brazil. He wants to return to Portugal and he wants me to take him back. He needs someone to care for him now in his old age. But I won't take him back. It's not right at all. I liked him once but that's all over now. The best part of the life of a couple is passed. I'm not interested in his returning. I'm not an object to be put away and then picked up, dusted off and used again. I am not an object. I am a person. I am human. I have the right to be treated like a person, don't you think? I managed to make a good life for myself and my children here, but he arranged nothing for himself there — nothing. He's got nothing there, but he's also got nothing here. He has never done anything for me or my daughters and now he wants to come back. Who does he think he is? I'm not crazy. He has no right whatsoever.

A CANADIAN GRADUATE STUDENT'S STORY

In my study of women's work and the social construction of gender, based on fieldwork in 1984-85 in rural Portugal, stories like Maria's exemplified how existing anthropological frameworks for describing and understanding rural women failed to represent the women as they would represent themselves (Cole 1991). The conventional framework of honour and shame, for example, that defined women of southern European societies in terms of their sexuality and in their roles as wives, mothers and daughters, apparently was not applicable to the fisherwomen of Vila Chã, the village on the north coast of Portugal where I had lived (Campbell 1964; Peristiany 1965). Women in Vila Chã consistently represented themselves as workers *(trabalhadeiras).*

Vila Chã women's stories revealed feminist "women and development" theoretical frameworks to be problematic as well for writing about women, work and rural development in Portugal. These frameworks sought both to critique liberal modernization theories of economic development and to introduce a gender consciousness to Marxist critiques of liberal theory (Etienne and Leacock 1980; Mies 1986). In my study I describe changes in women's work over three generations during which women have moved out of a household economy based on domestic fisheries production into transnational factories where they are industrial wage workers in food and fish processing and garment and electronics manufacture. Using a women-and-development framework Vila Chã women's experience might be interpreted as a case study of women's loss of autonomy as economic production is removed from their control in the household and as women become instead a cheap labour force in an international economy. But embedded in this kind of analysis and problematic for me now were universalist assumptions made by many Western feminist scholars about women's experience and about the global transformations required to end the oppression of women. How was I to interpret the narratives of young Vila Chã women who, for example, aspired to be housewives — a condition anathematic to Western feminists — in order to escape the exploitative working conditions of their present lives as factory workers or the poverty that had dominated the lives of their mothers and grandmothers? A new kind of subject-object opposition had been created in women-and-development theory: that between Western feminists (self/subject) and a universalized category of so-called "Third World Women" (other/object).

Recording fisherwomen's narratives was, I considered, a feminist method that might help ameliorate the intellectual imperialism of both of these analytical frameworks: the androcentric honour-and-shame model of gender relations that treated men as subjects and "woman" as man's "other," and the feminist women-and-development framework that assumed an ideal universal and autonomous female subject. Recording women's stories enabled me to hear about the diversity of women's experiences in Vila Chã and to recognize the existence of multiple subject-positions generated under even the very particular social, economic and historical conditions of a small village in rural Portugal. I hoped that presenting women's stories might ultimately contribute to the development of more appropriate frameworks for understanding (and, it was hoped, ameliorating) the conditions of women's lives worldwide. I also saw the systematic recording of women's stories as an effort to conduct research on more democratic terms and hoped that the women's words would keep me from arbitrarily imposing any totalizing scheme over their lives.[2]

The response of my graduate thesis committee at all stages of the project was instructive. Although the collection of life stories — what anthropologists until recently have called life histories — has a long tradition in anthropology, the method also has a long history of being criticized. Life histories have been considered too individual, subjective, idiosyncratic, anecdotal; the data they represent have been said to be non-comparable, non-generalizable, non-scientific (Langness and Frank 1981). More recently, the problems of translation, editing and the textual representation of other lives, other selves in life history have been highlighted (Mintz 1989). When I told my committee that I wanted to "do" women's life histories the response was, "Yes, we all do life histories, but that can't be all you do" — meaning that I would have to "collect" these stories while pursuing other more "scientific" methods of fieldwork: conduct a household census; collect data on household budgets and income strategies; collect genealogies; record the demographic data of births, marriages and deaths contained in the parish registers; and so on. And this is what I undertook to do.

When I returned from Portugal and began to write my thesis in the summer of 1985, I was further socialized to the ethnographic writing process that exorcises the personal subjective experience of fieldwork and yields the scientific monograph where the anthropologist is invisible yet omniscient. The material I was most comfortable writing about were the stories individuals had told me about their lives; these stories kept me in touch with my friends and with my own experience in Vila Chã. But when I took them to my thesis committee, their response was: "Very interesting and very enjoyable to read but you're not writing for *The New Yorker.* If you want to use them, put them in an appendix." Instead, my training was to write in the classic anthropological style that Jonathan Spencer has called "ethnographic naturalism": "the creation of a taken-for-granted representation of reality through the use of certain standard devices such as free indirect speech and the absence of any tangible point of view" (152). My resistance took the form of maintaining as central a place for the women's stories as I could: they did not go in the appendix. Nonetheless I was beginning to formulate an answer to literary critic Mary Louise Pratt's question about anthropologists. She asked: "How ... could such interesting people doing such interesting things produce such dull books? What did they have to do to themselves?" (1986:33). It appeared that what they had to do was seek to eliminate other possible understandings of the material. A standard means of achieving this authority in ethnography has been to homogenize the subjects (to speak of *"The* Andaman Islanders" or *"The* Nuer" for example) and to speak "objectively" about them. It is this kind of ethnography that has undergone such extensive rethinking since the mid-1980s.

Reflecting on my graduate experience now several years later in these self-conscious times in anthropology, in this paper I explore the relationship between the kind of ethnography that I was trying to write — which I call feminist — and the ethnographic writing that since then has become known as "new" ethnography in postmodernist circles in anthropology. I ask: Is feminist ethnography "new" ethnography? Do we want it to be? Does it matter?

FEMINIST ANTHROPOLOGISTS AND THE NEW ETHNOGRAPHY

Stephen Tyler defined new ethnography as "evocation ... for the world that made science and that science made, has disappeared, and scientific thought is now an archaic mode of consciousness ... The post-modern world is a post-scientific world. Post-modern ethnography captures this mood of the post-scientific world for it, too, does not move toward abstraction, away from life but back to experience" (1986:123).

New ethnography according to James Clifford rests upon new modes of authority that are "experiential," "interpretive," "dialogical," "intersubjective" and "polyphonic." Noting that all ethnographies are situated, that none are simply objective representations of reality, Clifford (1986) describes ethnographic writing as shaped and determined in at least six ways: (1) contextually (it draws from and creates meaningful social milieux); (2) rhetorically (it uses and is used by expressive conventions); (3) institutionally (one writes within and against specific traditions, disciplines, audiences); (4) generically (an ethnography is usually distinguishable from a novel or a travel account); (5) politically (the authority to represent cultural realities is unequally shared and at times contested); (6) historically (all the above conventions and constraints are changing) (Abu-Lughod 1990).

The new self-consciousness about textual production in anthropology encourages experimentation with form, the most acclaimed of which has been the dialogical and multivocal "new" ethnography — "a decolonization at the level of the text [that offers] the voice of the narrator/anthropologist [as] only one among many, and [allows] the voices of the subjects to be heard" (Abu-Lughod 1990:11). During the 1980s a standard handful of "new" or "postmodern" ethnographies was continually cited (Crapanzano 1980; Dwyer 1982; Rabinow 1979). Courses in ethnographic writing flourished; articles on the production of ethnography proliferated in journals; new journals, societies and institutes were founded; and rare was the ethnography published without at least a footnote acknowledging the author's awareness of questions of reflexivity and "authorial authority" (Paine 1989).

Feminism and postmodernism are both products of the cultural and political climate of postcolonialism and late capitalism, but in anthropology the work of postmodernists has achieved a legitimacy that the work of feminists has not. Feminist ethnographers have been at work in the discipline since the early 1970s, yet a corpus of what could be called feminist ethnography can not be as readily identified. In anthropology postmodernism dissociated itself from the writing of feminists which was explicitly excluded from 1980s debates about the "new" ethnography on the grounds that feminist texts didn't exhibit "textual innovation" (Clifford 1986:6, 19). Feminist anthropologists, however, have been experimenting with form and method and theory (Abu-Lughod 1986; Mascia-Lees et al. 1989; Wolf 1992). Feminist anthropologists also endeavour to recognize new modes of authority that are experiential, intersubjective and dialogical. And feminists also seek in their texts to recognize the possibilities of new and multiple subject-positions.

How can the marginalization of feminist writing in anthropology be explained when the (similar) postmodernist critiques of traditional ethnography are being taken seriously? I submit that at least four areas of difference between feminist and postmodernist ethnography can be identified that may also partially explain the peripheral place of feminist anthropology in the rethinking of ethnographic writing in the 1980s. The four areas I will discuss are: (1) the professionalization of ethnography; (2) the idea of feminist social science; (3) the definition of politics; and (4) the implications of what has become the "crisis of difference."

The Professionalization of Ethnography

Contrary to Tyler's assertion that the new ethnography moves away from abstraction toward experience, postmodernists in the discipline write at a high level of abstraction. They reject the rhetoric of social science but not in favour of more accessible language, rather in favour of a rarefied discourse that can be more exclusive than

conventional anthropology. The claim that the move "toward experience" in postmodernist ethnography is "new" is also arguable
when we acknowledge that there is a long tradition — a well-established subgenre — of anthropological writing that has been grounded
in personal experience. These are the letters, diaries, memoirs, nov-
els and prefaces written by anthropologists that subjectively describe
their day-to-day experiences and relationships during fieldwork
(Bowen 1954; Briggs 1970; Mead 1977; Malinowski 1967). These
works use many of the conventions now considered experimental in
the new ethnography: first-person narration, transcriptions of dialogues with "informants," reflection on the impact of the ethnographer's feelings and relationships with subjects, and so on. This
writing, although it has been recognized as useful for teaching
undergraduates about fieldwork, has been exorcised from the scientific monograph or only published subsequent to it in a fictionalized
account under a pseudonym, or even posthumously. Much of the
writing in this subgenre is by women (Briggs 1970; Fernea 1965;
Landes 1947; Shostak 1981; Smith 1954; Wolf 1968). Is it inci-
dental that when women were writing this kind of anthropology it
was considered self-indulgent, anecdotal and personal and that when
men began to write "toward experience" — for those who first
defined the new ethnography were men (Clifford and Marcus 1986;
Marcus and Fischer 1986; Tyler 1986) — they described this writing as new, experimental, reflexive and professional?[3]

In a recent essay responding to the assertion that feminist
anthropologists have not been involved in textual innovation, Lila
Abu-Lughod (1990) asks: "Where have feminist anthropologists
been?" She suggests that feminists have been engaged in the project
of persuading colleagues and superiors that anthropology that takes
gender into account is not only good anthropology but better anthropology and that this project might have encouraged a textual con-
servatism. She also notes, as I would, that feminist anthropologists
have been more concerned with representation in its political rather
than its literary sense. That is, we have been dedicated to making
sure that women's lives are represented in descriptions of societies
and that women's experiences and gender itself are theorized in our
accounts of how societies work. Thus the texts of feminist ethnog-

raphers have tended to be concerned less with textual analysis and experimentation and more with contributing to knowledge about women and gender. Feminist anthropologists have been concerned with collecting, organizing and presenting information. This purpose raises questions about our continuing relationship with science, about method, methodology and epistemology, and about the relationship between these questions and the kind of ethnography that feminists write.

Feminist Anthropologists are Social Scientists

Trained as social scientists, feminist anthropologists have been concerned with epistemological questions: how do we know what we know about women and gender? We have entered into debates in the discipline about subjectivity and assertions of objectivity about the history of androcentric bias, about whether there is or can be a feminist method of inquiry and about the role of politics in empirical research.[4] According to Sandra Harding three feminist epistemologies have developed in response to these concerns. The first, "feminist empiricism," seeks to account for androcentric bias while retaining as much as possible of the traditional epistemology of science. Much of the anthropology of women of the 1970s may be understood as feminist empiricism. Second are what Harding calls the "feminist standpoint epistemologies," which draw on the theoretically richer resources of Marxist epistemology — the women-and-development theoretical framework that flourished in the 1980s, for example. And third, are feminist forms of postmodernism that argue that feminist standpoint epistemologies ultimately "founder on the wrecks of no longer viable enlightenment projects" — the search for the one truth, for example. Harding argues that all of these epistemologies are flawed because of what they have borrowed from their nonfeminist ancestors, but that in spite of these flaws each is effective and valuable in the justificatory domains for which it was intended.

Harding then goes on to suggest that feminist scientists have been overly concerned with these questions of method, methodology and epistemology and that it is more useful to ask: what accounts for the undeniable fruitfulness and power of so much feminist research? What do feminist researchers *do?* She identifies three attributes of feminist research: (1) the "discovery" of gender and its consequences: feminist research is distinctive in its focus on gender as a variable and an analytic category (like race and class) and in its critical stance toward gender; (2) the incorporation of women's experience: feminist research asks questions that originate in women's experiences, designs research that is intended to provide explanations of social and biological phenomena women want and need, and uses women's experiences as a significant indicator of the "reality" against which hypotheses are tested; and (3) feminist research incorporates "a robust gender-sensitive reflexivity practice," which Harding describes as "insisting that the researcher be placed in the same critical plane as the overt subject matter, thereby recovering for scrutiny in the results of the research the entire research process" (1989:29). Feminist researchers, then, are committed not only to understanding the historical construction of race, class, culture and gender within which our subject matter moves but also to identifying how these same historical lenses shape our own beliefs and behaviours. It is this reflexivity that we hope will help us avoid the erroneous universalizing that has characterized some feminist work. The researcher thus appears in the analysis not as an invisible, anonymous, disembodied voice of authority but as a real, historical individual with concrete, specific desires and interests — and ones that are often in tension with each other. Since these characteristics of the researcher are part of the evidence readers need to evaluate the results of research, they are presented with those results.

Although postmodernists in the discipline rely heavily upon two of these characteristics in their writing — the focus on experience and the practice of reflexivity — they do so apparently without recognizing the parallels to feminist writing. Strathern has described this disjunction in contemporary anthropology as "awkward" (1987a). In my view, "awkwardness" in the relationship between postmodernism and feminism in anthropology can be attributed to at least two differences: different understandings of what constitutes "theory" and different views on the question of practice.

Feminist anthropologists place their research in the context of larger analytical frameworks (or theories). They maintain that there are things that we want (and need) to know about the logic of large social processes — how institutions came into existence and change over time, for example — that are not always visible through the lens of the consciousness of those historical actors (including the anthropologist's) whose beliefs and activities constitute such processes. And they maintain that some theories and analytical frameworks have proved to be more useful than others and that we need to continue to develop criteria for evaluating differing theories or generalizing frameworks. Feminist allegiance to the idea of theory places them in conflict not only with leading postmodernists who reject the possibility both of social totalities and of totalizing theories (theories of patriarchy and oppression, for example) but with postmodernists in our discipline who tell us that the new ethnography is "anti-science." Where postmodernism critiques theoretical and ethnographic assertions of unities or systematicity as homogenizing and dominating, feminist anthropologists, as scientists, continue to believe that some theoretical universalizing is necessary.

A third issue between feminist and postmodernist practitioners in the discipline is that feminists place their research in the context of a moral and political movement and see this as a strength of their work. Feminist anthropologists are concerned with the practical implications of what they write.

Text and Context: The Location of Politics

Feminist anthropologists locate their research and writing in the political context of feminism, a movement for social change. By contrast, postmodernists in the discipline locate politics at the level of the text and are concerned with politics as rhetorical activity aimed at subverting existing cultural meanings. This preoccupation more with the text and with *how* we represent and less with epistemological issues of how we know what we know sidesteps basic political issues in anthropology: the issue of Western knowers and representers and non-Western knowns and representeds (cf. Abu-Lughod 1990:11); and the relations of race, class and gender that pervade the postcolonial contexts in which anthropological research, fieldwork and writing are undertaken.

The tools of deconstruction and the increased awareness of the politics inherent in the production of texts have, at the same time, had an undeniably important impact on anthropology notably in challenging notions of static and universalist dichotomies such as subject/object, self/other, male/female upon which Western thought (including anthropology) historically has been based, and in urging instead the recognition of multiple and heterogeneous subjectivities. But in disclaiming the possibility of universals, postmodernism has had a double-edged impact on movements for social change, like feminism, which have been thought to depend upon achieving some unity of purpose, usually through recognition of commonalities and shared experiences — that is, through shared subject-positions and/or coalitional strategies. Feminists like Nancy Hartsock (1989), for example, ask why it is that just at this juncture in history when those who have been invisible or "other" (colonized, working-class, women, for example) are claiming their subjecthood, their right to "self-determination," it is now asserted that there can be no subjects or selves without violation to the conditions of multiplicity and heterogeneity. To many feminists, then, these concerns of postmodernist ethnography appear to represent a retreat into text rather than a move out toward context, as Strathern (1987b) put it.

Difference: The Crisis and the Promise

Postmodernist thought within feminism has tended to enhance the experience of "differences-within" and to diminish the importance of "differences-between" entities. Differences within the category "woman" have achieved analytical prominence as differences between categories (for example, between women and men) have receded in importance. Second-wave feminism now has almost two decades of experience with "differences-within." In the 1980s division occurred as the differences in the writing and practices of women of colour were recognized (see Stasiulis 1993). A decade earlier, the movement was divided when socialist feminism began to emphasize women's class oppositions to one another and to question the universal utility of founding concepts such as patriarchy. Where has the crisis of difference led?

Feminist theorists who note that the deconstruction of difference has had a contradictory impact on feminist practice note that

whereas sensitivity to and knowledge about the multiplicity of differences among (within) women has increased, the unity of categories like women, gender and patriarchy has been undermined.
Susan Bordo, in her recent essay "Feminism, Postmodernism and
Gender Scepticism" (1990), argues that postmodernist thought
which eschews generalizations about gender a priori on theoretical
grounds has had the effect of disarming — of taming — the critical
energy of feminism as a movement of cultural resistance and transformation.

The crisis of difference has challenged feminism to reconsider
where it should locate its theories, knowledges and practices.[5] Thus
some feminist postmodernists argue that we can't have totalizing
theories (like patriarchy) because they violate the heterogeneous and
multiple subjectivities that comprise the world and that we should
instead be concerned with the local and particular, that is, with the
differences among women (Nicholson 1990). Others argue that this
emphasis on the local leaves feminists in a state of "paralyzing anxi-
ety" (Bordo 1990:142) with no position from which to identify and
critique macrostructures of inequality and injustice and no position
from which to critique broad-based relations of dominance and subordination (along lines like gender, race and class). Perhaps, as literary critic Marlene Kadar suggests, we could think of this position as
necessarily a less secure one but not necessarily a state of paralysis?
"Postmodernism and feminism argue for [a] critical area somewhere
in between a feminism with clarity and a feminism that suffers its
own ignoble glitches and moves on" (1992:9).

CONCLUSION

Anthropology has long sustained critiques (both internally and
externally generated) that its ethnographies are too particular, too
local. Anthropologists have replied that our responsibility is to par-
ticularistic "thick" description, that theory hovers close to the
ground, and that in anthropology "small facts speak to large issues,
winks to epistemology" (Geertz 1973). The particular speaks to the
general whether we make this explicit in our writing or not.
Anthropologists share a postmodernist concern for the notion of

many truths. We are acutely aware of the dangers of theories that universalize and generalize, for we can always find a cultural exception. But we are also wary of how relativism (where multiple and heterogeneous subjectivities are considered equal) serves to maintain the world as it is. And feminist anthropologists, aware of the dangers of universalizing and essentializing women's experience, nonetheless believe that we need to continue to use categories such as women and gender and that dismantling these categories in favour of difference and multiplicity is also dismantling and undermining movements to end the oppressions of women in their diverse and multiple forms.

Anthropological discourse has its roots in the exploration and colonization of the rest of the world by the West. It defines itself primarily as the study of "other" people even though anthropologists have long recognized that what we wanted to know about "other" people emerged from questions that we wanted answered about ourselves (Burridge 1973). Some would argue that the idea of a Western self was constituted in part through this confrontation with a non-Western "other."

Where anthropology is rooted in the problem of historically constituted self/other distinctions based on race, Western feminism arises out of self/other distinctions based on gender. Western feminist discourse is, as Simone de Beauvoir pointed out, a discourse of the other. And it has been women's experiences as men's "other" that have taught us that self/other oppositions are necessarily hierarchical and about power. Nonetheless, feminism has been an attempt to turn those (women) who had been constituted as "others" into "selves" — into subjects. The crisis of difference within contemporary feminism, then, has been a painful re-experiencing of the "violence inherent in the business of creating selves" (Abu-Lughod 1990:25). Describing this as a time of "gender trouble," Judith Butler argues that the destabilization of the subject "woman" and of gender as a category "ought not to be lamented as the failure of feminism or of feminist theory but, rather, affirmed as the promise of the possibility of complex generative subject-positions, as well as coalitional strategies that neither presuppose nor fix their subjects in their place" (1990:339). Feminists thus are coming to terms with womanhood as a partial identity and the recognition that, as women, we work from fragmented selves and can work together as different selves who only partially intersect. According to Abu-Lughod (1990:25-26), feminist anthropologists working with the recognition of "difference in sameness, of a self that participates in multiple identifications, and an other that is also partially the self" are moving beyond the impasse of the fixed self/other or subject/object divide critiqued by postmodernist new ethnographers. Abu-Lughod continues: "What feminist ethnography can contribute to anthropology is an unsettling of the boundaries that have been central to its identity as a discipline of the self studying the other" (1990:26).[6] By showing us how we are always a part of what we study and always stand in definite relations to it, feminist anthropology thus challenges the assumption of anthropology that we can stand outside — a myth that the new ethnography sustains.

In the end it doesn't matter whether feminist ethnography is "new" ethnography or not. What matters is that feminist ethnographers maintain a "robust reflexivity" (Harding 1989) in method, purpose and text; that we write as people "with feelings, histories and desires — as well as information and knowledge" (Torgovnick 1990); that we recognize the continual possibilities of new subject-positions and coalitions; that we understand that not all subject-positions are equal or benevolent; and that we understand this through working toward global frameworks that recognize the historical basis of hierarchy and privilege and that seek knowledge as part of the work to abolish these.

NOTES

1.   An earlier version of this essay entitled "Is Feminist Ethnography 'New' Ethnography?: The Taming of the Shrew in Anthropology" was presented to the Southwest Ontario Women's Research Colloquium at McMaster University in March 1991. I am thankful to the participants for their comments as well as to Ruth Behar, Robert Paine and Lynne Phillips for their readings. I recorded Maria's narrative during fieldwork in Portugal in 1984-85 funded by the Social Sciences and Humanities Research Council of Cananda. It appears along with those of other Vila Chã women in my book *Women of the Praia: Work and Lives in a Portuguese Coastal Community.*

2.   In a recent essay entitled "U.S. Academics and Third World Women: Is

Ethical Research Possible?" Patai answers the question negatively. Exploring
the fragile border between appropriation and empowerment, between the
appropriation of women's words and experiences by the researcher and the
claim that feminist research, by "giving a voice" to those who would
otherwise remain silent, is empowering women, Patai concludes that "we
continue to function in an overdetermined universe in which our respective
roles ensure that *other* people are always the subjects of *our* research, almost
never the reverse" (1991:149). While I agree with Patai that ultimately it is
impossible to conduct research outside the social and economic relations of
power that define our respective places in the world, I argue that we
nonetheless need to recognize the absolute necessity of continuing to seek
ways to democratize the research process.

3.   Answering the title question of this essay properly requires a historical
       analysis of changing conventions in writing anthropology and changing
       definitions of what constitutes professionalism in ethnography. For second-
       wave feminists in the discipline were not the first to theorize gender, and
       postmodernists were not the first to write experiential, dialogical or
       multivocal ethnography. Ruth Benedict's students of "culture-and-
       personality," for example, experimented widely in their writing. My
       experience of the marginalization of feminist writing in anthropology during
       the 1980s described in this essay has led me to a study of the processes of
       canon making and marginalization in the history of anthropology and I am
       currently at work on a book about the life and work of Ruth Landes (1908-
       91), a student of Boas and Benedict whose career aptly illustrates these
       processes at work (Cole 1994; 1995; see also Harrison 1991; Lutz 1990;
       Morgen 1989).

4.   See the collection of essays in *Feminism and Science* (Tuana 1989) for a more
       thorough exploration of these issues than can be undertaken here. Some of
       the questions discussed are: Is there a feminist method? Because feminists
       are critical of scientific method are they therefore proposing some non-
       scientific method of inquiry? Or are they exposing characteristics that have
       always been present in scientific inquiry (subjectivity and false claims to
       objectivity, for example)?

5.   In a recent article in MS magazine, sociologist Kathleen Barry, remembering
       her experience as a working class woman in the women's movement of the
       early 1970s, argues: "No politics of difference intends to include. It is the
       making of the 'other.' When difference is our first recognition of each other,
       it becomes the primary basis of separating women from each other" (1990:
       85). And, she goes on, "in the context of social and economic realities,
       recognition of difference can translate into situations where individuals
       increasingly see themselves as responsible only for themselves and their kind
       — and that, for example, when 1 in 5 black teenagers become pregnant
       each year in the U.S., it is a problem that only African-American women
       need address."

6.   These boundaries are also being dismantled by indigenous or Native
      anthropologists, some of whom describe themselves as "halfies" — people
      between cultures, anthropologists who are also a part of the culture or
      society in which they do fieldwork (see, for example, Abu-Lughod 1986;
      Claudio 1991; Harrison 1991; Kondo 1990; Lavie 1990; Narayan 1989). In
      both feminist and "halfie" ethnography, the creation of a self through
      opposition to an other is blocked, and therefore neither the multiplicity of
      the self nor the multiple overlapping and interacting qualities of the other
      can be ignored (Abu-Lughod 1990). My experience in moving from
      research in rural Portugal to research with Portuguese in Canada (where
      Portuguese are constructed as "immigrant" and "ethnic") suggests that
      undertaking anthropology "at home" also forces us to dissolve dichotomies
      and boundaries (see Strathern 1987c).

BIBLIOGRAPHY

ABU-LUGHOD, Lila. 1986. *Veiled Sentiments: Honor and Poetry in a Bedouin Society.* Berkeley: University of California Press.

———. 1990. Can There be a Feminist Ethnography? *Women and Performance* 5(1):7-27.

BARRY, Kathleen. 1990. "Deconstructing Deconstructionism (or, Whatever Happened to Feminist Studies?)." *MS Magazine* 1(4):83-85.

BORDO, Susan. 1990. Feminism, Postmodernism, and Gender Scepticism. In *Feminism/Postmodernism,* ed. L. Nicholson. New York: Routledge, 133-56.

BOWEN, Elizabeth. 1954. *Return to Laughter: An Anthropological Novel.* New York: Anchor Books.

BRIGGS, Jean. 1970. *Never in Anger: Portrait of an Eskimo Family.* Cambridge: Harvard University Press.

BURRIDGE, Kenelm. 1973. *Encountering Aborigines: A Case Study: Anthropology and the Australian Aboriginal.* New York: Pergamon Press.

BUTLER, Judith. 1990. "Gender Trouble, Feminist Theory, and Psychoanalytic Discourse." In *Feminism/Postmodernism,* ed. L. Nicholson. New York: Routledge, 324-40.

CAMPBELL, John. 1964. "Honour and Shame in a Cypriot Highland Village." In *Honour and Shame: The Values of Mediterranean Society,* ed. J. Peristiany. Chicago: University of Chicago Press, 173-90.

CLAUDIO, Fernanda. 1991. "Native Anthropology: Some Reflections on Theory and Methodology." In *Immigrants and Refugees in Canada,* ed. Satya P. Sharma, Alexander M. Ervin and Deirdre Meintel. Saskatoon: University of Saskatchewan, 249-65.

CLIFFORD, James and George Marcus, eds. 1986. *Writing Culture: The Poetics and Politics of Anthropology.* Berkeley: University of California Press.

COLE, Sally. 1991. *Women of the Praia: Work and Lives in a Portuguese Coastal Community.* Princeton: Princeton University Press.

COLE, Sally. 1994. Introduction to *City of Women* by Ruth Landes [orig. pub. 1947]. Albuquerque: University of New Mexico Press.

————. 1995. "Ruth Landes and the Early Ethnography of Race and Gender." In *Women Writing Culture/ Culture Writing Women,* ed. Ruth Behar and Deborah Gordon. Berkeley: University of California Press.

CRAPANZANO, Vincent. 1980. *Tuhami: Portrait of a Moroccan Tilemaker.* Chicago: University of Chicago Press.

DWYER, Kevin. 1982. *Moroccan Dialogues.* Baltimore: Johns Hopkins University.

ETIENNE, Mona, and Eleanor Leacock, eds. 1980. *Women and Colonization: Anthropological Perspectives.* New York: Praeger.

FERNEA, Elizabeth. 1965. *Guests of the Sheik: An Ethnography of an Iraqi Village.* New York: Anchor.

GACS, Ute, et al., eds. 1989. *Women Anthropologists: Selected Biographies.* Chicago: University of Illinois Press.

Geertz, Clifford. 1973. "Thick Description: Toward an Interpretive Theory of Culture." In *The Interpretation of Cultures: Selected Essays by Clifford Geertz.* New York: Basic Books, 3-30.

HARDING, Sandra. 1989. "Is There a Feminist Method?" In *Feminism and Science,* ed. N. Tuana. Bloomington: Indiana University Press, 17-32.

HARRISON, Faye. 1991. "Ethnography as Politics." In *Decolonizing Anthropology: Moving Further Toward an Anthropology for Liberation,* ed. Faye Harrison. Washington, DC: American Anthropological Association, 88-109.

HARTSOCK, Nancy. 1990. "Foucault on Power: A Theory for Women?" In *Feminism/Postmodernism,* ed. L. Nicholson. New York: Routledge, 324-40.

KADAR, Marlene. 1992. "Coming to Terms: Life Writing — from Genre to Critical Practice." In *Essays on Life Writing: From Genre to Critical Practice,* ed. M. Kadar. Toronto: University of Toronto Press, 3-16.

KONDO, Dorinne. 1990. *Crafting Selves: Power, Gender, and Discourses of Identity in a Japanese Workplace.* Chicago: University of Chicago Press.

LANDES, Ruth. 1938. *The Ojibwa Woman.* New York: Columbia University Press.

————. 1947. *City of Women.* New York: Macmillan.

LANGNESS, Lewis, and Geyla Frank. 1981. *Lives: An Anthropological Approach to Biography.* Novato, CA: Chandler and Sharp Pubs.

LAVIE, Smadar. 1990. *The Poetics of Military Occupation: Mzeina Allegories of Bedouin Identity Under Israeli and Egyptian Rule.* Berkeley: University of California Press.

LUTZ, Catherine. 1990. "The Erasure of Women's Writing in Sociocultural Anthropology." *American Ethnologist* 17(4):611-27.

MALINOWSKI, Bronislaw. 1967. *A Diary in the Strict Sense of the Term.* London: Routledge & Kegan Paul.

MARCUS, George, and Michael Fischer. 1986. *Anthropology as Cultural Critique: An Experimental Moment in the Human Sciences.* Chicago: University of Chicago Press.

MASCIA-LEES, Frances E., Patricia Sharpe, and Colleen Ballerino Cohen. 1989. "The Postmodernist Turn in Anthropology: Cautions from a Feminist Perspective." *Signs* 15(1):7-33.

MEAD, Margaret. 1977. *Letters From the Field 1925-1975.* New York: Harper and Row.

MIES, Maria. 1986. *Patriarchy and Accumulation on a World Scale: Women in the International Division of Labour.* London: Zed Books.

MINTZ, Sidney. 1989. The Sensation of Moving, While Standing Still. *American Ethnologist* 16(4):786-96.

MORGEN, Sandra. 1989. "Gender and Anthropology. Introductory Essay." In *Gender and Anthropology: Critical Reviews for Teaching,* ed. Sandra Morgen. Washington, D.C.: American Anthropological Association, 1-20.

NARAYAN, Kirin. 1989. *Storytellers, Saints, and Scoundrels: Folk Narrative in Hindu Religious Teaching.* Philadelphia: University of Philadelphia Press.

NICHOLSON, Linda, ed. 1990. *Feminism/Postmodernism.* New York: Routledge.

PAINE, Robert. 1989. "On Authorial Authority." *Culture* 9(2):35-47.

PATAI, Daphne. 1991. "U.S. Academics and Third World Women: Is Ethical Research Possible?" In *Women's Words: The Feminist Practice of Oral History,* ed. S.B. Gluck and D. Patai. New York: Routledge, 137-53.

PERISTIANY, John. 1965. *Honour and Shame: The Values of Mediterranean Society.* Chicago: University of Chicago Press.

PRATT, Mary Louise. 1986. "Fieldwork in Common Places." In *Writing Culture,* ed. J. Clifford and G. Marcus. Berkeley: University of Chicago Press, 27-50.

RABINOW, Paul. 1979. *Reflections of Fieldwork in Morocco.* Chicago: University of Chicago Press.

SHOSTAK, Marjorie. 1981. *Nisa: The Life and Words of a !Kung Woman.* New York: Vintage Books.

SMITH, Mary. 1954. *Baba of Karo: A Woman of the Muslim Hausa.* London: Faber and Faber.

SPENCER, Jonathan. 1989. "Anthropology as a Kind of Writing." *Man* 24:145-64.

STASIULIS, Daiva. 1993. "'Authentic Voice': Anti-racist Politics in Canadian Feminist Publishing and Literary Production." In *Feminism and the Politics of Difference,* eds. Sneja Gunew and Anna Yeatmen. Halifax: Fernwood Publishing, 35-60.

STRATHERN, Marilyn. 1987a. "An Awkward Relationship: The Case of Feminism and Anthropology." *Signs* 12(2):276-92.

―――. 1987b. "Out of Context: The Persuasive Fictions of Anthropology." *Current Anthropology* 28(3):251-81.

―――. 1987c. "The Limits of Auto-anthropology." In *Anthropology at Home,* ed. A. Jackson. A.S.A. Monograph 25. London: Tavistock Pubs, 16-37.

TORGOVNICK, Marianna. 1990. "Experimental Critical Writing." *Profession* 90:25-27.

TUANA, Nancy, ed. 1989. *Feminism and Science.* Bloomington: Indiana University Press.

TYLER, Stephen. 1986. "Post-modern Ethnography: From Document of the Occult to Occult Document." In *Writing Culture,* ed. J. Clifford and G. Marcus. Berkeley: University of California Press, 122-40.

WOLF, Margery. 1968. *The House of Lim: A Study of a Chinese Farm Family.* Englewood Cliffs, NJ: Prentice-Hall.

———. 1992. *A Thrice-told Tale: Feminism, Postmodernism and Ethnographic Responsibility.* Palo Alto: Stanford University Press.

CHAPTER 11

Engendering the Mask

THREE VOICES

Rae Anderson

HREE "VOICES" CONVERGE TO TALK AROUND THE SAME issues. One voice speaks from her studio and is poetic and evocative. One voice speaks not in words but through images. One voice speaks from her training in the academy.

No voice can be more authoritative than the others: all contribute to our knowledge. It is only Convention who stills the Polyphony, who privileges one sort of discourse over another, who assigns that which is appropriate for the occasion.

Our voices complement, contradict and hence enrich each other. We each of us carry a multiplicity of voices inside one body. Should one voice deny another or can we in our writing express the creative tension in simultaneous re-presenting of a common theme?

I/we write as an artist.
I/we write as an anthropologist.
I/we speak through the visual.

Let us re-think presentation to honour sliding horizons.

Mask literature in general commonly reports women being excluded from coming into contact with masks in small-scale societies. It appears that while masking is well nigh a worldwide phenomenon, concomitantly women hardly ever wear masks on important public occasions, nor do they seem to make them, according to ethnographic accounts. To what extent is the apparently poor coverage of women in the masking literature a case of neglect of women's contributions? To what extent is it a case of active exclusion of women from masked ritual?[1] Such questions frame an appropriate arena for highlighting issues of essentialism, difference and our understandings of categories of knowledge.

While there has been theorizing about the relationships of material culture, ideology and questions of power, the political dimension of masks as performing *objects and the issue of gender power relationships in masked ritual have not been fully tackled. The tendency in many analyses of the mask has been to adopt a relatively uncritical and apolitical stance.[2] "Beneath sym-*

Masks? Hallowe'en? There is a certain question of the relevance of masks for North American society. We are too sophisticated perhaps for the "crude" embodiment of spirit within sculptural form. We are not able to suspend disbelief without scoffing cynicism at the gullibility of the "primitives" with their belief in their "masked devils." Even so, who hasn't been spooked by that moment when You turn and see the Other looking at you? And so we have lost the original meaning of our celebrations, and can't tell you why they should continue, only that they must.

Mask makers in Western societies do not work within the tightly defined traditions common to non-Westerners. There is no unifying command of myth to aid us in formulating our visions. The choices are broad. Our visual lexicon is enormous. Some artists treat the mask as a haunting device of decoration while others maintain that the mask is not fulfilled until it is worn. The *bolic systems, beneath ideas about sacredness and purity and religious duty, we need to see the realities of power: who has it, who uses it, in what ways, to what ends" (Keesing 1981:299).*

A number of theories have been put forth for the so-called exclusion of women from masking. The supposed impurity of women, due to the polluting dangers of contact with menstruation and childbirth (women's functions), is often cited in ethnographic accounts as one reason, and the sexual division of labour has also been cited as a possible explanation for the "rule of exclusion." In central West Africa, for instance, women have traditionally worked with soft materials — clay and textiles. The carving of wood and stone has been of the male domain.

The question of division of labour revolves further around the question of who has rights in making figurative works of ritual art. Men are the image makers: "Women are considered to produce utilitarian objects rather than works of art" (Jules-Rosette 1984:96). Such a theory suggests that women have babies, but only men carve images (Adams 1980). The remark implies that the mask may enjoy some link with male attempts to reinforce their rights in women's

gallery is our "ritual" space. Invitations, notices of the event are sent out to the community. The catalogue/brochure is printed. The curators (guardians) assemble to hang the show. We convene at a certain hour for the opening. The event takes place, and then is no more. Galleries have become our society's spiritual temples, the public laundromat for cleansing our souls. We remind ourselves of our transgressions and restate our ideals in symbolic form.

The art of "primitive" peoples has long captured Western imagination with its apparent depth and purity of feeling. Such art has at times exerted a strong influence on the art produced in the highly industrialized modern cultures of the West. Some artists have taken to outright copying through "affinity" (Clifford 1985:165). This term of kinship suggests some unspoken unconscious universal relationship between "the tribal and the modern." Other artists have justified the wholesale adoption of another culture's imagery by citing it as a tribute. Cultural appropriation is this century's form of colonialism.

I began my research looking for other mask makers, other

"natural" reproductive capacities. Masks, for instance, may aid in simulating the "rebirth" of an initiate as a fully integrated adult member of society.[3] *Yet another facet to this argument, based on women's supposed inherent link to nature and men's link to culture (Ortner 1974), is that men may show more of a predilection for elaborate institutionalized modes than women, with institutionalized modes being secret societies or cults. This reasoning follows from an argument first proposed by Mead (1949) and later extended by Chodorow (1978) such that women have only "to be" in order to assume adulthood, given the biological facts of reproduction. Women grow into their adult role in continuous association with their mothers. Men on the other hand must differentiate themselves from their mothers, must "do" in order to achieve adulthood. Thus masks, particularly masks used in initiation rites, can be seen as tools for intensifying gender identity, as markers for differentiating male from female in the transition from youth to adult.*

A number of researchers have sought an answer to questions about the apparent exclusion of women from masking by postulating a social structural correlation between masking and matrilineality,

women mask makers. How have women used the mask in other places — is there a common thread between their usage and mine? Strathern has referred to femininity as "universal womanness" (Strathern 1981:670). It is perhaps this essential "universal womanness" that I thought I was searching for.

This search for the elusive woman mask maker has been unrewarded. She seems not to exist. Even among the Mende, the Sande *sowei* mask, expressing the essence, the epitome of female beauty, power, grace and strength drawn from the ancestors, presents this package through the mediation, the interpretation of the male mask maker. It is a formula to which all subscribe, and to which all pay homage.

I find it ironic that in searching out inspiration for my own mask work I have unwittingly been inspired by a vocabulary developed by male mask makers, albeit a language supported and upheld by women. My visual work over the years has continued to circle round and round this theme of women, masks and exclusion.

She-Male was the first to play with a still groping vocabu-

with males suffering a certain degree of alienation under a matrilineal system — alienation which then leads to production of art, and of masks in particular (Haselberger 1961:351; Kroeber and Holt 1920: 453; Ottenberg 1975:202; Pernet 1979: 284; Tooker 1968:1172; Wolfe 1969:4)

The search for a possible correlation between mask use and matrilineality relies upon accepting that projected feelings of alienation would act as a causative agent for artistic production, and more specifically, masks. As one critic succinctly put it, the supposed feelings of alienation experienced by men operating within a matrilineal society "could just as easily produce ulcers as art" (Wolfe 1969:41).

The greatest number of explanations for the exclusion of women from masking have been founded on cultural elaborations of essential biological processes and on a system of opposing and dichotomous roles for women and men. While many of the theories are potentially valuable for their contribution to understanding gender dynamics inherent in masking, it has been comparatively easy to discount women's contributions to masking with the simplistic generalization that masks are of the male province.

If we broaden the bounds of lary of "fe/male" integration. I had but the glimmerings of a model of female and male elements in balance, integrated, inseparable and dependent upon each other. *Fish Woman* was an experiment on the theme of the "vagina dentata" — an archetypal threatening image which had appeared in one of my dreams years ago, before conscious knowledge of the named concept. The form of phallus took shape in the *Beehive* — a towering womb home for those creatures of industrious pollen transfer. From the entrance way to the "hive" extended out a luscious human-like tongue. The *Breastplate of Fertility* was a wearable torso piece of nine life-size breasts with nipples assertively pushed out. The series of masks was later purchased by one of Canada's well-known fashion designers for the finale of her annual fashion show — all that is, but the *Breastplate of Fertility*. There was some question of offending sensibilities, even though the designs had been passed in the proposal stage. In retrospect I find it ironic that this was a piece which I had intended as a celebration of female fertile energy, while the success of the fashion

The Dance of the Scarecrow Brides

Anderson farm, Maple, Ontario. Photo by Rae Anderson.

accessibility to the mask, it is clear that often it is not only women who are excluded from mask-related activities, but any who are uninitiated, for example, children as well as uninitiated males (Tonkin 1979: 8). Thus the character of the relationship between masks and women is part of a larger question of who has access to ritual knowledge and who does not. Urban and Hendricks (1983) have fruitfully used the concept of "indexing" to suggest that masking in Amerindian Brazil operates as a semiotic system and encodes a number of classes or categories of social identity: uninitiated and initiated, female and male, adult and child, as well as in-class distinctions. Whitbeck (1989) has critiqued such thinking which stresses dramatic dualistic oppositions. Thus at the very moment of considering the mask as a gendered object, "we [must] simultaneously recognize the need to deconstruct the category 'gender'" (Morgen 1989:8), and understand that "men and women ... [are] not ... opposed, unitary categories but ... [occupy] a number of different roles in each society, which in turn have a complex set of relationships" (Lamphere 1987:24).

Tonkin (1979:3) draws a useful analytical distinction between secular "power" in its social science

show depended very much upon the projection of the "idealized" female form — a distant object of desire. My interpretation was uncomfortably literal.

Crow.Bride. comprised a circle of nine cruciform figures clothed in bridal gowns and veils; a series of nine masks of "Crow" were set to hang in a slightly wider circle between each bride. One review of the *Crow.Bride.* show spoke about some visitors to the gallery having found the installation "tasteless": "[The viewers'] attachment to the gown-as-symbol must be so strong that any use (or misuse) other than for which they [sic] were intended amounts to blasphemy. Many fail to see that any ritual or icon — whether religious or secular rarely springs into being free from its ancient, even pagan, roots" (Mozel 1986:12).

The Dance of the Scarecrow Brides grew from an experiment with the art form of the scarecrow. I am fascinated by the fact that we take our old clothes, stuff them and place them out on the land as our representatives and watchdogs. When seen from a distance, they are startlingly human and alive. Where did all these dresses come from?

sense, as a quantity of political coercion and spiritual "Power" with all the sacred dimensions it can have, including growth, fertility and life-force. The mask is a symbol of spiritual Power (to use Tonkin's designation) in its capacity to transform within a religious context, through its manipulation of the living/not living paradox, that is, "I am what I am not." This control overflows into the wider social and political arena; knowledge of the mysteries of the mask signals attainment of secular power and status within the community. Those able to pay for the privilege can buy into the symbolic trappings of authority.

If we examine the degree to which women do participate in masked ritual, we discover a number of typologies for such participation. These may be identified as a series of gradations moving from a more passive to a more active role. While the gradations overlap to some degree, the most "passive" is characterized as the incorporation of elements associated with the "feminine" into the ritual at a symbolic level. For instance, origin myths for the mask often refer to women's involvement in the discovery or invention of the first mask. The place where the masquerade takes place, the materials for the making of the masks, the imagery of the mask may all hold specifically feminine associations. Women

Who wore these dresses, now yellowed with age? Do these brides not recall the day of your own wedding? Where is your wedding dress? Have you kept it carefully wrapped, hidden away as a sacred vestment, to be brought out perhaps for the marriage of your own daughter? Some of these scarecrow dresses are very old, the brides who once wore them may now be dead. Is this a circle of ghosts — pale reflections of youth, health and beauty? And yet they seem very alive. Every bride is beautiful, so the saying goes — and every bride is beautiful because of this "mask" that she wears. Hours of love and care were lavished upon this lacy whiteness, this veil of seduction which holds out the promise of ripeness and fitness to bear children. Remember the dance of the seven veils. The veil also reminds us of christening clothes; this same veil then encompasses the final of life's ceremonial robes, the shroud. Dichotomies reverberate: the black and the white; the dark side of the moon, the full moon; the male and the female; the ambiguity of Crow's androgynous nature, the scarecrows as equally androgynous with their phallic cross structure and female overlay; Crow of many faces, the brides faceless; the *may also contribute to the materials for making the mask, or may furnish part of the costume that is necessary to its manifestation.*

Some authors have been at pains to ascertain whether or not women know what's going on in a masquerade despite their "exclusion." Do women know the truth, and merely plead ignorance about the secret rituals?[4] This question, however, arises from our preoccupation with the mask as disguise. For us the mask is only a mask, and there is a human being beneath that mask, while the non-Western masker is convinced that he literally becomes whatever his disguise signifies.

More important than focusing on the argument of belief or disbelief, is the issue of differential access to the meaning of the ritual event. Men (initiated) and women (uninitiated) hook into different levels of meaning, as do the initiates themselves based on hierarchy of command, and right to acquire ritual lore (Bellman 1979:48). "Knowledge is a component of hierarchy" (Tonkin 1983:166).

Part of the continuum of support for the masquerade involves women actually acting as appreciative audience for the proceedings. The very presence and full co-operation of all members of the community contributes to the success of the

Crow's fertility as the mythical Creator of the world itself, the brides' circle as a pregnant image of fertility; Crow as harbinger of death and decay, an ill omen, echoes the brides' ghostly skeletal aspect. The concentric circles embody at once the womb that brings forth and the grave that swallows all things.

Raettlesnake featured a fifteen-foot ruin of a canoe with a figure of dried, shrivelled skin lying therein. From this figure extended a great length of umbilical cord. Masks hung suspended from the ceiling and radiated out from the canoe. It is often after the fact that I have uncovered some rationale for a visual image. I found a book entitled *The Serpent in Kwakiutl Religion* in which I discovered that the canoe was often one of the manifestations of the serpent, and further, the following tale was related to illustrate another manifestation of the serpent:

In several Kwakiutl myths occurs a woman who acts as a good adviser and warns the principal characters in the myth of danger. She is in the back part of the house of some supernatural beings and has this peculiarity that she is rooted to the

Snakebird and Egg

Mask from "Raettlesnake" series. Photo by Susan Ross.
(Papier-mâché, brass bells, gold leaf.)

celebration: *"The audience is the critical component of the context in which the mask is performed. It is highly significant that masks are never worn alone, so far as I know, but always vis-à-vis an audience. The audience is, in effect, part of the mask and necessary to its manifestation" (Halpin 1979b:11).*

One of the most common exceptions to the so-called "rule of exclusion" is that of the older woman, the woman past menopause. For instance, the Mbole of the West African Poro society guards the ritual pipe and razor used during initiation of new members. Women's participation as members of a mask society is often defined in terms of their reproductive role — thus they are "mothers" to the novices. The symbolic ambiguity inherent in a menopausal woman's state — that she is a woman but also, because non-menstrual, akin to a man — seems to allow for her symbolic crossing of culturally defined boundaries.

The most "active" degrees of participation in mask ritual involve the making or wearing of masks. While in many myths of mask origin women are believed to have discovered or been given the secret ritual knowledge, practically never are they cited as having made the first mask (Pernet 1979:211; see also Pernet 1982).

floor by a vein, which leaves her body between the legs. This vein belongs to the essence of her being, for, if it should be cut through, she would die. It is also impossible to dig the woman out, because the deeper one digs, the thicker the being becomes (Locher 1932:70).

Much later in my research I read that among the Mende, when a woman dreams of a serpent, it is believed she will become pregnant. Pregnant women also often tie a serpent skeleton at their waists to encourage a successful birth. "The great spirit of Temne Bondo ... [is] known as ... 'the Great Thing of the Sound of Thunder' [visually, lightning], which is said to allude to the crack of a hatching egg. It is this 'Great Thing,' represented by a serpentine procession of women ... which gives birth to the initiates, as new adult women, at their final ceremonies of 'coming out'" (Lamp 1985:38). This echo of imagery indeed seems to bespeak some great collective pool of symbolic images of which I partake. I do not see these images as great unchanging realities as suggested by Jung. Rather these images are called up in response to

Belly Belly mask shield
One of five eight-foot mask shields for R.E.D.: The Mens Club.

Installation and performance in collaboration with Marie-Josée Chartier,
choreographer, and Michael Baker, composer. Dancers: Tom Brouillette, Peter
Chin, Michael Quérin, Alejandro Ronciera, David Wood.
Photo by Cylla von Tiedemann.

The single most clear example of women making masks is provided by the Gajesa masks of the Iroquois Husk Face Society, which are made by women but worn by men. These masks are made of corn husks braided or twined together to form a face, usually encircled with a fringe of husk strands. There is a clear connection between women as the nourishers of society as a whole and the masks that they fashion as emblematic of that nourishment. The women's techniques of corn braiding are part of the manufacture of such items as shoes, mats, dishes and baskets. These corn husk masks seem to be regarded as a relatively recent development (Ritzenthaler 1969:32; Fenton 1982:340-41).

As with making, *women's* wearing *of the mask seems to be practically nonexistent. The example of the Mende (West African) Sande secret society shines forth as a rare example of a highly developed use of masks by women — the only known example of its type. It provides "the only known art tradition in the world in which women wear masks as they carry out important social tasks" (Adams 1980:9). (I would add here that a few other examples of women "wearing" do exist, but these seem to be chiefly in parody of men's rituals and are scarcely comparable in scale to the Sande example (e.g., Calame-Griaule 1966:299-300; Maybury-*

"recurrent experiences which cut across the boundaries of cultures and artistic media ... and ... reveal the preoccupations of an era" (Lauter 1984:x-xi).

"Raettlesnake" encompassed many strands of thought — paradoxical strands. My adherence to black and gold played with two qualities: black, a gaping hole into which one may fall forever; and gold, the epitome of utmost reflection, a gleam which comes to life with a ray of light. The series of masks was inspired by the mythical serpent which through its power of shedding its skin may live on forever; the masks then became as layers of skin, documenting life's experiences. The masks could also be seen as visual records of the birthing process. Many of them featured the process of emerging forth.

Images of fertility and life were juxtaposed next to decay and death. The *Serpent Mother* may at first have appeared to be but the remains of some human body laid to rest. What was lying in state, however, was just a skin — a cast-off shell, discarded, without substance, faint echo of a living form — but a skin with a rounded belly, a fecund pregnant form. The twisted cord could have been the umbilical cord, the rope of life;

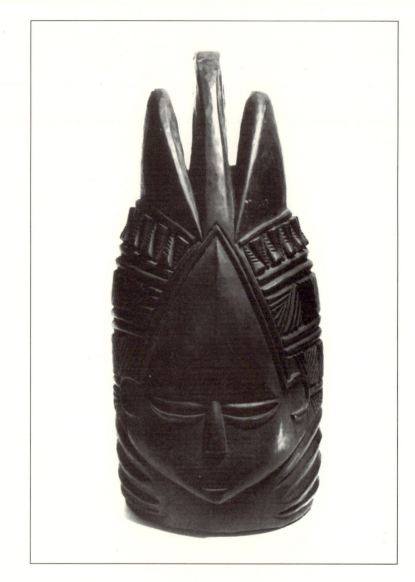

Mende sowei mask

Courtesy of the Royal Ontario Museum, Toronto, Canada. Cat. No. HA 385.
(On permanent loan from Capt. A.W. Boddy.) Height 19".

Lewis 1967:129; Osgood 1970:426).

There is but one principal kind of Sande mask, known as sowei — a helmet form with a large domed forehead and elaborate hair design, black in patina. The mask is commissioned from a male carver. It appears principally on two occasions — at the time of initiation of young women, and to exact justice at the transgression of Sande law.

Mende and West African women in general have consistently exercised a degree of independence, political authority and control of resources — these, it seems, within a system which traditionally favours patrilineal descent and patrilocal residence. The Sande society operates as an example of women's strength and solidarity. The mask is a symbol of power shared by both women and men. Yet while Sande women do indeed enjoy full participation in that which has the world over been part of the male domain, the mask in which they partake is a mediated image, for it is a mask carved by men alone.

We have then two critical examples worldwide — one in which women wear masks, but do not make them, and the other in which women make masks, but do not wear them. The making and the

it may also have been the serpent.

The canoe itself was also a metaphor for the serpent, a primordial and at once creative and destructive force. The very ribbing of its structure echoed the sleek snake's skeletal structure. The boat was at once an image of tomb and womb. Emblem of the journey from the land of the living to the land of the dead, a vehicle of transformation, it echoed the very function of the mask. For the mask provides the means for assuming another identity, an extra-ordinary identity, and in and by itself embodies paradox. The assumption of a mask implies the "death," the sublimation, of one persona to bring forth another.

R.E.D.: The Mens Club was inspired by a book entitled *The Island of Menstruating Men* (Hogbin 1970), which describes men's practice of lacerating the penis as a purificatory "menstrual" rite among the Wogeo of Papua New Guinea. The reinterpretation of the biological process of menstruation, as an act of purification and celebration (at odds with our society's conventional view of the process as unmentionable and "dirty")

Volva Volva. Part of *OS: The Love Darts of the Slug*

Dancer: Marie-Josée Chartier. Photo by Susan Ross.
(Papier-mâché, leather, bamboo, raffia.)

wearing do not converge.

The Sande example may go part way in answering the question of why women have apparently not used the mask. Without a high degree of publicly recognized status along with a ritual "support system" in the face of societal traditions favouring male descent, the symbolic trappings of power/Power (for example, the mask) may not exist for women in other societies. The Mende Sande society in part provides a solid front against male encroachment, and has embraced a very visible symbol of solidarity through its sowei *mask in an area well known for its masking traditions. At the same time the right to access the sacred knowledge of the society, and to dance the* sowei *mask is restricted to certain select lineages. We must then consider the intersection of gender with social status as well as age, for gender is not the only difference that makes a difference. Our understanding is determined by a "situated knowledge" (Haraway 1988).*

The extraordinary nature of the Mende Sande society becomes apparent given the context of the Gelede masquerade of the neighbouring Yoruba, which pays homage to the spiritual powers of women, especially older women. They are praised as "our mothers," "the gods

— this reinterpretation was a starting point.

In the process of menstruation is a model for life's conduct. Out of a seeming image of death, the loss of blood, we prepare anew for the next part of the cycle, with its potential for conception and growth — a hopeful vision. We bleed yet do not die. On a microcosmic level each female body passing through the phases of ovulation and menstruation echoes the larger rhythms of seasons passing, the relationship of earth and moon movement. By ignoring or shaming the rhythms of a living healthy body we poison our means of survival.

The mask shields were inspired in part by ceremonial and war shields of Papua New Guinea. The traditional shield is a symbol of masculine strength and protection, which we wished to infuse with female imagery. In *R.E.D.* the shield became an image of power mediating between outward trappings of corporate power and visions for societal change. There is a fitting convergence between the mask and menstruation for each requires the "death of self" in order to bring forth another persona, a new life.

I Sing. No One Hears Me.

From "Coma Amok" series. Photo by Susan Ross.
(Papier-mâché, leather, raffia, copper leaf.)

of society" and "the owners of the world" (Drewal and Drewal 1983:xv). Yoruba women control economics and trading, and may commission masks commemorating their roles in the Gelede society (society membership being open to all, both women and men); but they do not themselves wear the mask (Drewal and Drewal 1983:260).

The function of the mask within a given society may have some bearing upon how accessible the mask is. Masks of a "sacred" order often require more stringent prohibitions than those accorded a secular and theatrical entertainment role. For example, "man-regarding" (Cole 1970:7-8) kinds of self-transformation that enhance the status of the wearer (e.g., ceremonial dress, body decorations) seem to be primarily the sorts of masks that women access; Kwakiutl women, for example, wear headdresses during masked ceremonials (Hawthorn 1967: 116). In contrast the "spirit-regarding" transformations that cancel the wearer's identity temporarily (through the superimposition of a new "face" or "body") are the sorts of transformations which fall within the male domain (Cole 1970:7-8).

The analysis here has privileged the wearing or the making of the mask as of utmost prestige value, with such prestige as generally

Os: The Love Darts of the Slug drew its inspiration from studies of animal behaviour, in particular, courtship displays and mating dances of the snail family. "Os" comes from the Latin meaning mask, opening, mouth, face, innermost spirit, bones. The snail has been chosen as a fitting symbol for questioning and reinterpreting our social definitions of feminine and masculine, for many snail species are hermaphroditic (they possess a gland, the ovotestis, which produces both eggs and sperm).

The title takes its name from the habit of the Roman snail (Helix pomatia) and more common Garden snail (Helix aspersa) of shooting a calcium harpoon-like shaft, about 5/16" long into its partner as part of a courtship — this has come to be known as the telum amoris ("love dart"). Another species of snail, the Limax maximus, actually performs a complicated sequential mid-air "Liebespiel," with the partners suspended from a tree branch and entwined spiral fashion. Yet another species, the slipper limpet (Crepidula fornicata), begins life as a male, passes through a hermaphroditic stage and finishes as a female.

male oriented. It is important, however, to recognize that dancing is extremely important in masked performances, and women often participate whole-heartedly in dancing. It is possible that in non-Western societies dancing is at least as important an expression of communication of values as the actual wearing of the mask. Thompson (1974) argues very strongly that it is the dancing of the mask that renders it alive and active. To my knowledge little research has been done on the "native" values of worth attached to the various aspects of masquerade preparation and performance. The overriding role of women in mask ritual seems to be primarily symbolic, with men "using" the female image to define the boundaries of their identity. Masks featuring images of women can thus be seen as constructions of men's ideals and values for womanhood, for it is men who make masks, and generally men who wear them. Such images of women are mediated by men.

The study of masking necessarily becomes a study of gender power relationships, given the apparent fusions of gender categories within masked ritual — fusions which are "used, contested, and sometimes ... shifted over time" (Ortner 1990:56). The mask literature has concentrated on presenting (hostile) structural

Coma Amok. First a story. Near one of the busiest intersections in Toronto a circle of people was standing just outside a bank. I stopped, curious. They were all staring intently at something. There was complete silence. They were transfixed, incapacitated because there, down on the sidewalk, by the doorway of the bank, was a praying mantis. No one knew what it was. No one wanted to touch it. No one could enter or leave the bank. The mantis swayed unsteadily. One of its legs was injured. It glowed green green against the grey concrete. No one knew what to do. No one in the crowd had ever seen such a creature. It chattered defiance.

"Coma" means a state of profound insensibility, and is here pitted against "amok" (or amuck) in the sense of "possessed by a reckless mania." The inability to recognize a creature such as the praying mantis, so that its presence becomes an absurdity, a raw juxtaposition of living swaying green with concrete, epitomizes "coma amok." Yet within the senselessness or loss of control there may be some sort of symmetry. There is potential for balance within the unbalance symbolized by the *oppositions which have grown from differences and has then made the leap from oppositions to hierarchies. Although men have in most cases dominated the visible manifestations of masquerade, the possibility that the presence of women, even symbolically, is indispensable has been ignored. While the ideology of male dominance would seem to be hegemonic, to use Ortner's term (1990), the so-called exclusion of women is never total. Some degree of participation of women (however er subordinate or suppressed), is always present to complement the activities of the men. Female presence (material or symbolic) may provide what Bateson refers to as a "grandiose female matrix" (Bateson 1946:120) in which mas(k)uline performance has its locus.*

choice of such a palindrome as "coma amok." "Mantis" comes from the Greek meaning "prophet," and is a genus remarkable for its holding of its anterior legs like hands folded in prayer. There are many legends about the mantis because of its habit of remaining motionless or of swaying gently back and forth in supplicating pose. In fact "preying" rather than "praying" may be a more apt epithet for the mantis, for all mantids are voracious carnivores and will devour even their own kind. The mantis thus becomes a fitting metaphor for human capacity both to seek the richest of spiritual experience through prayer and to ravage beyond measure.

NOTES

1. Comparatively little attention has focused on the contributions of women to celebrations of masked ritual, with the exception of the recent full body of literature on West Africa's Sande society. Some other notable contributions have been made by Drewal 1977; Eder 1977; Maertens 1978; Pernet 1979, 1982; Tonkin 1979, 1983.

2. Part of the difficulty in formulating a general theory of masking is that the mask can simultaneously take many forms and function on many different levels. Researchers are not always careful to clarify their use of the word. Say the word mask, and more often than not people will mention, in addition to Hallowe'en masks or "primitive" tribal masks, veils, face makeup or tattoos. As Urban and Hendricks point out, however, "Masks are never worn as everyday social apparel" (Urban and Hendricks 1983:213). They usually are part of a special ceremonial occasion. For the purposes of this

study I have confined my interest to the mask as a transforming cover for the face or whole head.

3. Ortner in her research on Andaman Island society refers to senior men hand-feeding initiates: "Initiates were being reborn as adults, and ... it was the senior men who were symbolically claiming to deliver them into adulthood, as women delivered them into the world as infants in the first place" (Ortner 1990:59).

4. Interestingly, Hauser-Schaublin in her research among the Iatmul points out that in fact women and men may know the exact same stories. Although the Iatmul have separate names for the two sets of stories, she could see no clear distinction on the basis of content between the stories that women and children know and the men's "secrets." The ideology supported by all, however, is that only men know the true myths (Hauser-Schaublin 1977:259-60).

BIBLIOGRAPHY

ADAMS, Marie Jeanne. 1980. "Introduction. Masking in Sierra Leone and Liberia." *Ethnologische Zeitschrift* 1:9-12.

ARDENER, Shirley. 1975. "Sexual Insult and Female Militancy." In *Perceiving Women,* ed. Shirley Ardener. London: Malaby, 29-53.

BATESON, Gregory. 1946. "Arts of the South Seas." (exhibition review) *Art Bulletin* 28:119-23.

BELLMAN, Beryl L. 1979. "The Social Organization of Knowledge in Kpelle Ritual." In *The New Religions of Africa,* ed. Bennetta Jules-Rosette. Norwood, NJ: Ablex, 39-56.

CALAME-GRIAULE, Geneviève. 1966. *Ethnologie et langage.* Paris: Gallimard.

CHODOROW, Nancy. 1978. *Reproduction of Mothering: Psychoanalysis and the Reproduction of Mothering.* Berkeley: University of California Press.

CLIFFORD, James. 1985. "Histories of the Tribal and the Modern." *Art in America* (April):164-77, 215.

COLE, Herbert M. 1970. *African Arts of Transformation.* Santa Barbara: The Art Galleries, University of California.

DOMINGUEZ, Virginia R. 1987. "Of Other Peoples: Beyond the 'Salvage Paradigm'." In *Discussions in Contemporary Culture,* ed. Hal Foster. Seattle, WA: Dia Art Foundation, 131-49.

DREWAL, Henry John. 1977. "Art and the Perception of Women in Yoruba Culture." *Cahiers d'études africaines* 17(4):545-67.

————, and Margaret Thompson Drewal. 1983. *Gelede: Art and Female Power among the Yoruba.* Bloomington: Indiana University Press.

EDER, Milton. 1977. "Huts, Masks and Women: Marriage in Shavante Life." *El Dorado* 2(2):78-86.

FENTON, William N. 1982. "Masked Medicine Societies of the Iroquois." (Reprinted from Annual Report of the Smithsonian Institution, 1940: 397-430) In *Native North American Art History: Selected Readings,* ed. Zena Pearlstone Mathews and Aldona Jonaitis. Palo Alto, CA: Peek Publications, 325-600.

HALPIN, Marjorie. 1979a. "Confronting Looking-glass Men: A Preliminary Examination of the Mask." University of Northern Colorado, Greeley. Museum of Anthropology. Occasional publications in anthropology. Ethnology series no. 33, 41-61.

———. 1979b. "Self, Other, and the Mask." Paper presented in the Symposium, Masks and Masquerade in the Americas, Forty-third International Congress of Americanists, Vancouver.

HARAWAY, Donna. 1988. "Situated Knowledges: The Science Question in Feminism and the Privilege of Partial Perspective." *Feminist Studies* 14(3):575-99.

HASELBERGER, H. 1961. "Method of Studying Ethnological Art." *Current Anthropology* 2(4):341-55.

HAUSER-SCHAUBLIN, Brigitta. 1977. "Frauen in Kararau: Zur Rolle der Frau bei den Iatmul am Mittelsepik, Papua Neu Guinea." *Baseler Beitrage zur Ethnologie* 18.

HAWTHORN, Audrey. 1967. *Art of the Kwakiutl Indians.* Vancouver: University of British Columbia Press.

HOGBIN, Ian. 1970. *The Island of Menstruating Men: Religion in Wogeo, New Guinea.* Scranton, PA: Chandler Publishing.

JULES-ROSETTE, Bennetta. 1984. *The Messages of Tourist Art: An African Semiotic System in Comparative Perspective.* New York: Plenum Press.

KEESING, Roger M. 1981. *Cultural Anthropology: A Contemporary Perspective.* New York: Holt, Rinehart and Winston.

KROEBER, A.L., and Catherine Holt. 1920. "Masks and Moieties as a Culture Complex." *Journal of the Royal Anthropological Institute of Great Britain and Ireland* 50:452-60.

LAMP, Frederick. 1985. "Cosmos, Cosmetics and the Spirit of Bondo." *African Arts* 18(3):28-43, 98-99.

LAMPHERE, Louise. 1987. "Feminism and Anthropology: The Struggle to Reshape Our Thinking about Gender." In *The Impact of Feminist Research in the Academy,* ed. Christie Farnham. Bloomington: Indiana University Press, 11-33.

LAUTER, Estella. 1984. *Women as Mythmakers: Poetry and Visual Art by Twentieth-century Women.* Bloomington: Indiana University Press.

LOCHER, G.W. 1932. *The Serpent in Kwakiutl Religion: A Study in Primitive Culture.* Leyden: E.J. Brill.

MAERTENS, Jean-Thierry. 1978. *Le Masque et le miroir: Essai d'anthropologie des revêtements faciaux.* Paris: Aubier-Montaigne.

MAYBURY-LEWIS, David. 1967. *Akwe-Shavante Society.* New York: Oxford University Press.

MEAD, Margaret. 1949. *Male and Female: A Study of the Sexes in a Changing World.* New York: Dell.

MORGEN, Sandra, ed. 1989. *Gender and Anthropology: Critical Reviews for Research and Teaching.* Washington, DC: American Anthropological Association.

MOZEL, Howard. 1986. "A Look Into the Collective Unconscious." *Oakville Beaver* (May 23):12.

ORTNER, Sherry B. 1974. "Is Female to Male as Nature is to Culture?" In *Woman, Culture and Society,* ed. Michelle Zimbalist Rosaldo and Louise Lamphere. Stanford: Stanford University Press, 67-88.

———. 1990. "Gender Hegemonies." *Cultural Critique* (Winter):35-80.

OSGOOD, Cornelius. 1970. *Ingalik Material Culture.* (reprinted from 1940 edition) New Haven: Human Relations Area Files.

OTTENBERG, Simon. 1975. *Masked Rituals of Afikpo: The Context of an African Art.* Seattle, WA: University of Washington Press.

PERNET, Henry. 1979. "'Primitive' Ritual Masks in the History of Religions: A Methodological Assessment." Ph.D. thesis, University of Chicago.

———. 1982. "Masks and Women: Toward a Reappraisal." *History of Religions* 22(1):45-49.

RITZENTHALER, Robert. 1969. *Iroquois False-Face Masks.* Milwaukee Public Museum, Publications in Primitive Art 3.

STRATHERN, Marilyn. 1981. "Culture in a Netbag: The Manufacture of a Sub-discipline in Anthropology." *Man* 16:664-88.

THOMPSON, Robert Farris. 1974. *African Art in Motion: Icon and Act.* Washington, DC: National Gallery of Art.

TONKIN, Elizabeth. 1979. *Masking and Masquerading, with Examples from West Africa.* University of Birmingham Discussion Papers, Series C, Sociology and Politics (no. 36).

———. 1983. "Women Excluded? Masking and Masquerading in West Africa." In *Women's Religious Experience,* ed. Pat Holden. London: Croom Helm, 163-74.

TOOKER, Elisabeth. 1968. "Masking and Matrilineality in North America." *American Anthropologist* 70(6):1170-75.

URBAN, Greg, and Janet Wall Hendricks. 1983. "Signal Functions of Masking in Amerindian Brazil." *Semiotica* 47:181-216.

WALENS, Stanley. 1983. Analogic Causality and the Power of Masks. In *The Power of Symbols: Masks and Masquerade in the Americas,* ed. N. Ross Crumrine and Marjorie Halpin. Vancouver: University of British Columbia Press, 70-78.

WHITBECK, Caroline. 1989. "A Different Reality: Feminist Ontology." In *Women, Knowledge, and Reality,* ed. Ann Garry and Marilyn Pearsall. Boston: Unwin Hyman, 51-76.

WOLFE, Alvin W. 1969. "Social Structural Bases of Art." *Current Anthropology* 10(1):3-44.

CHAPTER 12

New Voices on Fieldwork

Clara Benazera
Elizabeth Houde
Marie-Hélène Bérard
Renée Ménard

*I*N 1989 A GROUP OF GRADUATE STUDENTS AT THE University of Laval formed a discussion and work group to consider the difficulties of defining and operationalizing the notion of household. Our concerns quickly extended beyond the notion of household to include other aspects of our research, most notably the question of women.

Our educational backgrounds in feminism were very different and we wondered if the mere fact of being interested in women and of wishing to convey their reality as accurately as possible made us feminist anthropologists. Fieldwork in one way or another provided us with the answer to our questions — or so we thought.

Generally, our reflections here concern the appropriateness of academic or institutional feminism in conveying and describing the day-to-day reality of women from elsewhere. These reflections are based on our fieldwork experiences in different geographical areas:

Marie-Hélène Bérard (Burkina Faso) ponders the appropriate analytic framework for rendering Sahelian women's notion of time; Elizabeth Houde (Costa Rica) argues in favour of a renewal of conceptual and methodological tools in order to better grasp "women's day-to-day experiences and negotiations"; Clara Benazera (Costa Rica) raises the question of the commitment of the feminist anthropologist and its implication for methodology; Renée Ménard (Colombia) addresses the question of the social responsibility of the researcher in the field toward other women.

These reflections in no way claim to be based on an exhaustive knowledge of the current literature on feminism or of anthropological research. Our intention is not to reject the heritage of feminist research of the seventies and eighties, but rather to make a modest contribution to the new challenges raised by both research and practice in feminist anthropology in the nineties.

MARIE-HÉLÈNE (BURKINA FASO)

The following comment reflects some questions which were raised during a research trip to Burkina Faso.[1] The study focused on the effects of income-generating activities on rural women's organization of time and work routines. I was particularly interested in the introduction of a new technology, the *karité* press.[2] The press was meant to lighten women's traditional workload while at the same time providing them with an income.

Feminist critique of development usually addresses the question of the heavy workload of Third World women: women generally work longer hours than do men; they work a double day; etc. Some have taken this workload to be an indicator of their social oppression, others an obstacle to the improvement of their economic conditions. For development workers in the field, time is often seen as an obstacle to women's participation in projects. For some it represents a constraint on their social and economic advancement: "Women's advancement is without a doubt most delayed by their lack of availability to cooperate with us" (Allan and Benihirwe, in Champagne 1989:291, my translation). As a consequence, the development workers I met are generally concerned about helping women to "better manage" their time.

I share this preoccupation for women's time, but from another perspective. During my fieldwork it always appeared important to me to try to capture women's reality from their own point of view. The Sahelian woman's notion of time involved a logic totally different from the production-oriented rationality developers seek to impose on them. The time-oriented preoccupations of Western feminists also seemed to me to be inappropriate, since they too are rooted in our socio-economic context where production predominates; our preoccupations may make sense to us but not necessarily to women elsewhere on the planet.

The Sahelian women I was able to talk to were clearly less worried about saving time than were the development workers whose job it was to introduce new technology into the community. For example, when I asked the village women what advantages they saw in the new *karité* press, they referred mostly to improvements in hygiene. Nevertheless they went on using the traditional method of transforming the *karité*,[3] which allows them to use the product in a traditional manner — either by selling it at the market in small quantities in order to ensure a modest but regular income or by giving it to other women in order to consolidate alliances with them.

It was through fieldwork that I came to see that the workload of Sahelian women must not be confused with "women's housework" in industrialized countries. The Sahelian women's preoccupation does not correspond to the preoccupations of women in the north. I imagine that many feminists in academia would be offended if they were told that they have much less control over their time than most rural women of Sahel, but my data leads me to believe that this is in fact the case.

I make this point despite the postmodern currents that run through present-day anthropology. Postmodernism involves a deconstruction not only of the validity of our interpretations but also of the relevance of our commitments. Adherents of this approach think that the desire to bear witness to the reality of others is an intellectual fiction. It is not that I do not recognize the subjective content of any research process, but I refuse to accept the dead end to which this paradigm ultimately leads us: a fin-de-siècle defeatism which refuses all commitment and/or bias. I personally feel that postmodernism leaves one in an ontological vacuum. Must I resign myself to conceptualizing women's time from a culturalist or psychological viewpoint? I think not.

ELIZABETH (COSTA RICA)

During my graduate studies I carried out two research trips in a fishing community in Costa Rica.[4] The focus of my research was on the complexity of the process of social differentiation in the Costa Rican milieu. I wanted to connect macro- and micro-social analyses and attempted to grasp the structural features of this process, by considering the internal organization of the household.[5] Although at first I did not intend to take a direct interest in women's roles within the community, my integration into Costa Rican households[6] enabled me to identify certain spaces occupied by women. This fieldwork revealed that the daily reality of women is much more complex and diversified than suggested by the concepts some feminists use (universal subordination of and the oppression of women). Let me briefly examine several examples.

In two of the households I studied, decisions concerning the socio-economic orientations of the household are generally based on a common agreement, the woman and the man speaking out and adopting positions on various issues. In one of these households, the woman often acts as the spokesperson for the household (she has an education, her husband never went to school). She is the one who goes to the capital to handle administrative matters or to accompany her husband for important transactions. The two women in these households also have direct access to the money their husbands earn and they have a say in the use of this money.

In another case, a young woman living in a low-income household participates very little in the choices made by her husband, and everything related to the purchase of food, clothing and material goods is almost exclusively the concern of her husband. She has no idea how much her husband earns and hardly ever sees a trace of his earnings.

In yet another household study, the information I collected from the wife of the man who owns the house shows variability in the type of economic contribution made by household members. The houseowner does not have absolute rights over the money earned by those living under his roof, nor does he have a say regarding their activities. It is interesting to note that the income earned by the only employed daughter of the household is not handed to the owner in order to cover certain costs related to food or electricity. However, when necessary, she might sometimes supports the other women of the household, in this case, her sister and her mother.

As these four cases indicate, the household presents rich oportunities for the observation of social processes. It was only through such fieldwork that I was able to catch a glimpse of the potential sphere of power and autonomy that women may indeed occupy within the household. Although I do not want to deny the existence of exploitation and oppression of women in the community, I believe that focusing initially on exploitation and oppression tends to conceal important aspects of social reality experienced by women. It seems considerably more enriching (as much for feminist studies as for the women in whose name we speak) to try to grasp women's daily experiences and negotiations with others than to limit ourselves to revealing only the oppression they experience. I believe that it is by seeking to understand the processes through which women organize and manage their lives, as well as the nature of their relationships (to other women and men), that we will be able to do them justice in our texts.

Even a brief look at internal household dynamics indicates that the notion of the universal oppression of women put forward by some academic feminists tends to oversimplify the complexity of women's condition. We must persevere in our search for concepts which more clearly express the voices and politics of women. Further explorations into the internal dynamics of households seem to me to be an important avenue for realizing this objective.

CLARA (COSTA RICA)

Following three research trips to Costa Rica in the context of a research project and of my master's project,[7] I began to question the relevance of academic feminism to the daily reality of Costa Rican women. My objective here is to consider the possible consequences on anthropological methodology[8] of the feminist commitment, a commitment which appears to me to be both "social" and "academic." My training has involved familiarizing myself with conceptual frameworks and methodological principles. Parallel to this I have become sensitized on a personal level to feminist politics. Are these two processes compatible? Does fieldwork nourish this complex combination or undermine it?

During fieldwork in Costa Rica I shared the life of a group of women and a village community and was witness to local gender politics and power struggles. Clearly each of my informants, men and women, young and old, rich and poor, had daily long-term political "objectives." To reach these objectives, various culturally specific means are used. As a feminist my understanding of women's needs does not necessarily complement that presented to me by informants. Hence there is the need to locate social and cultural informants so as to decipher these women's "political" goals. This task is not necessarily a simple and straightforward one, however.

During my stay in Costa Rica, I worked with a group of local male leaders who were involved in community development. They raised the question of "women's role" with regard to the setting up of a project specifically addressed to women. To these men "women's role" should first and foremost be "taking care" of the children and "doing housework." According to them, a project that would best fill the women's needs would be a sewing course, for instance. Such a project was in fact set up, without any prior consultation with the women concerned. This event reveals a certain type of gender relation and raises questions about how feminist anthropologists undertake data collection.

As a witness to this process, how do I disantangle my feminist principles from the prerequisites of anthropological methodology? As a feminist, how do I deal with the fact that a man speaks or decides for a woman without being delegated to do so? Can I maintain a distance between myself as a feminist and myself as an anthropologist? How can such a distance be maintained with all informants, both men and women? What best describes reality, men's discourse, our observations or women's comments? How do I choose among these realities and put order into this complex data?

These questions are not peculiar to feminist anthropology. Nevertheless, I feel that my university training led me to believe that an anthropologist is immune to political bias, whereas my fieldwork demonstrated quite the opposite. Both feminist anthropology as a discipline and the anthropological training offered to graduate and undergraduate students must take blame for this problem. Feminist anthropology has failed to sensitize us to the need for a careful analysis of the interplay between the researcher as a committed actor and the researcher as a scientific observer. Our anthropological training has failed to initiate us to the vagaries of concrete conflictual situations and how to deal with them.

However, the current literature on feminist anthropology (Mascia-Lees, Sharpe, and Ballerino Cohen 1989; Moore 1988) does provide promising avenues. The debate raised by the "new ethnography" also introduces interesting possibilities: "A fundamental goal of the new ethnography is ... to apprehend and inscribe 'others' in such a way as not to deny or diffuse their claims to subjecthood. As Marcus and Fisher put it, the new ethnography seeks to allow 'the adequate representation of other voices or points of view across cultural boundaries'" (Mascia-Lees, Sharpe, and Ballerino Cohen 1989:14). Implied in this new awareness is the need for every generation to question, debate and take a stand on basic political issues and feminist commitment.

RENÉE (COLOMBIA)

In 1989 I undertook a master's program at the University of Laval with an interest in exploring women's subordination. Having joined a research project[9] on rural development and the integration of women into development in Colombia, I concentrated on women's access to land. I hypothesized then that their lack of access to property ownership prevented their economic independence. This seemed at the time a relevant indicator to measure their subordinate position within the society. I was economically oriented in my approach to women's subordination. I arrived in the field with a mixed conceptual framework that included Marxist and feminist concepts and an array of conceptual tools to convey the reality of the women concerned.

I was not prepared for the fact that my chosen methodology could become a threat to the safety of the women I met. Here I am not talking about the threat of guerillas in the countryside, although it does exist, in which case it would be the men who could be endangered. In this particular instance I am referring to the daily terrorism exerted on women in their own daily family life. Although the safety of all the women I met and interviewed was not threatened, I am aware of a case in which a woman I interviewed was mistreated by her husband for having answered my questions. This one case was sufficient for me to question the social responsibility of the feminist researcher toward her informants.

My academic training had not prepared me to face such an eventuality. The teaching, the readings and other educational means had only marginally touched on the social responsibility of the researcher towards female informants. Can we justify endangering women's safety in the name of shedding light on their subordinate position? The other face of this question is of course: can I as feminist, that is, as a person wishing to abolish the inequalities to which women are subjected, justify not revealing such a situation? In my opinion, the answer to both these questions must be no. But is it possible to resolve such a paradox?

It seems to me that the methodology favoured by feminists does not necessarily take into account the question of the social responsibility of the researcher toward her informants. It appears to be assumed that a feminist researcher is implicitly predisposed to apprehend, without difficulties, the reality of all of the women in the world. My fieldwork experience has showed me that, on the contrary, there is often an abyss between the researcher's understanding of her reality and her understanding of the reality of others. It therefore seems urgent to concentrate on this aspect of feminist research. We must reflect and attempt to equip ourselves with a methodology that allows us to grasp, document and convey through our writings the reality of our informants. This must be done whether or not our writings aim at documenting the women's political, economic or social situation.

We will have to find new research methods, especially in the area of understanding different means of communication. Body language and visual expressions often reveal more than words. We have to learn to listen to women's voices whether they reveal themselves through speech or through silence.

Although it may sound odd, during my fieldwork women's "voices" often reached me through their eyes. I was constantly frustrated at not being able to translate these "conversations"; I had access to no suitable tools for doing so. Should I have trusted my intuition to give these "frightened eyes" a voice? Probably not, given my goal of scientific analysis. How could I convey the messages behind those eyes without endangering the women? For now all I can do is identify that void I was faced with and wrestle with that dilemma: to tell or not to tell, how, and at what cost to my informants?

CONCLUSION

Our field experiences have forced us to reflect on, and sometimes adopt, certain positions regarding the methodologies, concepts or practices of feminist anthropology. We are well aware that we have raised here many more questions than we have answered. The contributions reveal the divergent views in our group. In this respect we reflect the larger academic debate which is marked by an array of points of view. But more interesting is the fact that this heterogeneity actually draws out the ambiguous situation of feminist commitment when confronted with the reality of field work.

Reflection on the notion of "household" and the notion of "time" has made us aware of how theoretical universalisms take us away from the contextualized reality of women. But does rejecting these universalisms confront us with a mass of culturally relative information which cannot be used comparatively? We think that feminist anthropology might provide us with a solution to that problem: by taking the point of view of women we can reread theoretical universalisms such as the notions of "household" and "time." This is an important project, but we are still left with the problem of what we mean by "the point of view of women."

Consider also the two contributions on the social responsibility and feminist commitment of researchers. Here we have two points of view which seem alike, but in fact they are not always necessarily so. One addresses the safety (physical or otherwise) of women informants, a very basic, daily situation. The other questions the very uncomfortable position of a person with two hats, committed feminist and anthropologist, who must relate to politically marked informants (men or women). We are faced in these articles with the distinction between ethics and action. Ethics for whom or what? Action by whom and for whom? In the field the fine line between these positions is not always obvious. This is especially the case when the education we receive does not specifically address these questions. As women embedded in the arena of male/female relations in our own societies, we have to take stock of the lenses of our vision of the world before identifying "other" women. Political commitment has consequences, something to which we should be sensitive. Moral commitment seems to be a matter of personal choice, but is it? We hope that these thoughts will help to provide new avenues which will permit all of us to speak more adequately to the reality of "other" women.

NOTES

1.   Made possible by a grant from the Centre Sahel at the University of Laval.

2.   Karité is a fruit growing naturally in some countries of western Africa. The fruit's almond is used to produce butter and soap for the local market. The karité press is a technology designed to cut down on time and energies while extracting karité butter from the crushed almonds.

3.   Suffice to say for the purpose of this article that the traditional method to transform the karité is long and strenuous. At the same time the harshness of these operations seems to be partially compensated by the working "ambiance" which exists throughout the transformation process (Beij 1986:85). The women come from the same concessions or are neighbours. In fact the traditional process of karité transformation is an opportunity for networking and mutual aid. This mutual aid is compensated by a gift of karité butter and implies a relation of reciprocity.

4.   I stayed in Costa Rica from June to August in both 1989 and 1990 in the context of a project directed by Professor Yvan Breton and subsidized by FCAR (Fonds pour la Formation de Chercheurs et l'Aide à la Recherche) and SSHRC (Social Sciences and Humanities Research Council of Canada).

5.   I define the household as a place of residence in which a series of social relationships in part determine the internal dynamic and the form it will take as a social group.

6.   I studied four households from different economic bases, three fishing households and one merchant household. The social composition of the households also differ.

.7.   The research project, directed by Professor Yvan Breton, focused on the socio-economic dynamics of small-scale fishing in Costa Rica. I made three trips from May to August in 1989, 1990 and 1991. These research trips were made possible by grants from FCAR and SSHRC.

8.   The notion of methodology is understood here as "the systematic study of the principles guiding anthropological investigation and the ways in which theory finds its application; an articulated, theoretically informed approach to the production of data, [...]" (Ellen (ed.), 1984:9). When I refer to anthropological methodology I am primarily referring to the practice of participant observation.

9.   This project is headed by Professor Marie France Labrecque, and the funds for the research come from both FCAR and SSHRC.

BIBLIOGRAPHY

BEIJ, A. 1986. *Femmes et karité: l'importance du karité pour les femmes dans un village Gourounsi au Burkina Faso.* Leiden: Université d'Etat de Leiden, Pays Bas.

CHAMPAGNE, Suzanne, éd. 1989. *Les femmes et le développement: stratégies, moyens, impact. Des coopérantes témoignent de leur expérience avec des femmes au Sahel.* Québec: Centre Sahel/Université Laval.

ELLEN, R.F., ed. 1984. *Ethnographic Research. A Guide to General Conduct.* Research Methods in Social Anthropology 1. London: Academic Press.

MASCIA-LEES, F.E., P. Sharpe, and C. Ballerino Cohen. 1989. "The Postmodernist Turn in Anthropology: Cautions from a Feminist Perspective." *Signs* 15(1):7-33.

MOORE, Henrietta. 1988. *Feminism and Anthropology.* Minneapolis: University of Minnesota Press.

CHAPTER 13

Conversation between Cultures Outrageous Voices?

ISSUES OF VOICE AND TEXT IN FEMINIST ANTHROPOLOGY

Judith M. Abwunza

*I*N A CONTEXT OF FEMINIST ANTHROPOLOGY AND engendered power, Amadiume, an African anthropologist, says some Western women anthropologists take "the universal social and cultural inferiority of women [as] a foregone conclusion.... These post-doctoral women anthropologists had not de-anthropologized themselves before embarking on their gigantic project of assessing women's condition in societies chosen haphazardly from all over the Third World" (1987:4).

Outraged voices are demanding to be heard. Are their voices outrageous? Privileged access to cultural knowledge no longer alludes to the anthropologist engaged in fieldwork, the hallmark of the discipline. Voices with lived cultural expertise inside the profession (e.g., Amadiume above) and outside (e.g., Logoli women below[1]) demand the privilege. A postcolonial critique such as Amadiume's, is directly levelled against "experts" from academe who, from their positions of power, provide the "truth" of cultures for members of the academy and (less so) members of the culture itself. The following presentation of voices is investigatory in that the writer seeks a path. The presentation turns on this white and Western woman anthropologist's dilemma in regard to two ethical "technicalities" in anthropology's representation of the other. Who speaks for whom? and In whose interest are spoken voices heard?

DISCIPLINE(D) VOICES

Ethnographic texts, Clifford (1988) says, are "orchestrations of multivocal (and unequal) exchanges occurring in politically charged situations." Ultimately all voices become, "constructed domains of truth, serious fictions"(10). For the most part, cross-cultural representation is, as Clifford describes his own recent work, "written from within a 'West' whose authority to represent unified human history is now widely challenged"(13). "The predominant mode of modern fieldwork authority is signaled: "You are there ... because I was there"(22). But today, "the silence of the ethnographic workshop has been broken — by insistent, heteroglot voices, by the scratching of other pens"(26). The participant observer offering "a dialectic of experience and interpretation"(34) is threatened, even when experience may subdue interpretation, in that a paradox is evident. Of whose experience are we speaking? Whose interpretation is the authority?

Authority in ethnographic texts has relied on the subjective experience of the participant-observing scholar, who *collects* data from *informants* rather than recognizing where the action belongs: the scholar *receives* data from *those who inform*. Interpretation in ethnographic texts turns on interesting objectifying meanings like "looking at culture as an assemblage of texts to be interpreted" and "ethnography is the interpretation of cultures." It is further self-serving as the ethnographer takes the text and leaves the field, thus "a generalized 'author' must be invented to account for the world or context within which the texts are fictionally relocated," for example, "the native point of view," "the Trobrianders," "the Nuer" (Clifford 1988:38-40). Dialogue and context are left behind in the relocation. Interpretive texts are thus labelled "unreciprocal," coming under attack by the critics of colonial representation where the ethnographer has all the power to present the cultural "truth." Ethnography is, in "truth," a "constructed negotiation" between subjects: the ethnographer, who has a conscious, political agenda, and cultural members who have a similar agenda. Experience and interpretation fail any test of "authority." They are one sided and must yield, Clifford says, to the authority of dialogue and polyphony.

Dialogue has been described as a "shared vision of reality" (cf. Crapanzano 1977, 1980). However it is a shared vision that is not really dialogical in structure, as the writer retains control and provides the dialogue of certain individuals to act as representative or "typical" of their culture. The polyphonic mode is openly built up from quotations with some emphasis on "privileged informants" who break the "post-Malinowski professional taboo" as they are accorded a form of cultural expertise (yet via a benevolent dominance). The polyphonic mode is a "virtuoso orchestration by a single author of all the discourses in his or her text"(Clifford 1988:50). An additional textual strategy may be included in the polyphonic mode, one which Clifford describes as "a utopia of plural authorship that accords to collaborators not merely the status of independent enunciators but that of writers." But utopian for two reasons: first, the ethnographer is the editor, choosing which voice to include and which to delete. Second the ethnographer as editor prescribes the order of the text, giving voice to the other at his or her will and in his or her context. The text ultimately becomes the "intention of a single author" (1988:51) (but see below), and polyphonic authority with its strategy of plural authorship is branded a text of stolen words (cf. Amadiume below).

Yet another new ethnography is in order, one that denies any ingredient of "authority." Barbara Tedlock says,

Being, being present, being absent, being there documenting, being back here inscribing: how does one collect or display such an existence? Can "self" and "other" ever be gathered together into a single cohesive (or at least partly cohesive) text or film? Perhaps an ethnographic text or film should reveal its own contingency and tell of an overanxious ambition to control that must be continually deferred, a desire that must be frustrated.... If holders of cameras and holders of pens cannot trace a reality totally outside the self (one's personal gendered social history) why can we not simply admit, document, even celebrate the fact that we have generated a new reality, the reality of an encounter between a specific ethnographer and specific subjects? (Tedlock 1991:1)

Stating the encounter as the reality may allow the true state of affairs to be presented, that a conversation between cultural subjects is taking place that assumes *no* authority.

But positions of power remain on both personal and discipline levels. First, the Western and white anthropologist is a "privileged refugee" (Tedlock 1991:1) unpacking what McIntosh calls the invisible knapsack of white privilege, which puts her or him at an advantage (1989:10). The conversation between cultures takes place on unequal terms. Is it enough to call attention to this privilege and go on with the presentation? Second, positions of power unfold within constraints imposed by the discipline. Members of the discipline must adhere to the "rule" of the discipline itself, the disciplinary components of academe. According to Clifford, "Now that naïve claims to the authority of experience have been subjected to ... suspicion, we may anticipate a renewed attention to the subtle interplay of personal and disciplinary components in ethnographic research" (1988:54).

The main concern as I see it is, *there is no "single author" in academe.* While receiving data from the lived cultural expertise provided by others when I was a "privileged refugee," and also while "writing up" the research (anthropological tasks of professionalization), personal and disciplinary components were less "subtle interplay" and more obtrusive conflict. Let me demonstrate the dilemma in regard to the two key ethical issues in anthropology's representation of the other: who speaks for whom? and In whose interest are spoken voices heard?

First, a field story. Picture a group of women sitting in a yard on a hot afternoon in the middle of the dry season in Maragoli, Western Kenya. The anthropologist, part of the group, attempts to explain to the gathered Logoli women what "telling their story" by "writing their words" means, as a justification for taking up their valuable time by interviews. I show them a recent publication on African women, neighbours of theirs. The women examine and comment on the few photographs in the volume. They then ask me to show them the women's words. I tell them to look through the book for inverted commas, drawing them on the ground, preparing to read them the words of their neighbours. Most words, phrases, paragraphs they point out belong to others, not to the women in the culture under study. I find a few women's words scattered here and there. A frustrating, guilt-provoking personal component settles on me.

Second, a discipline story: a couple of examples attached to the disciplinary component. The personal narratives approach is suggested in an effort to allow women to represent themselves (cf. Personal Narratives Group 1989). Voices from the Personal Narratives Group say, "In anthropology, a younger generation questioned the absence of people in ethnographies. They noted the absence of either the ethnographer or the subject from anthropological accounts, claiming that gender, emotion, informal power, and cultural conceptions of the self were absent. Since feminist theory is grounded in women's lives and aims to analyze the role and meaning of gender in those lives and in society, women's personal narratives are essential primary documents for feminist research. These narratives present and interpret women's life experiences" (1989:3-4).[2] For example, forms of this method have recently produced: *Each In Her Own Way* (Levy 1988), *Three Swahili Women* (Mirza and Strobel 1989), *Life Histories of African Women* (Romero 1988) and *Voices from Mutira* (Davison et al. 1989). A personal narrative approach attempts to assist in circumventing what Moore describes as the "political and theoretical complexities of trying to speak *about* women, while avoiding any tendency to speak *for* them ... Feminist anthropology, unlike the 'anthropology of women,' has made some progress in this area, because while it acknowledges that 'women are all women together' it also emphasizes that there are fundamental differences between women" (Moore 1988:191-92).

But two "suggestions" by representatives from the discipline were made in the light of my written presentation of Logoli women's personal narratives. The first voice said something like this: "You have not told me why I should read these women's words and you have not provided the explanation of how their words fit in the text and are important for the analysis." The women's voices should be framed by mine, providing incentive for the reader to read their words, and then providing an interpretation so that the reader may understand those words. The action and the agency in their voices (their agenda) must be framed by mine (discipline agenda). In addition, my frame may not be "unsophisticated," as an unsophisticated analysis is not reflective of the discipline. Clarity and conciseness are to be sacrificed for academic convolution. Simply stated, the tension that exists here is between theorizing women and presenting women. I am forced to engage in benevolent dominance if I analyze, present, analyze. Benevolent because I insist their voices remain. Dominance because I interpret their voices. As Tedlock (1991) has said, we kill the women's voice by our own, we pin them like butterflies to the wall, as we provide the interpretation. In whose interest are these spoken voices heard?

Second is in my presentation of Logoli women's power. Again a voice from a representative of the discipline: "By saying, 'This is a study of women's power,' you set up a question in my mind, what about men's power?" This thesis — which presents women's oppressive circumstances while yet presenting their power, which focuses on their power rather than their powerlessness — may not be academically sound. Women's power must be framed by men even though there is a long history of men's power in ethnography that totally neglects women. A graduate student, dealing with a thesis committee, is not in a position to insist that women's power need not be framed by men's. Not so benevolent a dominance here! In whose interest are spoken voices heard? Logoli women's power in the thesis was salvaged by my vulnerable insistence and by an "other," a woman academic with power.

Let me provide as further example theoretical presentations of African women, most particularly as these presentations are portrayed in language use that in turn supports an analytical panorama. As a brief background, more than two decades of theoretical and empirical attention to women's place in African societies has forced acknowledgment of widespread diversity in women's roles and statuses. Much of the research has been directed to economic issues and development initiatives involving women who are embedded in sets of socio-culturally contextualized relationships. Models in current usage arise from three basic critical strategies. First is the criticism of the optimism about economic progress of women through modernization, or the imposition of a capitalist economic system. Second is the re-evaluation of the role of women to reflect their changing status in contexts where an underlying emphasis on patriarchal ideology endured and expanded through changing economic practices and deliberate state policies. The third approach, connected to the second and crucial for my current work, emphasizes a theme which is absent or incipient in early research, that is, the association of women's power in economic, social and political roles with gender and class inequalities.

Investigations on women are now narrowed to detailed case studies (cf. Amadiume 1987 on Igbo women of Eastern Nigeria; Oboler 1985 on Nandi women of Western Kenya; Robertson 1984 on Ga women of Central Accra, Ghana) and/or centre on pertinent analytic categories: colonization (Etienne and Leacock 1980), work (Leacock and Safa 1986), class (Robertson and Berger 1986), patriarchy and class (Stichter and Parpart 1988), and the state (Parpart and Staudt 1989). The emerging literature speaks about women's continuing hard work within changing systems of production and women's contribution to economics and development issues. Women's actual power in work and decision making however, may not be given sufficient representation. If it is given representation, power may be implicitly denied to women through the imposition of confined theoretical perspectives epitomized by language use that assigns a secondary status to women's work and decision making. Economic language has trivialized both men and women noncapitalist producers. Although the language was initially developed in peasant studies before women's work was problematized or even included, there is no justification for its continued usage in an African era when lines between capitalist and noncapitalist production are not easily drawn. Listen to the language these voices use.[3] For example, note the use of the term "subsidiary" for "subsistence production" (mainly women's work) or in the usage of "petty" for commodity production in selling goods (say market goods) or providing services (say through women's group work or, on an individual basis, say through sex in prostitution) when held up against an assumed superior capitalist mode of production. Women's decision-making power is dismissed as mere "strategy" or as attempts to "outwit the system." "System" in this context refers to some form of patriarchal structure said by some researchers to be evident in a historical "patriarchal mode of production" continuing today in a "capitalist mode of production" that relegates women to a class structure labelled as "oppressed."

My voice, based on my personal experience as "privileged refugee," says that this verbal (thus analytical) assignment of second class status to the value of women's labour in contrast to what are considered "real wages" in the "formal sector" of capitalism, presumably engaged in primarily by men, does not reflect the actual contribution of women to production. African women engage in all forms of productive labour, particularly in today's economic circumstances in which men as well as women have limited access to something depicted as "real wages" in capitalism. Similarly, verbally (thus analytically) designating women as an "oppressed class" does not adequately reflect their power position in decision-making processes attached to their involvement in all productive forms of labour or in their vested interest in permitting a patriarchal ideology to continue. It is necessary to challenge and change the language and to extend the theoretical perspectives to reflect women's power in work and decision making. It is no longer possible to assume that women are powerless or marginal actors "strategizing" in situations dictated by men and that there is a reified world economic structure in which the will of capitalism always wins. Indeed, more realistic attention is required in empirical and theoretical investigations, recognizing that during the course of the many researches life goes on for women as they rationally assess their needs and the means to fulfil them. Robertson says, "African women have ... capacity ... to organise themselves and set their own priorities.... The international community, and especially those interested in women in development, are getting wise in terms of attitudes and practices regarding Third World women. The matriarchal attitude that entailed telling such women what to do and predicating that advice on Western norms and experiences is giving way to listening to them and serving as facilitators in terms of resources" (Robertson 1988a:427-28).

Robertson is criticizing the attitude of some Western researchers, in particular Western women, who have assumed a superior or privileged knowledge position in their investigations of African women. Hence her phrase "matriarchal attitude." See also Davison et al. (1989:4), Lyons (1988), Stamp (1986), and Wipper (1972, 1988) for similar criticism, as they suggest that Western researchers and development workers listen to rural women, write *their* words and take heed of their experience and suggestions. The message is clear. As Robertson points out in a recent essay directed to African women's history, "Never Underestimate the Power of Women" (Robertson 1988b). A new position is necessary, that women's voices along with their actions, will assist in revealing women's power. But is conversation between cultures possible without dominance, benevolent or otherwise?

VOICES WITH LIVED CULTURAL EXPERTISE

bell hooks, in an American context, says, "Much feminist theory emerges from privileged women who live at the center, whose perspectives on reality rarely include knowledge and awareness of the lives of women and men who live in the margin. As a consequence, feminist theory lacks wholeness, lacks the broad analysis that could encompass a variety of human experiences.... At its most visionary, [feminist theory] will emerge from individuals who have knowledge of both margin and center" (hooks 1984: Preface). Feminist ethnographic gaze is depicted in Carrillo's (1981) poem cited by Tedlock (1991), "And When You Leave, Take Your Pictures With You," where "white sisters" who "love to own pictures of us" should "think again" because "No one smiles ... cleaning up after our white sisters radical friends.... And when our white sisters radical friends see us in the flesh not as a picture they own, they are not quite as sure if they like us as much" (Tedlock 1991:24-25).

Amadiume, in an African context, says the ideal presentation of the experience of African women's lives would be entirely their own:

There is a need for material about women, collected and explained by African and other Third World women themselves, from which adequate and suitable theories and methodology can be worked out.... It can be argued that because of their plural and multicultural backgrounds as a result of the colonial heritage, Third World women are best qualified to carry out comparative studies and make generalized statements about women's position in their societies. (Amadiume 1987:10)

For example, Amadiume criticizes conflating the experiences of women in different societies for general purposes, "development," or "co-operation for political action and solidarity," that is, the general notion of "sisterhood." She uses as one example Pat Caplan and Janet Bujra, *Women United, Women Divided — Cross-Cultural Perspective on Female Solidarity* (1978). She particularly criticizes the incorporation of Nelson's article in this volume, refering to Nelson's use of Mathare (Kenya) women, women whom Nelson describes as "not [having] learnt to operate effectively as a group in the political arena." Amadiume says, "The choice of harassed and powerless beer-brewers using every means to survive reinforces the racist notion that African women prostitute themselves to survive" (1987:5). Further, Amadiume has depicted the personal narrative approach as "inglorious," in that it is "collecting and publishing what Third World women are saying, as if Western women originated the thoughts or arguments.... Given the monopoly on resources [for African women to engage in research] this is, unsurprisingly, another form of exploitation; it is stealing words from the horse's mouth!" (Amadiume 1987:10).

All the above voices add to my dilemma in seeking a path. The reality of the situation is that feminist anthropology and feminist anthropologists are constrained on a number of personal and academic levels, not the least of which are gender, colour and class. Interestingly, our (greater?) concentration on these levels likely stems from our personal and disciplinary positions as "others." Hence our awareness of and attention to voice and text. From our position of "others" we are compelled to sensitivity.

In conclusion, I steal words about engendered power from the mouths of "others" without pinning butterflies to the wall, but with a position of power because I have selected who will speak and in what order they will be heard.

From the time of the ancients, we have always done so. It is rooted in the past with Imungu [God] and in the cave at Muwg'oma that the man will be the commander (Field interview, Margoli, October 27, 1987).

The man is *omwene hango,* the commander, he is the owner, he is in charge. Although we all have a higher authority who makes the ultimate decisions, it is a man's duty to be in charge of his home, his wife, his children (Field interview, Margoli, November 17, 1987).

Women have forgotten their place and so have men. When the ancients went to war it was the men who went first, but it was the women who dragged the rocks. Without the rocks the men could not fight the war (Field interview, Margoli, February 17, 1987).[4]

Last evening Mudasia came back drunk with two of his brothers. He yelled and told all the children to leave the house. He came after me with a *panga* [machete]. One of his brothers stayed at the back door of the house and one stayed at the front. This was to stop me from leaving and to hear how he would teach his wife a lesson as they are saying I am too independent. I took the *panga* away from him. I said, "If you want to fight with *pangas* I have the sharpest one in the house" (Field interview, Margoli, March 9, 1988).

Outraged, outrageous voices. *But you are only hearing them because I was there!* A conversation between cultures took place. Who do they/I speak for, them or me? And in the context of this presentation, where outraged and outrageous voices are perceptible among those who perpetuate the misunderstandings as well as among those who would transform them, the question still hangs: In whose interests are all these spoken voices heard?

NOTES

1. The Avalogoli (the people of Logoli) are a horticultural society of 200 thousand, reliant on both subsistence production and wage and casual labour, who live in Maragoli, Western Kenya, East Africa. My most recent fieldwork with Avalogoli was conducted in 1987-88, 1992 and 1994. Citations from field interviews in this paper are taken from a more detailed study on Logoli women's lives that displays contradictions of gender and local political economy (Abwunza 1991).

2. Mbilinyi's article in this volume is a superb example of a conversation between cultures.

3. The words emphasized by inverted commas are taken from "Introduction: Towards a Materialist Perspective on African Women." They are found in section C., which provides a summary of the articles in the edited volume (Stichter and Parpart 1988:14-23).

4. The words of a very old woman at an early morning assistant chief's *barazza* (meeting). This "Mummy" refused me permission to "take her name to Canada."

BIBLIOGRAPHY

ABWUNZA, Judith M. 1991. *Logoli Women of Western Kenya Speak: Needs and Means.* Ph.D. thesis, University of Toronto.

AMADIUME, Ife. 1987. *Male Daughters, Female Husbands. Gender and Sex in an African Society.* London: Zed Books.

CAPLAN, P., and J.M. Bujra, eds. 1978. *Women United, Women Divided — Cross-Cultural Perspectives on Female Solidarity.* London: Tavistock.

CARRILLO, Jo. 1981. "And When You Leave, Take Your Pictures With You." In *This Bridge Called My Back: Writings by Radical Women of Color,* ed. Cherrie Moraga and Gloria Anzaldua. New York: Kitchen Table, Women of Color Press, 63-64.

CLIFFORD, James. 1988. *The Predicament of Culture. Twentieth-Century Ethnography, Literature, and Art.* Cambridge, MA: Harvard University Press.

CRAPANZANO, Vincent. 1980. *Tuhami: Portrait of a Moroccan.* Chicago: University of Chicago Press.

———. 1977. "The Writing of Ethnography." *Dialectical Anthropology* 2(1):69-73.

DAVISON, Jean, with the women of Mutira. 1989. *Voices from Mutira. Lives of Rural Gikuyu Women.* Boulder and London: Lynne Rienner Publishers.

ETIENNE, Mona, and Eleanor Leacock, eds. 1980. *Women and Colonization.* New York: Praeger.

HOOKS, bell. 1984. *Feminist Theory from Margin to Center.* Boston: South End Press.

LEACOCK, Eleanor, Helen I. Safa, and Contributors. 1986. *Women's Work.* South

Hadley: Bergin and Garvey.

LEVY, Marion Fennelly. 1988. *Each In Her Own Way.* Boulder and London: Lynne Rienner Publishers.

LYONS, Harriet. 1988. Introductory Note. *Canadian Journal of African Studies* 22(3):422-26.

McINTOSH, Peggy. 1989. "White Privilege: Unpacking the Invisible Knapsack." *Peace and Freedom,* (July/August):10-12.

MBILINYI, Marjorie. 1989. "I'd Have Been a Man": Politics and the Labor Process in Producing Personal Narratives." In *Interpreting Women's Lives,* ed. Personal Narratives Group. Bloomington: Indiana University Press, 204-27.

MIRZA, Sarah, and Margaret Strobel, eds. and trans. 1989. *Three Swahili Women.* Bloomington: Indiana University Press.

MOORE, Henrietta L. 1988. *Feminism and Anthropology.* Minneapolis: University of Minnesota Press.

OBOLER, Regina Smith. 1985. *Women, Power and Economic Change: The Nandi of Kenya.* Stanford, CA: Stanford University Press.

PARPART, Jane L., and Kathleen A. Staudt. 1989. *Women and the State in Africa.* Boulder and London: Lynne Rienner Publishers.

Personal Narratives Group, eds. 1989. *Interpreting Women's Lives. Feminist Theory and Personal Narratives.* Bloomington: Indiana University Press.

ROBERTSON, Claire. 1984. *Sharing the Same Bowl.* Bloomington: Indiana University Press.

———. 1988(a). "Research on African Women since 1972: A Commentary." In *Canadian Journal of African Studies* 22(3):427-28.

———. 1988(b). "Never Underestimate the Power of Women." *Women Studies International Forum* 11(5):439-53.

———. and Iris Berger, eds. 1986. *Women and Class in Africa.* New York: Africana Publishing.

ROMERO, Patricia W., ed. 1988. *Life Histories of African Women.* London: Ashfield.

STAMP, Patricia. 1986. "Kikuyu Women's Self-Help Groups: Toward an Understanding of the Relation Between Sex-Gender System and Mode of Production in Africa." In *Women and Class in Africa,* ed. Claire Robertson and Iris Berger. New York: Africana Publishing, 27-46.

STICHTER, Sharon B., and Jane L. Parpart. 1988. *Patriarchy and Class. African Women in the Home and the Workforce.* Boulder: Westview Press.

TEDLOCK, Barbara. 1991. "The Ethnographic Gaze." Unpublished paper presented at the University of Western Ontario, Department of Anthropology.

WIPPER, Audrey. 1988. "Reflections of the Past Sixteen Years, 1972-1988, and Future Challenges." *Canadian Journal of African Studies* 22(3):409-21.

———. 1972. "The Roles of African Women: Past Present and Future." *Canadian Journal of African Studies* 8(2):143-46.

CHAPTER 14

Reading the 'Montreal Massacre'[1]

IDIOSYNCRATIC INSANITY OR THE MISREADING OF CULTURAL CUES?

I.P. (Trish) Wilson

TEXT: THE 'MONTREAL MASSACRE'

*A*T A FEW MINUTES PAST FIVE ON THE AFTERNOON OF Wednesday, December 6, 1989, a twenty-five-year-old man methodically parked his car in a tow-away zone on the campus of the University of Montreal in the province of Quebec, Canada. He walked unobtrusively through the doors of L'Ecole Polytechnique (Montreal's School of Engineering) carrying a semi-automatic rifle. In a second-floor hallway, he shot an employee; in the cafeteria, three students; in a spray of bullets in one classroom, four more students. The gunman guaranteed his "fifteen minutes of fame," however, in room 303. Smiling as he interrupted a dissertation on heat transfer mechanics, he asked the women present to line up on one side of the room, and the men to leave. His request was greeted with laughter, a laughter which subsided only when he fired two rounds into the ceiling. He shouted: "You're all a bunch of feminists, and I hate feminists!"[1] The four dozen men in attendance left quietly, without protest. Six of the women died in the ensuing barrage of bullets.

'The worst single-day massacre in Canadian history'[2] resulted in the death of fourteen women, twenty-seven injuries, and the violent suicide of the perpetrator, Marc Lepine. Lepine justified his actions in a three-page suicide note found on his body and published almost a full year later, in which he blamed feminists for "spoiling my life" (*Sunday Sun* November 25, 1990).

Mass media coverage of what are considered to be newsworthy violent situations has emphasized the fictionalized stereotype of violent behaviour as mere individual idiosyncrasy. Violence against women in North American cultures, specifically, has been conventionally portrayed as merely the 'insane' behaviour of psychologically disturbed individuals. This paper explores avenues of explication for this phenomenon which rely on the definition of violent behaviour not as isolated insanity but rather as expressive of interactive ideological processes. Through an exploration of the meaning media coverage has given to the understanding of the 'Montreal Massacre,' this paper is an attempt to explain how particular ideologies interact in their contribution to violence against women.

SUBTEXT I: INSANITY AS EXCUSE

In the ensuing media coverage, this event was immediately portrayed as the 'Montreal Massacre,' a term which became standard in public discourse pertaining to the killings. Analysis of Lepine's actions focused on the murder as the violent, idiosyncratic act of an insane individual. Headlines and conversations bristled with words such as 'revenge,' 'savagery' and 'obsession' in descriptions of Lepine as the 'alienated loner.' For weeks, even months, afterwards, public and media discourse debated Lepine's motivations in his apparently 'senseless' rampage. Psychiatrists, psychologists, media contributors — each appraised what one called this 'stereotypical mass killer' — apportioned the causes of Lepine's ostensible 'mental breakdown' almost evenly among a battered childhood, a broken home, an unfortunate personal relationship and a fascination with war games, videos and movies. The victims were portrayed only as 'targets of a primal and mysterious rage.'

As I will outline later in this paper, it can be seen that Lepine carefully and, in his estimation, logically chose his target group. Thus, contrary to public and media labelling, Lepine's act was no random 'massacre'; it was not an indiscriminate killing. It is, as well, a misconception to portray violent episodes as performed by socially isolated (i.e., insane) individuals, since violent behaviours are other-directed acts occurring in the context of shared experience and culture. In categorizing them as idiosyncratic, insane performances, we are mislabelling them since individuals ultimately derive legitimation, not from internal personal categories of self-esteem, but from the values of the culture in which they live (see, for instance: Bell 1968; Gergen and Davis 1985; Luhmann 1990; Shweder and Levine 1984).[3] Such behaviours, then, can only be understood through analysis of the nature of inter-personal and institutional relationships and within the context of the encompassing social order. Social-scientific research evaluation thus exposes and emphasizes the analytical inadequacies of categorizing Lepine's lethal behaviour as merely the isolated performance of an individual insane subject on a blindly driven rampage.

SUBTEXT II: INSTITUTIONAL RELATIONSHIPS

Several social constructions are implicated in Lepine's murderous 'extravaganza.' Sociological or anthropological analysis of Lepine's behaviour thus requires an exploration into the relationship between societal norms and institutions and intentioned individual behaviour. Of special interest, given the specific target group for Lepine's violence, are the interrelationships between gender, class, ethnicity — and violence. Although I restrict this paper primarily to the processes which interact between the sex/gender system and individual and collective male behaviour, it is to be noted that research findings show correlations between low socioeconomic status and psychological 'symptom patterns' of disorder (Dohrenwend and Dohrenwend 1969, for instance) analogous to explicit correlations between occupation, education, gender and status itself. As well, contemporary ideology functions to justify differences in the opportunities and rewards available to people of different classes, races and sexes and to make these differences appear to be rational, rather than arbitrary, and just, rather than unjust. Although the lives of individual women are influenced through the allocation of an inferior social status to them in relation to men, the recognition of other power structures,[4] also based on systemic inequality, is necessary to present an adequate theoretical analysis. Structures of class, race and sexuality "are not mutually exclusive but interactive.... The position of men and women, however, vary [sic] on the key dimension of gender, so that while some men may be less valued because of their race, class or sexuality, all men by virtue of their gender have power as men in relation to all women" (Hanmer, Radford, and Stanko 1989:6-7).

Social scientists recognize that members of Western societies, regardless of class and ethnic background, endeavour to realize upward social mobility through "prestige-securing achievement and social ascent" (Dohrenwend and Dohrenwend 1969:51), although both the assessment of personal mobility potential and the meaning of such achievement results differ between individuals. Differences in individual alternatives in meaning-attachment occur because, although basic human meanings are derived from common experience and communication, individual members of any specific society to some extent share the meanings, ideas and beliefs prevalent in that society.[5] Thus racism and sexism, both of which include class distinctions, can be seen as intertwining oppressive structures which operate under Western systems displaying "patriarchal prerogatives" (Bradbrook et al. 1987:9).

CONTEXT I: GENDER REALITIES

Feminist condemnation of Lepine's crime as an illustration of the subordinate position of women in contemporary Canadian society initially led to widespread denial by both the media and the general public. Those negatively affected by Marc Lepine's actions (and here I include men, as well as women) refused to acknowledge this event as descriptive of the nature of the culture with which they felt most familiar and in which they felt most secure.[6] In an attempt to personally distance themselves from a society in which such an 'atrocity' could take place, men and women in English Canada emphasized the supposed significance of aggression within the culture of nationalism in Quebec (*Toronto Star* December 12, 1989; *Calgary Herald* December 10, 1989).[7] It was difficult to address this question with any plausibility, however, since in one particular recent year (1985), Quebec's homicide statistics totalled 143, compared with 534 in the province of Ontario (Statistics Canada 1986). Homicide appeared in the dinnertime evening news more often in Ontario than Quebec.

Canadians believed that Canada evidenced none of the backward, patriarchal attitudes they freely attributed to less developed countries; nor, they argued, was Canada so violence-prone as her more aggressive southern neighbour. Many Canadians were heard to say that they could understand something like this happening in 'the States' (*Globe and Mail* December 8, 1989; *Montreal Gazette* December 10, 1989),[8] but that it was incomprehensible that such 'senseless' violence could take place in their homeland. In these proclamations, Canadians felt justified by the statistical evidence. In 1984, for instance, the homicide rate in Canada was 2 per thousand, compared with a U.S. homicide rate approaching 20 per thousand (Statistics Canada 1986; U.S. Bureau of the Census 1988).

It is true that contemporary Canadian society is represented as liberal and egalitarian: this representation is accepted as reality in national, as well as international, circles. Once women had won the battle to be considered persons they obtained the vote in various provinces between 1916 and 1922 (Burt et al. 1988). It seems indisputable that women's status has been enhanced since the conflicts prevalent in the late nineteenth century between the suffragettes and the dominant (male) culture over legal recognition of women as sentient beings (persons/citizens). As early as 1967 the Canadian Government established the Royal Commission on the Status of Women in order to address the issue of women's inequality. The first director of the Canadian-inaugurated Women and Development Programme of the Commonwealth Secretariat was a Canadian. In 1987, having completed two four-year terms on the United Nations Commission on the Status of Women, Canada solicited reelection (Burt et al. 1988). Canada's recent history with respect to national and international policy decisions, then, is commendable.

Within woman's daily lived experience in Canada itself, however, there still exist traditional social structures of gender differentiation and gender opposition. These are among the first social constructs we should explore. They are maintained through a world view which, to avoid trite, timeworn debate, I will characterize not as patriarchal but as androcentric (or andro-archical) power structures. These terms should be seen as defining a set of interdependent social relations among men, relations which enable them to dominate women. Although in this sex/gender order men do occupy different positions within the hierarchy due to racial, ethnic or class differences, they are united in their shared relationship of dominance over women and are dependent on each other for the maintenance of that domination.

CONTEXT II: THE INDIVIDUAL REALITY OF MARC LEPINE

Marc Lepine was born Gamil Rodrigue Gharbi, the son of a Québecoise mother and Algerian father. He legally adopted his mother's maiden name and a new first name at the age of eighteen (*Newsweek* December 18, 1989). Although his parents separated in 1970, upon their divorce in 1976 Lepine became a recognized part of a growing statistical group, the children of single parent households.[9] He grew up a 'francophone,' a member of a social group which in Canada has historically suffered from a lower socio-economic status than the encompassing 'anglophone' culture (Hunter 1980; Blishen 1986). An 'unemployed electronics buff,' he had planned to attend the engineering school at which the 'Massacre' took place (*Newsweek* December 18, 1989).

Canadian labour force changes and post-World War II changes in value orientations have been accompanied by relatively high unemployment, especially for those under twenty-five who have little or no post-secondary education. Without post-secondary education, Lepine was at a socio-economic disadvantage: he intellectualized this as "continu[ing] my studies in a haphazard way for they never really interested me, knowing in advance my fate." He claimed to have been turned down for military service for being "asocial." Marc

Lepine's suicide note embodies the sense of failure and frustration he felt with his continued existence, which was "only to please the government."

Lepine's family profile records that his father (his primary role model and mentor during his formative years) considered women "the servants of men,"[10] said that women were not men's equals, and was not averse to punishing his wife physically if she arrived home late (*Chatelaine* June 1990, based on divorce report proceedings). If we profess the importance of primary group socialization processes, we have to assume Lepine's view of women to incorporate, at the least, their devaluation with respect to men's hierarchical position.

Traditional economically-based institutional frameworks, in Canada as in the United States, support sexual intimidation and violence as some of the more extreme (yet accepted) mechanisms in the social control of women. These frameworks are supported by similar historically specific sanctions and encouragements within the two cultures (Collier and Rosaldo 1981; Edwards 1987; Radford 1987; Rosaldo 1980; Ramazanoglu 1987). As social constructs, they need to be explored further.

CONTEXT III: THE REALITIES OF CULTURAL INTER-RELATIONSHIPS

Recognition of an androcentric/andro-archical[11] system encompasses recognition that men's violence to women is a political issue, one which expresses existing power relations that maintain and reproduce both men's domination and women's subordination. Male violence toward women can be best understood through the evaluation of male power as a dynamic structural dimension in which gender differentiation locates men in a primary position and assumes women to be the Other, the not-men and, therefore, the inferior gender.

"If the personal is political, what are the politics?" (Ramazanoglu 1987). This question is appropriate in the context of the politics of gender differentiation and gender opposition relating to Lepine's vengeful retribution against those he characterized as "viragos" — feminists to whom he wished to "put an end."

In Canada, as in the United States, the ideal female role has been conventionally restricted to either the venerated domestic position or to public assignments which utilize woman's supposedly nurturing domestic nature (nursing, teaching, table waiting, cooking and so on).[12] In existence is a set of ideological beliefs about both the sanctity of the family and the inherent nature of woman, which is utilized, ultimately, in the justification of woman's subordination. These culturally sanctioned views of Woman and her role are embodied in legal, economic and financial discriminations against women. Women are, for instance, culturally (and sometimes legally) defined solely by their relationship to men.[13] Although women's labour force participation rate rose from 38 percent in 1970 to approximately 53 percent in 1983 (Statistics Canada 1983), this statistic does not acknowledge that this participation is accounted for by the increasing number of deskilled, low paying clerical and service jobs in a post-industrial society; positions which are both horizontally and vertically segregated (i.e., by occupation and by sex).[14] These ideological views also prevail in social institutions and processes in such domains as education, healthcare, social welfare policies and the criminal justice system.

In education, younger women are still presumed to be marriage-bound, and even if members of the white middle or upper class, they are thought to be marking time in post-secondary education (see, for instance Batcher 1987; Tavris 1977; Hanmer, Radford, and Stanko 1989). Women are still a minority in educational programs which prepare students for many of the expanding technological jobs, and it is still the case that it has "proven easier for women to succeed educationally in traditional subjects than to achieve a significant transformation of the mainstream curricula" (Rich 1980 cited in Norris 1987:79). In the area of health care, the control of women's reproductive rights lies in the hands of the male-dominated political and medical establishments, and social class and economic factors determine available choices (see, for example, Dreifus in Jagger and Rothenberg 1984; Greer 1984; Norris 1987). Social welfare policies stigmatize single-parent families (which commonly consist of a woman and her children) as the most substantial utilizers of the welfare economy (Hanmer, Radford, and Stanko

1989), and in Canada, "lone parent mothers make up about 30 percent of the poor population each year" (Ross and Shillington
1989:19).[15] Finally, systems of protection and criminal control conventionally consider the household a private domain where a man
has the right to abuse a woman without constabulatory or judicial
interference (Hanmer and Maynard 1987; McCaughan 1977). Such
sanctioned views of women's position within Canadian society
specifically, and North American societies generally, define women
as an inferior class in need of paternalistic protection or control in
various instances.

COMMUNICATION I: FEMINISM, FRUSTRATION AND LEGITIMATION

In contemporary Western societies, women in non-traditional occupations, or with non-traditional career goals, have been categorized
as feminists in media and public analysis. The label has taken on, for
some, the connotations of a pejorative epithet, perhaps founded in
the public perception of feminists' surrender of respectable, pater-
nalistically protected powerless roles in favour of rebellious, strong,
masculine, oppositional ones. As presumptive actors in environments that previously belonged solely to men, women who accept
the challenge of nonstereotypical roles or behaviour have, especially
in the fluctuating economic aftermaths of the second World War,
tempted categorization as the expropriators of men's economic positions through their participation in fields which are customarily
conceived of as the exclusive realms of men. In Lepine's opinion,
feminists "wanted to keep the advantages of women ... while seizing
for themselves those of men."

Where gender-specific behaviours, aspirations and achieve-
ments are the only socially sanctioned behaviours, we should not be
surprised to find men such as Marc Lepine assuming that there is
something innately natural in their right to attain status and life-sat-
isfactions that should be denied women. If we listen to anthropologist Elliott Leyton, we should also not be surprised to find that Marc
Lepine resorted to mass murder in order to communicate his alienation and frustration.

Leyton has described the 'typical' mass murderer as a middle-class white male who is convinced that a particular social group has deprived him of his rightful chance to achieve status and power (Leyton 1986). For Leyton, a "mass killing is always a 'suicide note' in which the killer states his grievance against his supposed persecutors" (quoted in *Chatelaine* July 1990).

Lepine had academic and career aspirations that could not be met. He claimed to have been turned down by the military for being 'asocial.' His application to study at L'Ecole Polytechnique du Montréal had been rejected. He voiced his self-perceived failure and frustrations within the social hierarchy and his inability to meet or maintain his personal and career goals as a grievance against feminists, his 'supposed persecutors.' For Mark Lepine, women — feminist women, specifically — had crossed the borders into what he considered exclusive male territory. Gender-specific powers related to his rights as a member of the superior (male) class could legitimate, for Lepine, his right to eradicate those more negatively valued in society than himself, providing the patriarchal prerogative upon which he could eventually justify his categorical choice of woman as victim. To again quote Leyton, mass murderers "find a target group on which they can blame their failure, so that in their minds, the reason they're failing is not because they're inadequate, or have no network, or don't understand the system, but because it's the fault [of others]" (Leyton 1990). In this ominous first case of its kind, the fault is that of women.

I noted earlier that Lepine's murderous actions negatively affected men as well as women. That men, as well as women, are adversely affected as a result of the entrenchment of gender socialization systems is often disregarded in social analysis. In the late twentieth century, North American men are products of cultures which valorize and celebrate vengeance and retribution as the norms of masculinity. Violence is portrayed as an easy, socially sanctioned option and is reinforced as an appropriate response to frustration. Mass media and sadistic pornography provide representations of brutality, bloodshed and carnage, whether in images of reality or of the fictionalized ideal. For more men than we care to admit, these representations justify their use of violent action in the solution of their problems. For not only women, but men as well, are victims of oppressive socialization processes.

It is true that Marc Lepine's individual biography includes many incidences of personal disappointments, failures and futilities; from the early breakup of his parents' marriage and his father's subsequent disinterest in the family to Marc's rejection by both the military and the engineering school. He also experienced difficulty in establishing good interpersonal relationships and in dealing with success (*Chatelaine* June 1990). Such patterns are not unique to Lepine's life history: they do not consistently result in 'murderous rampage.'

It is also true that Marc Lepine was a member of a socio-economic class which finds itself in a relatively inferior position in Canadian society, those visibly different from others in the dominant culture. Although in Canada the "clear trend has been in the direction of progressively decreasing ethnic inequalities over time" (Hunter 1980:159), educational levels, employment opportunities, average income and occupational status still vary between ethnic groups. Hunter's (1980) text on ethnicity and class analyzes the difference between some of the most prominent ethnic groups in Canada during the 1970s — the British, French, German, Jewish, Ukranian, Indian and Inuit. This analysis of necessity omits the effects of massive immigration policies later directed toward those of Middle Eastern, Asian or South East Asian descent. It concludes, however, that "in terms of wealth, the fact which stands out most prominently is the relatively poor position of Francophone Canadians" (Hunter 1980:159). The realities of ethnic inequalities, like those of personal frustration, however, do not consistently produce individuals whose final acts are the 'savage' extermination of others.

Lepine's family and social history incorporate an ideology of women as second-class citizens: as objects of male dominion and control, women were "not men's equals"[16] and so were fated to endure, if necessary, violent punishments at the hands of male authority. This particular subtext was augmented by implicit approval of the dominant ideology in the "stereotypical images of women marketed via women's magazines, television advertisements, and other media," emphasizing an objectification of women which "constitute[d] social support for an ideological construction of women as objects ... [and] ... object-victims" (Kuhn 1982:5). Millions of men are audience to this organization of meaning construction: not all mark women as victims, however.

The inter-relationships between individual and cultural realities provide clues to the nature of what may be termed Lepine's political agenda. A socio-psychological view of the multiple murderer (Leyton 1986) provides us with the following profile: the multiple murderer is most often on the margins of upper-working or lower-middle classes, usually a profoundly conservative figure who comes to feel excluded from the class he so devoutly wishes to join. There are significant contradictions embedded in the social order — contradictions between the killer's aspirations and the actuality of his socio-economic potential. These contradictions help to construct gaps in the borders of the individual's identity, leading to what might be labelled emotional preconditions for homicidal action — action in support of a political cause,[17] cultural statement or religious crusade. All multiple murderers share a self-absorption and simple-mindedness and a sense of a protest which seems to be more than entirely personal. There is the appearance of ideologically alternative political action on behalf of others (219). Mass murderers have absorbed a revolutionary rhetoric and style in order to carry out a personal vendetta, an individualized protest against their exclusion as "marginal" men (209). There is also a theatrical atmosphere attending the final catastrophe, one which is entirely in keeping with the fashionable violent codes of our current culture.

The killer is suicidal, according to Leyton, in the sense that he is willing to sacrifice himself for the cause, and the killings may be seen as a form of suicide note in which the killer states clearly which social category has excluded him. In an extended campaign of vengeance, he murders people unknown to him, but who represent to him (in their behaviour, their appearance or their location) the class that has rejected him (Leyton 1986:23). Force or violence utilized in this way is generally termed terrorism, a phenomenon in which "the 'victims' of such attacks are usually intended to be a mere vehicle, or medium, for making another point, establishing a symbolic victory.... The mass media are often the implicit or explicit rationale for such acts; getting the message out is important for those individuals committed to a cause" (Altheide 1985:261).

CONCLUSIONS: THE READING OF TEXT, SUBTEXTS AND CONTEXTS

In articulating cultural as well as individual processes in the construction of violent behaviour, we are better able to gain a perspective on the mutually reinforcing hierarchies of class, race and gender within North American societies. These hierarchies affect those interactive areas on the borders of personal identities, areas where the individual's character, personality and individuality articulate with his or her cultural environment. In the case of Marc Lepine these cultural articulations provided the context for his profound sense of personal alienation and frustration and can be seen as definitive influences on his ultimate intention. Recognizing the primary role of the media in the transmission of culture and its values, it is impossible to deny the consequence of this function for the maintenance of a context-specific sex/gender system and the legitimation of violence as a valid, universal tool in the communication of conflict and confrontation. Ideology makes that which is "cultural and therefore historically variable appear natural and therefore immutable" (Barthes, cited in Kuhn 1982:77), and media may be seen to "embody a series of ideological operations through which woman is constructed as ... 'a sign within a patriarchal order'" (Kaplan, cited in Kuhn 1982:77).

In academic discourse of the period before the 'Montreal Massacre,' the role of gender dichotomies and hierarchies in the socialization of men had been generally ignored, although exceptions to this statement can be noted (see, for instance, David and Brannon 1976; Doyle 1983; Pleck 1981; Tolson 1977). The focus has been on women as gendered objects, especially in North American societies. There has been an implication that the study of gender is a study of women only and a refusal to see men as also gendered subjects and objects. Male violence against women has been defined as a problem for women, with members of the dominant culture (men) refusing to define their own behaviour as problematic.

Violence as a conscious, intentioned form of social control, may be seen to support, rather than to disrupt, the set of relations between institutional and hierarchical stability. The official disregard of such violence, therefore, has served to maintain the status quo which Lepine so heartily defended.

I suspect, however, that Lepine would not approve of these new readings of his actions. A consequence of what one headline characterized as Lepine's 'misogynist murder' spree has been a new, critical evaluation of the meaning, in Canadian society, of violence toward women. Analysis of newspaper and magazine approaches to the story, as well as of public opinion, indicates a gradual change in the Canadian public's initial conviction that Lepine's act of violence had been an instance of 'individual insanity.' A conception that violence against women is a socially sanctioned phenomenon has gradually invaded the media's initial portrayal of the event as an isolated incident.

This new public discourse indicates a slightly elevated national consciousness concerning the magnitude and consequences of an entrenched system of androcentrism for female individuals. An assessment of the ramifications of such systems for male individuals has still to be made.

Feminist proposals, and the feminist commitment to personal and political action, led Lepine to append a list of the names of nineteen women who also came close to being victims on the day of his killing spree. These nineteen "radicals," as Lepine called them, survived by default. For Geneviève Bergeron, Hélène Colgan, Nathalie Croteau, Barbara Daigneault, Anne-Marie Edward, Maud Haviernick, Barbara Maria Kleuznick, Maryse Laganière, Maryse Leclair, Anne-Marie Lemay, Sonia Pelletier, Michèle Richard, Annie St.-Arneault, and Annie Turcotte — the almost anonymous women who died — their crime was against a man whose position in society was potentially theirs through their participation in the public economic arena, and, in his eyes, their overt expropriation of male rights.

NOTES

1. This paper is part of an M.A. thesis defended in the Department of
    Anthropology, McMaster University, in March 1992.

2. Words, phrases and sentences presented within single quotation marks [']
    are quotes from newspaper and magazine accounts of, not only the event
    itself, but also Lepine's personal life history and projected psychological
    profile. The text of the actual event is edited from *Newsweek,* December 18,
    1989.

3. Contemporary epistemologies of the social construction of the self follow
    the early texts of Benedict (1934) and the proponents of the culture and
    personality theories of the 1960s in their assertions. For anthropologists,
    Benedict's "emphasis on the psychological coherence of the varied
    institutions which make up a society" (Gorer 1953) led to the re-evaluation
    of previous studies of the relationships between culture and the construction
    of individual identity. For feminist anthropologists in the 90s and beyond,
    Benedict's accomplishments are an integral facet to the reclamation of the
    heritage of women in the discipline.

4. "Particularly those of heterosexuality, monogamy, motherhood and the
    public/private dichotomy contribute to the maintenance of male dominance
    and capitalist patriarchy" (Edwards 1987:23).

5. This is further explored in the sociological arguments surrounding the
    concept of deviance, which focus on the meanings inherent in social action
    and interaction. Douglas, for instance, begins with the assumption that
    "man [sic] shares symbols and is, therefore a member of a shared symbolic
    universe." In this analysis, the problems concerning social order are
    essentially problems involved in producing a shared cultural meaning under
    individual situational circumstances, allowing "an adequate fulfilment of
    societal members' requirements and aspirations in everyday circumstances"
    (Douglas 1971:3).

6. "59% Call Massacre Only Random Act; Poll Finds" (*Toronto Star,*
    December 29, 1989).

7. "Ontario, Quebec See Massacre Differently" (*Toronto Star,* December 12,
    1989). Also "U.S. 'Coverage' Speaks Volumes" (*Calgary Herald,* December
    10, 1989).

8. "Speaking About the Unspeakable: The Massacre in Montreal" (*Globe and
    Mail,* December 8, 1989). Also "How Did We Become So Sick? Or Were
    We Always Like That?" (*Montreal Gazette,* December 10, 1989).

9. Divorces in Canada rose from 621.0 in 1970 to 1051.4 per 100,000 in
    1979 (Statistics Canada 1983).

10. Marc Lepine's father, divorce proceedings record, 1976.

11. As stated above, these terms should be seen as defining a set of
    interdependent social relations among men, relations which enable them to

dominate women. These interdependent institutions encompass social and cultural power, as well as individual interests.

12.   In Canada the co-efficient of female representation (relationship of the female share of an occupational group to the female share in total employment) showed an over-representation of women of 1.32 in service-oriented occupations and 1.90 in clerical occupations, with an under-representation in agriculture, production and administration averaging 0.55 (Norris 1987:65).

13.   Social definitions are illustrated by media reports of women's accomplishments, for example, where they are customarily endorsed as the daughter, wife or mother of a male family member: this practice is not common in media references to men's accomplishments. Statutory reform of the Married Woman's Property Act (Canada) designated married women as separate persons in their own right, but the rule still exists that a wife has no domicile except her husband's, solely by virtue of the fact of the marriage (McCaughan 1977). Alberta (as of 1977) was the only province in which, after a judgment of legal separation, a woman could acquire a new domicile separate from that of her husband: in Saskatchewan, Nova Scotia and Prince Edward Island, a husband is still expressly liable for his wife's prenuptial debts (55); and, despite the absence of legal authority, it is tacitly implied in some legislation and administrative practices that a married woman's official name is that of her husband, and the obstacles in the path of any married woman who attempts to assert the contrary may be considerable (45).

14.   Hunter also elucidates the sex segregation in the workforce due to the increasing demand for female labour which has, for the most part, involved the recruitment of hitherto unemployed segments of the adult female population into new jobs, which have tended to become sex-typed as female jobs (1980:129). A further explanation of horizontal and vertical segregation can be found in Norris 1987, chapter 4: "The Economic Position of Women."

15.   However, the "average single recipient of social assistance remains on the roll for about seven months, and the average lone-parent mother for about three and a half years" (Ross and Shillington 1989:19). Annual income for households receiving social assistance in Canada (1988) varied as follows:

Province	Mother with 2 children	Employable couple, no children
Newfoundland	$9,396	$10,344
P.E.I.	9,720	11,328
Nova Scotia	10,368	10,560
New Brunswick	8,364	8,772
Quebec	8,688	10,836
Ontario	11,916	12,516
Manitoba	10,236	12,108

Province	Mother with 2 children	Employable couple, no children
Saskatchewan	10,980	13,320
Alberta	11,184	12,984
British Columbia	11,052	11,676

Source: (Ontario Social Assistance Review Commission 1988:58)

Although poverty is understood as a relative concept, recipients of social assistance are far below the putative poverty line in Canada.

16. Quoted from the testimony of Monique Lepine; divorce proceedings report, 1976.

17. "Political" is used here in the broadest sense of the term, to refer to social organization as a whole.

BIBLIOGRAPHY

Note: Various key words which appear in this paper as quotes from newspaper articles and headlines appear in coverage of the 'Montreal Massacre' during the period November 1989 to July 1990 in the following venues:

> *Calgary Herald* (Calgary, Alberta)
> *Chatelaine* (Toronto: McLean Hunter)
> *Hamilton Spectator* (Hamilton, Ontario)
> *McLean's Magazine* (Toronto: McLean Hunter)
> *Montreal Gazette* (Montreal, Quebec)
> *Newsweek* (Canadian Edition; Toronto, Ontario)
> *Sunday Sun* (Toronto, Ontario)
> *Globe and Mail* (Toronto, Ontario)
> *Toronto Star* (Toronto, Ontario)

ALTHEIDE, David L. 1985. *Media Power.* Beverly Hills: Sage.

BATCHER, Elaine. 1987. "Building the Barriers: Adolescent Girls Delimit the Future." In *Women and Men: Interdisciplinary Readings on Gender,* ed. Greta Hofmann Nemiroff. Vancouver: Fitzhenry and Whiteside, 150-64.

BELL, W. 1968. "The City, The Suburb, and a Theory of Social Choice." In *The New Urbanization,* ed. Scott Greer, et al. New York: St. Martin's Press, 132-68.

BENEDICT, Ruth. 1934. *Patterns of Culture.* Baltimore: Penguin.

BLISHEN, Bernard. 1986. "Continuity and Change in Canadian Values." In *Politics of Gender, Ethnicity and Language in Canada,* ed. Alan Cairns and Cynthia Williams. Toronto: University of Toronto Press, 1-26.

BRADBROOK, Pauline, et al. 1987. *Violence against Women: Abuse in Society and Church and Proposals for Change.* The Report to the General Synod of the Anglican Church of Canada. Toronto: Anglican Book Centre.

BURT, Sandra D., et al., eds. 1988. *Changing Patterns: Women in Canada.* Toronto: McClelland & Stewart.

CHATELAINE. 1990. "Why Did Mark [sic] Lepine Kill 14 Women?" 63(6):42-44, 74-76.

CLATTENBAUGH, Kenneth C. 1990. *Contemporary Perspectives on Masculinity: Men, Women and Politics in Modern Society.* Boulder: Westview Press.

COLLIER, J.F., and M.J. Rosaldo. 1981. "Politics and Gender in Simple Societies." In *Sexual Meanings,* ed. S.B. Ortner and H. Whitehead. Cambridge: Cambridge University Press, 275-320.

DAVID, Deborah S., and Robert Brannon. 1976. *The Forty-nine Percent Majority: The Male Sex Role.* Reading MA: Addison-Wesley.

DOHRENWEND, Bruce P., and Barbara Snell Dohrenwend. 1969. *Social Status and Psychological Disorder: A Causal Inquiry.* Toronto: Wiley-Interscience.

DOUGLAS, Jack D. 1971. *American Social Order: Social Rules in a Pluralistic Society.* New York: The Free Press.

DOYLE, James A. 1983. *The Male Experience.* Dubuque, IA: Wm. C. Brown.

DREIFUS, Claudia. 1984. "Sterilizing the Poor." In *Feminist Frameworks: Alternative Theoretical Accounts of the Relations between Women and Men,* ed. Alison M. Jagger and Paula S. Rothenberg. Toronto: McGraw-Hill, 58-66.

EDWARDS, Susan S.M. 1987. "'Provoking Her Own Demise': From Common Assault to Homicide." In *Women, Violence and Social Control,* ed. Jalna Hanmer and Mary Maynard. New Jersey: Humanities Press International, 152-68.

FRIEDMAN, Richard C. 1988. *Male Homosexuality: A Contemporary Psychoanalytic Perspective.* New Haven: Yale University Press.

GERGEN, K.J., and K.E. Davis, eds. 1985. *The Social Construction of the Person.* New York: Springer-Verlag.

GORER, Geoffrey. 1953. "The Concept of National Character." In *Personality in Nature, Society, and Culture,* ed. Clyde Kluckhohn and Henry A. Murray. New York: Alfred A. Knopf, 246-59.

GREER, Germaine. 1984. *Sex and Destiny: The Politics of Human Fertility.* London: Secker and Warburg.

HANMER, Jalna, and Mary Maynard, eds. 1987. *Women, Violence and Social Control.* New Jersey: Humanities Press International.

———, Jill Radford, and Elizabeth A. Stanko, eds. 1989. *Women, Policing, and Male Violence: International Perspectives.* London: Routledge.

HEARN, Jeff, and David Morgan, eds. 1990. *Men, Masculinities and Social Theory.* (Critical Studies in Men and Masculinities: 2). London: Unwin Hyman.

HUNTER, Alfred A. 1980. *Class Tells.* 2nd ed. Toronto: Butterworth.

JAGGER, Alison M., and Paula S. Rothenberg, eds. 1984. *Feminist Frameworks: Alternative Theoretical Accounts of the Relations between Women and Men.* Toronto: McGraw Hill.

KUHN, Annette. 1982. *Women's Pictures: Feminism and Cinema.* London: Routledge and Kegan Paul.

LEYTON, Elliott. 1986. *Hunting Humans: The Rise of the Modern Multiple Murderer.* Toronto: McClelland & Stewart.

———. 1990. *Speaking Out: Special Edition On Multiple Murderers and Modern Society.* Toronto: TV Ontario.

LUHMANN, Niklas. 1990. *Essays on Self-Reference.* New York: Columbia University Press.

McCAUGHAN, Margaret M. 1977. *The Legal Status of Married Women in Canada.* Toronto: Carswell.

MESSNER, Michael A., and Don F. Sabo, eds. 1990. *Sport, Men and the Gender Order: Critical Feminist Perspectives.* Champagne, IL: Human Kinetics Press.

MOORE, Robert L., and Douglas Gilette. 1990. *King, Warrior, Magician, Lover: Rediscovering the Archetypes of the Mature Masculine.* San Francisco: Harper.

NORRIS, Pippa. 1987. *Politics and Sexual Equality: The Comparative Position of Women in Western Democracies.* Colorado: Rienner.

Ontario Social Assistance Review Commission. 1988. *Transitions.* Toronto: Government of Ontario.

PLECK, Joseph H. 1981. *The Myth of Masculinity.* Cambridge MA: MIT Press.

PRONGER, Brian. 1990. *The Arena of Masculinity: Sports, Homosexuality, and the Meaning of Sex.* Toronto: Summerhill Press.

RADFORD, Jill. 1987. "Policing Male Violence — Policing Women." In *Women, Violence and Social Control,* ed. Jalna Hanmer and Mary Maynard. New Jersey: Humanities Press International, 30-45.

RAMAZANOGLU, Caroline. 1987. "Sex and Violence in Academic Life or You Can Keep a Good Woman Down." In *Women, Violence and Social Control,* ed. Jalna Hanmer and Mary Maynard. London: Macmillan, 61-74.

ROSS, David P., and Richard Shillington. 1989. *The Canadian Fact Book on Poverty.* Ottawa: The Canada Council on Social Development.

SHWEDER, R.A., and R.A. LeVine, eds. 1984. *Culture Theory: Essays on Mind, Self and Emotion.* Cambridge: Cambridge University Press.

Statistics Canada. 1983. *Statistics Canada Annual Report / Rapport annuel de statistique Canada.* Ottawa: Statistics Canada.

———. 1988. *Statistics Canada Annual Report / Rapport annuel de statistique Canada.* Ottawa: Statistics Canada.

STOLTENBERG, John. 1989. *Refusing to be a Man: Essays on Sex and Justice.* Portland, OR: Breitenbush Books.

TAVRIS, Carol. 1977. "Stereotypes, Socialization, and Sexism." In *Beyond Sex Roles,* ed. Alice G. Sargent. New York: West, 178-87.

TOLSON, Andrew. 1977. *The Limits of Masculinity.* London: Tavistock.

UNITED STATES Bureau of the Census, Statistical Research Division. 1988. *Statistical Abstract of the United States [The American Almanac].* Washington, DC: United States Print Office.

CHAPTER 15

By Way of Conclusion

A SHARED PURPOSE OF THE PAPERS IN THIS BOOK WAS TO develop cross-cultural understandings of "the paths women choose in their struggles to make better lives for themselves" (Judd, this volume). Motivating this volume is the question posed by Marie-Andrée Couillard in her contribution: as translators of women's struggles, how can feminist anthropologists identify what is at stake for women in social contexts that are radically different from their own? The challenge for feminist anthropologists is to recognize both the unity *and* the diversity of "feminism" across cultural boundaries. Developing cross-cultural feminisms leads feminist anthropologists to place in question the field methods, theorizing and ethnography that define anthropology as a discipline.

We interpret the multivocal and heterogeneous approaches to these issues in this volume as one of its strengths. Several of our

papers adopt an autobiographical voice as the author reflects upon
her own theoretical development as a feminist anthropologist over a
period of years (Abwunza, Couillard, Judd). Other contributors
question the utility of our feminist theoretical categories, which
may inhibit cross-cultural field research and international economic
development initiatives by preventing us from seeing the day-to-day
reality of particular women in specific contexts. Some authors argue
that we need to "reread" feminist theoretical constructs — the
notions of household or reproduction, for example — by taking the
point of view of the women with whom we work (Abwunza,
Benazera et al). On the other hand, constructs such as "household"
are found to continue to offer rich theorizing, as we see in Max
Hedley's paper. And the consideration of how gender operates as a
cultural category in the Canadian political landscape nurtures the
feminist vision of Trish Wilson in her contribution to this volume.

The creative and critical impetus of feminist scholarship in
Canadian anthropology maintains a long-standing alliance with
Canadian social sciences, especially the theoretical frameworks of
political economy. Several papers critique the literature and the
practice of "women and development." Others study the intersections of culture, gender and economy in the world of women's work
defined in the broadest sense. Papers in this volume explored, for
example, global perspectives on breastfeeding and technology (Van
Esterik); Navajo women's weaving and its commodification
(M'Closkey); women and the art of maskmaking (Anderson);
industrial homework in Ontario (Leach); and women and unionization (Baker).

The intersections of politics and practice in our work requires
that feminist anthropologists negotiate a theoretical space between
the cultural relativism that is a hallmark of anthropology and the
universalism that tends to circumscribe academic feminism. In our
research and writing the contributors in this book sought, on the
one hand, to theorize cultural differences in a way which will be useful to those with whom we work. On the other hand, we continue
to search for and document what Ellen Judd in her chapter calls "a
historically grounded basis for an oppositional vision." That is, we
hope to recognize, understand and make visible women's struggles

within their particular social and historical contexts, and to consider the ideological and material places within which women have been able to work toward a better life for themselves.

A POST-MORTEM: MISSING IN ACTION

We would like, as feminist editors, to reflect briefly upon our experience of the manuscript review process because we think the process itself illustrates the place of feminist scholarship in the discipline of anthropology. Our manuscript, like most Canadian academic books, went through two separate review processes: first, by the publisher's anthropology reader; and, second by a reader for the Social Science Federation of Canada/Canadian Federation of Humanities' Aid to Scholarly Publications Programme. The manuscript was first read and rejected by our alma mater's publishing house. It is interesting to compare the different readers' comments, for they portray both the ambivalence of the discipline toward feminist work (whether of theory or practice) and the "awkwardness" that Marilyn Strathern identified in the relationship between anthropology and feminism. The reader for Carleton University Press consistently applauded the volume, noting the accessibility of feminist theory in the writing and the need for a book that makes available a wide range of feminist research in anthropology. The University of Toronto reader, however, described the text's engagement with postmodernism as "theoretically unsophisticated" and viewed as "complaining" the postgraduate reflexivity of several of the papers. The reader for the Aid to Scholarly Publications Programme insisted upon a lengthier, more authoritative, master introduction and the addition of a conclusion — structural characteristics which as feminist editors we resisted but have tried to provide. The book's inclusion of senior, junior and just-emerging scholars and its welcoming of the different strategies taken on by authors approaching similar issues was interpreted by the Federation's reader as "unevenness" in the "quality" of the papers. The Federation reader also considered that "polemics often masquerade as theory," a point similar to the University of Toronto Press reader.

In a number of the papers we *do* critically re-think our experiences as woman graduate students seeking feminist spaces in the discipline. We view this attribute positively — especially as many students tell us that these reflexive moments in our papers (regretfully) mirror their own experience in anthropology departments in the 1990s. That women's re-thinking is called "complaining" and not legitimate challenges to the canon should not surprise us however, given the gendered nature of discourse in the social sciences (Fox Keller 1990; Harding 1986; Tuana 1989; see also Harding 1993, on the "racial economy" of science) and given our own experience in anthropology. The extent to which the process of anthropological canon making continues to undermine feminism as theory is indicated by the response of the discipline's academic gatekeepers. They see the pushing at the boundaries of anthropology from a feminist perspective and disparage it as "polemics" and "politics."

The discipline's lack of recognition of feminist theorizing confirms this apprehension and dismissal. Feminist research and theory was absent from issues of the *Annual Review of Anthropology* until 1988. None of the articles in the seven volumes of the University of Wisconsin's "History of Anthropology" series consider the contribution of feminism to anthropology. Feminist research and theory is absent from a major retrospective on theory in anthropology since the 1960s (Ortner 1984), the postmodernist prescription for anthropology for the twenty-first century (Clifford and Marcus 1986), a Canadian perspective on the rebirth of anthropological theory (Barrett 1984), and from an important attempt to negotiate the political (theoretical) terrain between postmodernism and political economy (Ulin 1991).

Feminist anthropologists continue to meet resistance to feminist theorizing at a time when surely the question of "real" theory in anthropology is very much a moot one. In a recent article entitled "The Gender of Theory," Catherine Lutz (1995) suggests that feminist and postcolonialist theory is being managed by assertions (like the ones from the expert readers of our manuscript) that such work is political and not theoretical. Lutz describes the contemporary academy as a hierarchy of "high" theory (that of white males), "middlebrow" theory (that of women and people of colour) and the uneducated masses (students). She suggests that the academy's identification of the "middlebrow" as political action and not theory is a way of containing feminist and postcolonial critiques. Lutz cites, as an example of the effacement of feminist theory, a recent ad for an academic appointment that asked for a "feminist or a theorist." Like the gradations of "high" versus "low" culture, the hierarchical ranking of theory says more about those doing the ranking than it does about theory making itself (cf. Rosaldo, 1989).

At the 1994 annual conference of the Canadian Anthropology Society/Société canadienne d'anthropologie, a session focused on "Women's Work in Canadian Anthropology" and was intended as a forum to explore the history of women's contribution to Canadian anthropology. Papers included autobiographical memoirs, biographical essays, textual analyses of women's writing, women anthropologists' relationships with husbands and/or with women informants and so on. The intersection of "life" with anthropology was foregrounded in all cases. As has long been recognized by feminist theorists, women's lives and identities have not adopted linear or singular patterns. The "quest" is rarely a woman's analogy or metaphor for her life. Rather women's lives tend to be fragmented and intersected by multiple identities. Women's multiplicity embraces all the requirements of their life courses (cycles) mitigated by the external structuring of women's place(s) in societies. Coming to theory requires recording and theorizing these endless (for there is no end to women's experiences) details. Yet during the discussion period after these papers were given, a senior male anthropologist lamented what he saw as a validation of "gossip" in this project (see Cole, 1995).

Catherine Lutz's comment that, within the context of anthropological theory, feminism is "missing in action" seems to best express the current situation. Militaristic overtones aside, feminist anthropologists *are* missing in action — in our families, in our communities, in our jobs, in our lives. This is where we may always be (or at least for the foreseeable future), but it is also where most of us would want to be: where the action — living the political — is. This is the basis of our endorsing Marilyn Strathern's (1987:268) attribution of feminist scholarship's success to "the relationship as it is represented between scholarship and the feminist movement," a relationship that we choose to describe as that between "genre" and "life." The goal for feminist anthropologists, as we see it, is for writing (and anthropology) to be tied to life (and politics).

It is perhaps this orientation that explains why it troubles us to discern a tendency of some feminists toward creating a canon to parallel the malestream one. In our view this is a trend that is related to the continuing polarization of theory and practice by intellectuals. Jane Flax, for example, chastises feminist theorists for their "dangerously blind innocence" and argues that "politics requires a morality and knowledge appropriate to its *unique domain*" (1992: 459, our emphasis). It is this kind of argumentation that we think relieves feminist scholars from answering fundamental questions about how we understand women's lives and how we translate women's concerns into our political and theoretical practices for women. Such questions become the domain of fieldworkers (methodology) and activists (politics), arbitrary distinctions that feminist critiques of scientific knowledge have attempted to break down.

We identify the project to create a feminist canon as an elitist one as well, one that encourages a separation of feminist anthropology from life and from the concerns of nonacademic women. Perhaps it is because we locate our feminist anthropology in the Canadian political economy tradition that we lament not only the gendered nature but also the classist bias of the academic canon. A feminist canon that ironically reproduces class divisions is contrary to our participation in life and politics in the world, to our methodological concerns, and to our raison d'être as feminist anthropologists. We seek alternatives to classist, gendered canon in anthropology. This may mean we will continue to be missing in action, but for many of us, this is where the action is.

We think this volume offers access to the richness of feminist work in Canadian anthropology and gives cause to be optimistic about the future of feminist anthropology. Nonetheless, we anticipate that, as feminists, we will continue to work at the margins of the discipline of anthropology. Being on the margins is a double-edged position: on the one hand, frustration is built into interactions with the disciplinary canon and its practitioners; on the other hand, it is precisely this outsider status that will help to ensure that our theorizing articulates our political practice and that our practice articulates the lives of women.

BIBLIOGRAPHY

ABU-LUGHOD, L. 1990. "Can there be a Feminist Ethnography?" *Women and Performance* 5(1):7-27.

BARRETT, S. 1984. *The Rebirth of Anthropological Theory.* Toronto: University of Toronto Press.

CLIFFORD, J., and G. Marcus, eds. 1986. *Writing Culture.* Berkeley and Los Angeles: University of California Press.

COLE, S. (1995). "Women's Stories and Boasian Texts: The Ojibwa Ethnography of Ruth Landes and Maggie Wilson." *Anthropologica* 37(1): 3-25.

CONKEY, M., and J. Gero. 1991. "Tensions, Pluralities and Engendering Archaeology: An Introduction to Women and Prehistory." In *Engendering Archaeology,* ed. J. Gero and M. Conkey. Cambridge: Blackwell, 3-30.

FLAX, J. 1992. "The End of Innocence." In *Feminists Theorize the Political,* ed. J. Butler and J. Scott. New York: Routledge, 445-63.

FOX KELLER, E. 1990. "Gender and Science." In *Feminist Research Methods,* ed. J. McCarl Nielsen. Boulder, CO: Westview.

HARDING, Sandra. 1986. *The Science Question in Feminism.* Ithaca: Cornell University Press.

————. 1993. *The "Racial Economy" of Science: Toward a Democratic Future.* Bloomington: Indiana University Press.

LUTZ, C. 1995 (in press). "The Gender of Theory." In *Women Writing Culture/Culture Writing Women,* ed. R. Behar and D. Gordon. Berkeley: University of California Press.

ORTNER, S. 1984. "Theory in Anthropology Since the Sixties." *Comparative Studies in Society and History* 26(1):126-66.

ROSALDO, Renalto. 1989. *Culture and Truth: The Remaking of Social Analysis.* Boston: Beacon Press.

SILVERMAN, M. 1991. "Dispatch 1. Amongst 'Our Selves': A Colonial Encounter in Canadian Academe." *Critique of Anthropology* 11(4):381-400.

STRATHERN, Marilyn. 1987. "Out of Context: The Persuasive Fictions of Anthropology." *Current Anthropology* 28(3):251-81.

TUANA, N., ed. 1989. *Feminism and Science.* Bloomington: Indiana University Press.

ULIN, R. 1991. "Critical Anthropology Twenty Years Later: Modernism and Postmodernism in Anthropology." *Critique of Anthropology* 11(1):63-89.

RESOURCE BIBLIOGRAPHY

This bibliography is designed to serve as a resource for research on feminism and anthropology. Although not exhaustive, it contains representative works from five areas of investigation that influence or comprise feminist anthropology: interdisciplinary writing in feminist method and theory; feminist perspectives on the place of feminist and gender studies in anthropological research; explorations of the questions of translation and representation in the writing of feminist ethnography about "other" women's lives; and recent work in two substantive and enduring themes of feminist research in anthropology: women and international development issues and the politics of women and work.

I. FEMINIST METHOD AND THEORY

BARRETT, Michele. 1980. *Women's Oppression Today: Problems in Marxist Feminist Analysis.* London: Verso.

BURTON, Clare. 1985. *Subordination: Feminism and Social Theory.* Sydney: Allen & Unwin.

DuBOIS, Ellen Carol, and Vicki L. Ruiz, eds. 1990. *Unequal Sisters: A Multicultural Reader in U.S. Women's History.* New York: Routledge.

EICHLER, Margrit. 1987. *Nonsexist Research Methods: A Practical Guide.* Boston: Allen & Unwin.

FARNHAM, Christie, ed. 1987. *The Impact of Feminist Research in the Academy.* Bloomington: Indiana University Press.

FLAX, Jane. 1987. "Postmodernism and Gender Relations in Feminist Theory." *Signs* 12(4):621-43.

————. 1989. *Thinking Fragments: Psychoanalysis, Feminism and Postmodernism in the Contemporary West.* Berkeley: University of California Press.

GEIGER, Susan. 1990. "What's so Feminist About Women's Oral History?" *Journal of Women's History* 2(1):169-81.

HARAWAY, Donna. 1988. "Situated Knowledges: The Science Question in Feminism as a Site of Discourse on the Privilege of Partial Perspective." *Feminist Studies* 14(3):575-600.

HARDING, Sandra. 1986. *The Science Question in Feminism.* Ithaca: Cornell University Press.

————, ed. 1987. *Feminism and Methodology.* Bloomington: Indiana University Press.

————, and Merrill B. Hintikka, eds. 1983. *Discovering Reality: Feminist Perspectives on Epistemology, Metaphysics, Methodology and Philosophy of Science.* Dordrecht, Holland: D. Reidel.

————, and Jean O'Barr, eds. 1987. *Sex and Scientific Inquiry.* Chicago: Chicago University Press.

HESS, Beth B., and Myra Marx Fleece, eds. 1987. *Analyzing Gender.* Beverley Hills: Sage.

HOOKS, bell. 1990. *Yearning: Race, Gender, and Cultural Politics.* Toronto: Between the Lines.

KADAR, Marlene, ed. 1992. *Essays in Life Writing: From Genre to Critical Practice.* Toronto: University of Toronto Press.

KUHN, Annette, and Ann Marie Wolpe, eds. 1978. *Feminism and Materialism: Women and Modes of Production.* London: Routledge & Kegan Paul.

MINER, Valerie, and Helen E. Longino, eds. 1987. *Competition A Feminist Taboo?* New York: Feminist Press.

NICHOLSON, Linda, ed. 1990. *Feminism/Postmodernism.* New York: Routledge.

OAKLEY, Ann. 1981. "Interviewing Women: A Contradiction in Terms." In *Doing Feminist Research,* ed. Helen Roberts. London: Routledge & Kegan Paul, 30-61.

REINHARZ, Shulamit. 1992 *Feminist Methods in Social Research.* New York: Oxford University Press.

ROWBOTHAM, Sheila. 1989. *The Past is Before Us: Feminism in Action Since the 1960s.* London: Penguin.

TORGOVNICK, Mariana. 1990. *Gone Primitive: Savage Intellects, Modern Lives.* Chicago: University of Chicago Press.

TUANA, Nancy, ed. 1989. *Feminism and Science.* Bloomington: Indiana University Press.

II. FEMINISM AND ANTHROPOLOGY

BRETTELL, Caroline, and Carolyn Sargent, eds. 1993. *Gender in Cross-Cultural Perspective.* Englewood Cliffs, NJ: Prentice-Hall.

CAPLAN, Pat, ed. 1987. *The Cultural Construction of Sexuality.* London: Routledge.

COONTZ, Stephanie, and Peta Henderson, eds. 1986. *Women's Work, Men's Property: The Origins of Gender and Class.* London: Verso.

DI LEONARDO, Micaela, ed. 1991. *Gender at the Crossroads of Knowledge: Feminist Anthropology in the Postmodern Era.* Berkeley: University of California Press.

GACS, Ute, Aisha Khan, Jerrie McIntyre, and Ruth Weinberg, eds. 1989. *Women Anthropologists: Selected Biographies.* Urbana: University of Illinois Press.

GERO, Joan, and Margaret Conkey, eds. 1991. *Engendering Archaeology: Women and Prehistory.* Oxford: Basil Blackwell.

GOLDE, Peggy, ed. 1986. *Women in the Field: Anthropological Experiences.* 2nd. ed. Chicago: Aldine.

HARAWAY, Donna. 1989. *Primate Visions: Gender, Race and Nature in the World of Modern Science.* New York: Routledge.

HARRISON, Faye, ed. 1991. *Decolonizing Anthropology: Moving Further Toward an Anthropology for Liberation.* Washington: American Anthropological Association.

LEACOCK, Eleanor. 1981. *Myths of Male Dominance.* New York: Monthly Review Press.

LUTZ, Catherine. 1990. "The Erasure of Women's Writing in Sociocultural Anthropology." *American Ethnologist* 17(4):611-27.

MARTIN, Emily. 1987. *The Woman in the Body: A Cultural Analysis of Reproduction.* Boston: Beacon.

MASCIA-LEES, Frances E., Patricia Sharpe, and Colleen Ballerino Cohen. 1989. "The Postmodernist Turn in Anthropology: Cautions from a Feminist Perspective." *Signs* 15(1):7-33.

MOORE, Henrietta. 1988. *Feminism and Anthropology.* Minneapolis: University of Minnesota Press.

MORGEN, Sandra, ed. 1989. *Gender and Anthropology: Critical Reviews for Teaching.* Washington, DC: American Anthropological Association.

PAREZO, Nancy, ed. 1993. *Hidden Scholars.* Albuquerque: University of New Mexico Press.

ROSALDO, Michelle Zimbalist. 1980. "The Use and Abuse of Anthropology: Reflections on Cross-cultural Understanding." *Signs* 5(3):389-417.

SANJEK, Roger, ed. 1990. *Fieldnotes: The Makings of Anthropology.* Ithaca: Cornell University Press.

SAYERS, Janet. 1982. *Biological Politics.* London: Tavistock.

SCHEPER-HUGHES, Nancy. 1992. *Death Without Weeping: The Violence of Everyday Life in Brazil.* Berkeley: University of California Press.

STRATHERN, Marilyn. 1981. "Culture in a Netbag: The Manufacture of a Subdiscipline in Anthropology." *Man* 16:665-88.

———. 1987. "An Awkward Relationship: The Case of Feminism and Anthropology." *Signs* 12(2):276-92.

———. 1988. *The Gender of the Gift: Problems with Women and Problems with Society in Melanesia.* Berkeley: University of California Press.

ULIN, Robert. 1991. "Critical Anthropology Twenty Years Later: Modernism and Postmodernism in Anthropology." *Critique of Anthropology* 11(1):63-89.

WOLF, Margery. 1992. *A Thrice-told Tale: Feminism, Postmodernism and Ethnographic Responsibility.* Palo Alto: Stanford University Press.

III. WRITING FEMINIST ANTHROPOLOGY

ABU-LUGHOD, Lila. 1990. "Can There be a Feminist Ethnography?" *Women and Performance* 5(1):7-27.

AHENAKEW, Freda, and H. C. Wolpert, eds. and trans. 1992. *Our Grandmothers' Lives as Told in Their Own Words.* Saskatoon: Fifth House Publishers.

ANZALDÚA, Gloria, ed. 1990. *Making Face, Making Soul: Creative and Critical Perspectives By Women of Colour.* San Francisco: Aunt Lute Foundation Books.

BEHAR, Ruth. 1993. *Translated Woman: Crossing the Border with Esperanza's Story.* Boston: Beacon.

———, and Deborah Gordon, eds. 1995 (in press). *Women Writing Culture/Culture Writing Women.* Berkeley: University of California Press

BROWN, Karen McCarthy. 1991. *Mama Lola: A Vodou Priestess in Brooklyn.* Berkeley: University of California Press.

CRUIKSHANK, Julie, in collaboration with Angela Sidney, Kitty Smith, and Annie Ned. 1990. *Life Lived Like a Story: Life Stories of Three Yukon Native Elders.* Vancouver: University of British Columbia Press.

GLUCK, Sharon, and Daphne Patai, eds. 1991. *Women's Words: The Feminist Practice of Oral History.* New York: Routledge.

GORDON, Deborah. 1988. "Writing Culture, Writing Feminism." *Inscriptions* 3(4):7-26.

MOHANTY, Chandra Talpade. 1991. "Under Western Eyes: Feminist Scholarship and Colonial Discourses." In *Third World Women and the Politics of Feminism,* ed. Chandra Talpade Mohanty, Ann Russo, and Lourdes Torres. Bloomington: Indiana University Press, 51-80.

OKELY, Judith, and Helen Callaway, eds. 1992. *Anthropology and Autobiography.* London: Routledge.

Personal Narratives Group, ed. 1989. *Interpreting Women's Lives: Feminist Theory and Personal Narratives.* Bloomington: Indiana University Press.

SCHEIER, Libby, Sarah Sheard and Eleanor Wachtel, eds. 1990. *Language in Her Eye: Views on Writing and Gender by Canadian Women Writing in English.* Toronto: Coach House Press.

STRATHERN, Marilyn. 1987. "Out of Context: The Persuasive Fictions of Anthropology." *Current Anthropology* 28(3):251-81.

TORGOVNIK, Marianna. 1990. "Experimental Critical Writing." *Profession* 90:25-27.

TRINH T. Minh-ha. 1989. *Woman, Native, Other.* Bloomington: Indiana University Press.

VISWESWAREN, Kamala. 1988. "Defining Feminist Ethnography." *Inscriptions* 3(4):27-46.

———. 1995 (in press). *Fictions of Feminist Ethnography.* Minneapolis: University of Minnesota Press.

IV. FEMINIST ANTHROPOLOGY AND INTERNATIONAL CONTEXTS

BOURQUE, Susan C., and Kay Barbara Warren. 1981. *Women of the Andes: Patriarchy and Social Change in Two Peruvian Towns.* Ann Arbor: University of Michigan Press.

BRYDEN L., and S. Chant, eds. 1989. *Women in the Third World: Gender Issues in Rural and Urban Areas.* New Brunswick, NJ: Rutgers University Press.

CHAMPAGNE, Suzanne, éd. 1989. *Les femmes et le développement: stratégies, moyens, impact. Des coopérantes témoignent de leur expérience avec des femmes au Sahel.* Québec: Centre Sahel/Université Laval.

CREEVEY, Lucy E., ed. 1886. *Women Farmers in Africa: Rural Development in Mali and the Sahel.* Syracuse: Syracuse University Press.

CROLL, Elisabeth. 1978. *Feminism and Socialism in China.* London: Routledge & Kegan Paul.

DAGENAIS, H., and D. Piche, eds. 1994. *Women, Feminism and Development/Femmes, féminisme et développement.* Montreal, Kingston: McGill University Press.

DAVISON, Jean. 1988. *Agriculture, Women, and the Land: The African Experience.* Boulder, CO: Westview Press.

EHLERS, T. 1990. *Silent Looms: Women and Production in a Guatemalan Town.* Boulder, CO: Westview Press.

ETIENNE, Mona and Eleanor Leacock, eds. 1980. *Women and Colonization: Anthropological Perspectives.* New York: Praeger.

GALLIN, Rita S., and Anne Ferguson, eds. 1991. *The Women and International Development Annual,* vol. 2. Boulder, CO: Westview Press.

———. 1993. *The Women and International Development Annual,* vol. 3. Boulder, CO: Westview Press.

HARCOURT, W., ed. 1994. *Feminist Perspectives on Sustainable Development.* London: Zed Books.

JAYAWARDENA, Kumari. 1986. *Feminism and Nationalism in the Third World.* London: Zed Books.

JUDD, Ellen. 1994. *Gender and Power in Rural North China.* Stanford: Stanford University Press.

KHASIANI, Shanyisa A., ed. 1992. *African Women as Environmental Managers.* Nairobi: ACTS Press.

LABRECQUE, M.F., éd. 1994. *Développement international: l'étude des rapports sociaux de sexe.* Ottawa: CRDI.

LIDDLE, Joanna, and R. Joshi. 1986. *Daughters of Independence: Gender, Caste and Class in India.* London: Zed Books.

MERNISSI, Fatima. 1985. *Beyond the Veil: Male-Female Dynamics in Modern Muslim Society.* rev. ed. Bloomington: Indiana University Press.

MIES, Maria. 1986. *Patriarchy and Accumulation on a World Scale: Women in the International Division of Labour.* London: Zed Books.

MOHANTY, Chandra, Ann Russo, and Lourdes Torres, eds. 1991. *Third World Women and the Politics of Feminism.* Bloomington: Indiana University Press

NASH, June, and Patricia Fernández-Kelly, eds. 1983. *Women, Men and the International Division of Labor.* Albany: SUNY Press.

ONG, Aihwa. 1987. *Spirits of Resistance and Capitalist Discipline: Factory Women in Malaysia.* Albany: SUNY Press.

ROGERS, Barbara. 1980. *The Domestication of Women.* London: Tavistock.

RUIZ, Vicky, and Susan Tiano. 1987. *Women on the U.S.-Mexico Border: Responses to Change.* Boston: Allen & Unwin.

SEAGER, Joni, and Ann Olsen. 1986. *Women in the World: An International Atlas.* New York: Simon and Schuster.

SEN, Gita, and Caren Grown. 1987. *Development, Crises, and Alternative Visions: Third World Women's Perspectives.* New York: Monthly Review Press.

STAMP, Patricia. 1989. *Technology, Gender, and Power in Africa.* Ottawa: International Development Research Centre.

STAUNTON, Irene, ed. 1990. *Mothers of the Revolution: The War Experiences of Thirty Zimbabwean Women.* Bloomington: Indiana University Press.

STICHTER, Sharon, and Jane Parpart, eds. 1990. *Women, Employment and the Family in the International Division of Labour.* London: Macmillan.

TINKER, Irene, ed. 1990. *Persistent Inequalities: Women and World Development.* New York: Oxford University Press.

TOULMIN, Camilla. 1992. *Cattle, Women and Wells: Managing Household Survival in the Sahel.* Oxford: Clarendon

VICKERS, Jeanne. 1991. *Women and the World Economic Crisis.* London: Zed Books.

WARD, K., ed. 1980. *Women Workers and Global Restructuring.* Ithaca: ILR Press.

YOUNG, Kate, Carol Wolkowitz, and Roslyn McCullagh, eds. 1981. *Of Marriage and the Market: Women's Subordination in International Perspective.* London: CSE Books.

V. WOMEN'S WORK AND POLITICS

BENERÍA, L., and M. Roldán. 1987. *The Crossroads of Class and Gender.* Chicago: University of Chicago Press.

———, and S. Feldman, eds. 1982. *Unequal Burden: Economic Crises, Persistent Poverty, and Women's Work.* Boulder: Westview Press.

BOOKMAN, Ann, and Sandra Morgen, eds. 1988. *Women and the Politics of Empowerment.* Philadelphia: Temple University Press.

BRISKIN, Linda, and Patricia McDermott, eds. 1993. *Women Challenging Unions: Feminism, Democracy, and Militancy.* Toronto: University of Toronto Press.

BUNSTER, Ximena, and Elsa Chaney. 1985. *Sellers and Servants: Working Women in Lima, Peru.* New York: Praeger.

CALAGIONE, J., D. Francis, and D. Nugen, eds. 1992. *Women's Expressions: Beyond Accomodation and Resistance.* Albany: SUNY Press.

COBBLE, Dorothy Sue, ed. 1993. *Women and Unions: Forging a Partnership.* Ithaca: ILR Press.

DI LEONARDO, Micaela. 1984. *The Varieties of Ethnic Experience: Kinship, Class, and Gender Among California Italian-Americans.* Ithaca: Cornell University Press.

FERNÁNDEZ-KELLY, Patricia. 1983. *For We are Sold, I and My People: Women and Industry on Mexico's Frontier.* Albany: SUNY Press

KAHNE, Hilda A., and Janet Z. Giele, eds. 1992. *Women's Work and Women's Lives: The Continuing Struggle Worldwide.* Boulder: Westview Press.

LAMPHERE, Louise. 1987. *From Working Daughters to Working Mothers: Immigrant Women in a New England Industrial Community.* Ithaca: Cornell University Press.

LEACOCK, Eleanor, and Helen Safa, eds. 1986. *Women's Work.* South Hadley, MA: Bergin & Garvey.

LUXTON, Meg. 1980. *More Than a Labour of Love: Three Generations of Women's Work in the Home.* Toronto: Women's Press.

————, and Harriet Rosenberg. 1986. *Through the Kitchen Window: The Politics of Home and Family.* Toronto: Garamond.

NADEL-KLEIN, Jane, and Dona Lee Davis, eds. 1988. *To Work and to Weep: Women in Fishing Economies.* St. John's, Newfoundland: Institute of Social and Economic Research, Memorial University of Newfoundland.

NASH, June. 1989. *From Tank Town to High Tech.* New York: SUNY Press.

————. 1992. *We Eat the Mines and the Mines Eat Us.* 2nd. ed. with new preface. New York: Columbia University Press.

PHIZACKLEA, A. 1990. *Unpacking the Fashion Industry: Gender, Racism and Class in Production.* London: Routledge.

REDCLIFT, Nanneke, and Enzo Mingione, eds. 1985. *Beyond Employment: Household, Gender and Subsistence.* Oxford: Blackwell.

SACKS, Karen. 1988. *Caring by the Hour: Women, Work, and Organizing at Duke Medical Center.* Urbana: University of Illinois Press.

SANJEK, R. and S. Colen. 1990. *At Work at Home: Household Workers in World Perspective.* American Ethnological Society, Monograph Series No. 3. Washington, DC: American Anthropological Association.

STICHTER, S.B. and J.L. Papart. 1988. *Patriarchy and Class: African Women in the Home and Workforce.* London: Westview Press.

STOLLER, Ann. 1985. *Capitalism and Confrontation in Sumatra's Plantation Belt, 1870-1979.* New Haven: Yale University Press.

TIANO, Susan. 1986. "Women and Industrial Development." *Latin American Research Review* 21(3):157-70.

WARING, Marilyn. 1988. *If Women Counted: A New Feminist Economics.* San Francisco: Harper Collins.

WHITE, Julie. 1993. *Sisters and Solidarity: Women and Unions in Canada.* Toronto: Thompson Educational Publishing.

ZAVELLA, Patricia. 1987. *Women's Work and Chicano Families: Cannery Workers of the Santa Clara Valley.* Ithaca: Cornell University Press.

SOME QUESTIONS FOR STUDY
AND DISCUSSION

1.   Marie-Andrée Couillard (chapter 4) describes Islam as a "structuring difference" in Malay women's lives. Ellen Judd (chapter 3) argues that we cannot understand Chinese women's politics without looking at the state. How do these structural differences in women's lives provide the contexts for local feminisms?

2.   Penny Van Esterik (chapter 5) identifies oppositions within which Western analyses take place (production vs. reproduction, public vs. private, nature vs. culture, mind vs. body, work vs. leisure, self vs. other, maternal vs. sexual). Take one of these oppositions and discuss how it shapes how we understand women's lives.

3.   In chapter 7 Max Hedley shows how analyses of expanding market relations assume women's work to be "domestic" work and render it invisible. Kathy M'Closkey (chapter 6) argues that despite the fact that Navajo women's weaving was fully public and visible, its worth was never recognized. What is women's work? What are the processes that hide women's work?

4.   Pat Baker in chapter 9 describes how strikes organized by women often "fail" to achieve their goals but that many of the women she interviewed gained personal empowerment through their political activity in unionization. What does this analysis tell us about women's politics?

5.   Sally Cole (chapter 10) and Judith Abwunza (chapter 13) discuss the problems they faced in writing with "women's voices." What are some of the concerns when writing and representing women's experience across cultures? Is the role of feminist anthropology to translate women's experiences across cultural borders or do power differences make this project unrealizable?

6.   Focussing upon differences among women can lead to arguments that other women's realities are "none of our business." Yet some feminists argue for the importance of defending women's rights, as human rights, cross-culturally. What are the ethical dilemmas that feminists face on these issues?

7.   Several of the essays maintain the analytical utility of the category "woman." Rae Anderson (chapter 11) discusses how women are excluded from the ritual practice of wearing masks. Penny Van Esterik (chapter 5) argues that if we begin our critical thinking from the standpoint of women's breasts, we can begin to analyze the world in a very different way. And Trish Wilson

(chapter 14) focuses on the social control of women through violence. On the other hand, Marie-Andrée Couillard (chapter 4) and Benazara et. al (chapter 12) stress the important differences in women's lives cross-culturally. What are the implications of these differences and unities for a global feminism?

8.   The challenge for feminist anthropology is the challenge of anthropology: to recognize unity *and* diversity in human experience. How do the essays in this volume help us to face this challenge by providing guidelines for understanding "women's point of view" in different cultures?

NOTES ON CONTRIBUTORS

Judith Abwunza is Assistant Professor in the Department of Sociology and Anthropology at Wilfred Laurier University. Her research interests have included issues of development, ethnicity and political economy in rural areas of Kenya, East Africa. Her current research extends to Kenyan urban living, particularly urban women's poverty. Her most recent publication is "Ethnonationalism and Nationalism Strategies: The Case of the Avalogoli in Western Kenya," in Michael Levin (ed.) *Ethnicity and Aboriginality: Case Studies in Ethnonationalism,* University of Toronto Press, 1993.

Rae Anderson has spent the last decade working as a professional visual artist (sculptural installations), and is interested in contributing new perspectives to the discipline of visual anthropology as one who is a practitioner. She completed an M.A. (1989) in interdisciplinary studies at York University with a thesis focusing on the relationship between masks and women in small-scale societies, and a Ph.D. (1993) on social and spatial boundaries in two artists' housing cooperatives in Toronto. She is presently a postdoctoral fellow at York University.

Patricia Baker is an Assistant Professor in the Departments of Sociology/Anthropology and Women's Studies at Mount Saint Vincent University in Halifax, Nova Scotia. Her main research interest is in the experience of women in unions, particularly in Canada's financial industry. She is also interested in the development and application of feminist methodology. Recent publications include "Some Unions are More Equal than Others: A Response to Rosemary Warskett's 'Bank Worker Unionization and the Law,'" *Studies in Political Economy* 34, 1991, and "Reflections on Life Stories: Women's Bank Union Activism" in Linda Briskin and Patricia McDermot (eds.) *Women Challenging Unions: Feminism, Democracy and Militancy,* University of Toronto Press, 1993.

Clara Benazera is a doctoral student in anthropology at the University of Laval. She has been working for three years on a research project, headed by Professor Yvan Breton, concerning the social differentiation of Costa Rican small-scale fisheries. She is presently a member of a research team working on social changes in Brazilian fishing villages.

Marie-Hélène Bérard obtained her Master's degree in anthropology from the University of Laval in 1993 under Marie-Andrée Couillard's supervision. Her thesis concerns the notion of time as "enjeux" in the WID projects in Sahelian villages. She is currently working in a community network context in the city of Quebec.

Sally Cole is Associate Professor at Concordia University in the Department of Sociology and Anthropology. In her research she has recorded the life stories of Inuit teenagers in the Canadian Arctic, of Portuguese fishermen on the Newfoundland Grand Banks, of Portuguese immigrant workers in the Lake Erie commercial fishery and, in her book *Women of the Praia: Work and Lives in a Portuguese Coastal Community* (Princeton University Press 1991), of women in rural northern Portugal. She is at work on a book about the life and writing of anthropologist Ruth Landes.

Marie-Andrée Couillard is a professor of anthropology at the University of Laval. She has been working in Insular Southeast Asia since 1975, writing a Ph.D. thesis on rural Malay women and social transformations. She has been interested in issues of women and development as the head of a research group on women of Sahel, Africa, and as co-director for the Atelier international sur les femmes et le développement at the University of Laval. She is now working on a study of power and solidarity in women's groups, especially in Quebec, and further developing her concerns with culture and gender.

Max Hedley has his Ph.D. from the University of Alberta and is an Associate Professor in the Department of Sociology and Anthropology at the University of Windsor. He has a number of articles on farming communities in Canada and New Zealand and has been a Research Fellow with the Institute for Social and Economic Research at Memorial University, Newfoundland. He maintains his interests in aboriginal issues through his ties with the research unit at the Walpole Island Reserve in Ontario. He is currently working on a comparative study of fishing, farming and trapping in Canada.

Elizabeth Houde obtained her Master's degree in 1992 in anthropology. She made two research trips to Costa Rica as a member of a research team studying the social diversity of small-scale fishing. In the summer of 1991, she carried out a two-month research trip in Colombia and Ecuador as a consultant in the formulation of a project aimed at improving the socio-economic conditions of women in the Amazonian region. She is presently a doctoral student in anthropology at the University of Laval. Her research now concerns filiation among the Inuit of Quebec.

Ellen Judd teaches anthropology at the University of Manitoba. Her early research was on political symbolism in Chinese drama. Since the mid-1980s she has been exploring the social and symbolic construction of gender in contemporary China. See *Gender and Power in Rural North China* (Stanford University Press, 1994). Her current research project, on the politics of culture in China after 1989, includes an examination of women's organizing in the north China countryside. Her original home is Kingston, Ontario.

Belinda Leach is Assistant Professor in the Department of Sociology and Anthropology at the University of Guelph. She obtained a B.A. as a mature student from Carleton University, and M.A. and Ph.D. from the University of Toronto. She has worked as a staffperson with the National Action Committee on the Status of Women and as a volunteer on gender and development policy issues with Oxfam-Canada. Her research focusses on gender and family relations, informalization and class consciousness in the context of economic restructuring in Ontario.

Kathy M'Closkey is currently a doctoral candidate in the Department of Social Anthropology, York University. Until returning to university in 1989, she was an avid weaver, specializing in indigenous looms and weaving techniques. She has published papers on the economic and/or symbolic aspects of textile production in the Canadian Arctic and among the Navajo. She curated the historic portion of "Fibre: Tradition/Transition" which toured Ontario from 1988-1990, and is currently curating "Fields and Flowers: Fabric Landscapes of Prince Edward Island".

Renée Ménard obtained her Master's degree in anthropology from the University of Laval in 1993. Her thesis, a case study set in two rural Andean communities in Colombia, addresses international development's preoccupation with the sexual division of labor and women's economic conditions. She has been a member of the research team, Colombia: Development, Peasantry and WID, for three years and has completed two fieldwork trips to Colombia. She has written an article on the social impact of technology transfer on women participants and their households. She is currently a consultant in International Development for a private Quebec City-based consulting group.

Lynne Phillips is Associate Professor in the Department of Sociology and Anthropology at the University of Windsor. Her research interests include health concepts in the tropics, the impact of neoliberalism on rural households in Latin America, and post-colonial research methodologies. Her current research on the discourses of disease and development in Ecuador, Chile and Argentina is supported by a grant from the Social Sciences and Humanities Research Council of Canada.

Penny Van Esterik is Associate Professor of Anthropology and co-director of the Thai Studies Project at York University, Toronto. Her teaching and research interests include gender and development in Southeast Asia, refugee studies, nutritional anthropology, and breastfeeding research. Most of her fieldwork has been in Thailand, where she has published on the Thai food system, infant feeding practices, and women and Buddhism. Recent publications include *Beyond the Breast-Bottle Controversy* (Rutgers Press, 1989) and *Taking Refuge: Lao Buddhists in North America* (York Lanes Press, 1993). She is currently writing a book on gender ideology in Thailand.

I. P. (Trish) Wilson completed her M.A. in anthropology at McMaster University. At the time of her sudden and premature death she was revising her thesis "Metanarrative and Media: Retrospective on the Montreal Massacre" for publication and preparing to enter a Ph.D. program in educational administration. She was a member of the editorial board of *Nexus,* the Canadian Student Journal of Anthropology, and a member of the Professional Network and Support Coalition of Women in Anthropology, a division of the American Anthropological Association. With her husband, John Bregenzer, she was also working on a book about virtual communities.